SENSIBLE RELIGION

Sensible Religion

Edited by

CHRISTOPHER LEWIS
Christ Church, University of Oxford, UK

DAN COHN-SHERBOK
University of Wales, UK

ASHGATE

Published by
Ashgate Publishing Limited
Wey Court East
Union Road
Farnham
Surrey, GU9 7PT
England

Ashgate Publishing Company
110 Cherry Street
Suite 3-1
Burlington, VT 05401-3818
USA

www.ashgate.com

British Library Cataloguing in Publication Data
A catalogue record for this book is available from the British Library

The Library of Congress has cataloged the printed edition as follows:
Sensible religion / edited by Christopher Lewis and Dan Cohn-Sherbok.
    pages cm
Includes index.
ISBN 978-1-4094-6808-0 (hardcover : alk. paper) — ISBN 978-1-4094-6809-7 (ebook) — ISBN 978-1-4094-6810-3 (epub) 1. Religion--Philosophy. 2. Religions. 3. Religious life. I. Lewis, Christopher, editor.
BL51.S469 2014
  200—dc23

                                                                      2014006142

ISBN 9781409468080 (hbk)
ISBN 9781409468097 (ebk – PDF)
ISBN 9781409468103 (ebk – ePUB)

Printed in the United Kingdom by Henry Ling Limited, at the Dorset Press, Dorchester, DT1 1HD

Contents

Notes on Contributors

Dan Cohn-Sherbok is Professor Emeritus of Judaism at the University of Wales. He was ordained a Reform rabbi at the Hebrew-Union College-Jewish Institute of Religion and received a PhD from Cambridge University. He was Director of the Centre for the Study of Religion at the University of Kent.

Mary Grey is a Roman Catholic liberation theologian, until 2005 D.J. James Professor of Pastoral Theology at the University of Wales, Lampeter and formerly Professor of Contemporary Theology at the University of Southampton, based at La Sainte Union (1993–97). Before that she was Professor of Feminism and Christianity at the Catholic University of Nijmegen, the Netherlands (1988–93). Until summer 2013 she was Visiting Professor at St Mary's University College, Twickenham, London, and Honorary Professor at the University of Winchester. Now she is a freelance writer and lecturer.

Dawoud El-Alami is a Palestinian born in Jerusalem and brought up in Egypt. He holds the Licence en Droit from Cairo University and a PhD from Glasgow University. He worked as a researcher at the Universities of Kent and Oxford and taught at Al al-Bayt University in Jordan and for sixteen years at the University of Wales Lampeter. He is currently a Senior Teaching Fellow at the University of Aberdeen.

Sara Khan is director and co-founder of Inspire, a counter-extremism and human rights organization which seeks to address the inequalities facing British Muslim women. Sara has an M.A. in Understanding and Securing Human Rights and has over 20 years' experience as a human rights activist. She has campaigned, written, appeared on numerous media outlets and as part of her work with Inspire and has helped empower Muslim women to champion their rights. In 2009 Sara was listed in the Equality and Human Rights Commission Muslim Women's Power List.

Rabbi **Michael Lerner** is editor of *Tikkun Magazine*, chair of the Network of Spiritual Progressives, rabbi of Beyt Tikkun Jewish Renewal Synagogue Without Walls in Berkeley California and author of 11 books including Jewish

Renewal: A Path to Healing and Transformation; *The Politics of Meaning*; *Jews and Blacks* (with Cornel West); *Spirit Matters*; *The Left Hand of God: Taking Back Our Country from the Religious Right*; and *Embracing Israel/Palestine: A Strategy for Middle East Peace*.

Christopher Lewis is Dean of Christ Church, which is both a college of the University of Oxford and the cathedral of the Anglican diocese of Oxford. He is a Christian priest who has taught doctrine in an Anglican seminary and worked in parishes and three cathedrals. He has collaborated with Dan Cohn-Sherbok on a number of projects including an inter-faith book on life after death: *Beyond Death*.

Dr **Nokuzola Mndende** is the Director of Icamagu Institute of African Traditional Religion in South Africa. She holds a PhD in Religious Studies from the University of Cape Town. She is also a qualified diviner/traditional healer, a practitioner and leader of African Traditional Religion. She is a national Deputy Chairperson in the Commission on Traditional Leadership Disputes and Claims in South Africa. She has taught African Traditional Religion, Religion in Education and Feminist/Womanist Theology at the University of Cape Town, and Religious Education at the University of South Africa. She has written extensively on issues relating to African Traditional Religion. She has presented papers both nationally and internationally.

Dr. **Anantanand Rambachan** is Professor of Religion at Saint Olaf College, Minnesota, USA. Professor Rambachan is the author of several books, including *Accomplishing the Accomplished*; *The Limits of Scripture*; *The Advaita Worldview: God, World and Humanity*; and *A Hindu Theology of Liberation: Not-One is Not Two* (State University of New York Press, forthcoming). The British Broadcasting Corporation transmitted a series of 25 lectures by Professor Rambachan around the world.

Melissa Raphael is Professor of Jewish Theology at the University of Gloucestershire. She is the author of numerous articles and books, including *Thealogy and Embodiment: The Post-Patriarchal Reconstruction of Female Sacrality* (Sheffield Academic Press, 1996); *Rudolf Otto and the Concept of Holiness* (Oxford University Press, 1997); *The Female Face of God in Auschwitz: A Jewish Feminist Theology of the Holocaust* (Routledge, 2003); and *Judaism and the Visual Image: A Jewish Theology of Art* (Continuum, 2009); and is currently working on a new book on gender, idol-breaking and liberation.

The Revd **Hozan Alan Senauke** is a Soto Zen Buddhist priest, activist, writer, and musician, honored as a 'pioneer' of socially engaged Buddhism. He is vice-abbot of Berkeley Zen Center, where he lives with his family. From 1991 to 2002 Alan was Executive Director of the Buddhist Peace Fellowship. He serves on International Network of Engaged Buddhists' Advisory Committee. In 2008 Alan founded the Clear View Project, focusing on social change and training in Asia, particularly in Burma and among the India's Ambedkarite Buddhists. His books *The Bodhisattva's Embrace: Dispatches from Engaged Buddhism's Front Lines* and *Heirs To Ambedkar: The Rebirth of Engaged Buddhism in India* are published by Clear View Press. And Alan's CD of 'buddhistic' music, *Everything Is Broken*, was released in 2012.

Professor **Rita D. Sherma**, PhD, is the Swami Vivekananda Visiting Professor of Hindu Studies at the University of Southern California School of Religion and holds an M.A. in Religion, and PhD in Religious Studies (2002), from Claremont Graduate University. She has taught and researched on Hindu Theology, Women and Religion, Hindu Philosophy, Indic Dharma Traditions and related fields. Rita Sherma is the founding Vice-President, and Director of Programs of DANAM (Dharma Academy of North America), the first scholarly association in North America to offer a dedicated forum for the study of the global expressions of the religious traditions that emerged in India, in terms of their divergences, commonalities, shared categories and historical and conceptual interrelationships. Sherma has published five edited volumes including *Woman and Goddess in Hinduism: Reinterpretations and Re-Envisionings*; *Contemporary Issues in Constructive Dharma: Epistemology and Hermeneutics*; *Dying, Death, and Afterlife in Dharma Traditions and Western Religions*; and *Hermeneutics and Hindu Thought: Toward a Fusion of Horizons*. Forthcoming in 2014 are *Prayer and Worship in Indic Religions*; and *Engaged Hinduism: Service as a Spiritual Path*. She is currently writing two monographs, on ecological theology, and methodology in the study of religion. A contributing author for a number of edited volumes, Dr. Sherma is the Editor of Hinduism for the *Encyclopedia of Indian Religions*, and founding editor-in-chief of the *International Journal of Dharma Studies*.

Dharmachari Subhuti was born Alex Kennedy in Chatham, Kent, in the UK in 1947. He studied philosophy at what is now the University of North London. During a period of wide-ranging exploration in that time of explorations, the late 1960s, he came across a book of Buddhist scriptures and immediately recognized that he was a Buddhist. Seeking to learn meditation, he encountered Urgyen Sangharakshita, an English-born monk who had spent 20 years in India, studying and teaching. Towards the end of his time in India Sangharakshita had worked with Dr. B.R. Ambedkar, who had revived Buddhism in the land of its birth, leading the conversion of millions of his fellow 'untouchables.' In 1973, Subhuti was ordained by Sangharakshita into what is now the Triratna Buddhist Order, a non-monastic community, now numbering some 2,000 men and women worldwide. Subhuti has worked closely with Sangharakshita since his ordination, taking on many responsibilities from him as a leading member of the College of Preceptors, which carries out ordination into the Triratna Buddhist Order. He has published a number of books, including, *The Buddhist Vision*; *Sangharakshita: A New Voice in the Buddhist Tradition*; *Buddhism and Friendship*; and a recent compilation of essays on the fundamentals of Sangharakshita's teaching, *Seven Papers*. He now spends half of each year teaching Buddhism and leading retreats in India. Much of the rest of his time is spent in his mountain hermitage in north Wales, meditating, studying, and writing.

Opinderjit Kaur Takhar completed her PhD in Religious Studies looking at Sikh identity by examining a number of sects/groups amongst Sikhs. These included the Namdharis, Ravidassias, Valmikis, Guru Nanak Nishkam Sewak Jatha and Sikh Dharma of the Western Hemisphere/3HO. Since then she has carried out research into the egalitarian teachings of the Guru Granth Sahib in relation to women and caste. Her current research interests explore the issue of caste and identity amongst Punjabi dalits and Sikhs. She is Senior Lecturer in Religious Studies at the University of Wolverhampton, UK.

Keith Ward is a Fellow of the British Academy and a priest of the Church of England. He has been, among other things, Dean of Trinity Hall, Cambridge, Professor of the History and Philosophy of Religion, King's College London, and Regius Professor of Divinity, Oxford. He is now a Professorial Research Fellow at Heythrop College, London. He has written a 5-volume Comparative Theology, and other books in the Philosophy of Religion and in Theology. His most recent is *Morality, Autonomy, and God*, published by Oneworld Publications.

Tim Winter gained his first degree in Arabic from Cambridge University in 1983, after which he studied for six years in traditional Islamic institutions in the Middle East. He has held his present post in Cambridge since 1997. His publications include translations of ethical and mystical texts by al-Ghazali (d.1111), a series of articles on Islamic theology and Muslim-Christian relations, and two theological books in Turkish. In 2006 he published *Abraham's Children*, co-edited with Bishop Richard Harries and Rabbi Normon Solomon. He is the editor of the *Cambridge Companion to Classical Islamic Theology* (2008). He has been a Muslim for over 30 years.

Foreword
Sensible Religion – the Start of an Important Debate

Peter Vardy

This is an important book which deserves to be widely read. It brings together significant figures from a very wide range of religious traditions including African Traditional Religions as well as the major world religious and all the authors show sensitivity and present their respective positions clearly and well. If for no other reason, this volume would give the reader a distinctive 'feel' for the centre ground of the world religions and how this centre ground can be presented with clarity, logic and good argument.

Religion is under threat not only from celebrity atheists but also, within its own ranks, from the rise of fundamentalism, which is increasingly attractive to many people in a post-modern world dominated by relativism and a lack of concern for absolutes. Even more important than these forces, however, is the lack of clarity as to what religion really stands for.

W.B.Yeats put the position all too clearly:

> Turning and turning in the widening gyre
> The falcon cannot hear the falconer;
> Things fall apart; the centre cannot hold;
> Mere anarchy is loosed upon the world,
> The blood-dimmed tide is loosed, and everywhere
> The ceremony of innocence is drowned;
> The best lack all conviction, while the worst
> Are full of passionate intensity.

The worst, the fundamentalists, particularly the textual literalists, are indeed full of passionate intensity. This book is about the centre – about holding onto what is of enduring value in the great religious traditions of the world. The problem is that this centre has few voices to defend it and there is lack of clarity about what exactly it stands for. In this sense the problem is deciding what sensible religion is and how it can define itself against the rising indifference of the modern world.

Tim Winter makes clear that 'To be sensible is, all too often, to be perceived as prudent, moderate, consensual, and cautious about stepping into the unknown. It is, usually, to be uninspiring. It is not much of an exaggeration to claim that few people, historically, have had their lives profoundly changed by this kind of sensible person'. (p. 45). But he continues: 'What religion offers, at its most prophetic and authentic, may nonetheless be seen as sensible'. This is undoubtedly true but it is often far from clear precisely what such sensible people stand for and, perhaps perceptively, this book does not make the issue much clearer. All the authors present a view of their respective positions that avoid fundamentalism and eschew extremism. They are all likely to appeal to open minded, liberal readers. Sadly, however, those who adhere to religious practices are no longer drawn from this centre position; growth lies at the extremes where the centre position may appear unappealing.

Sara Khan maintains that 'One of the current crises facing Muslims today is the dominance of literal, decontextualised readings of Islam's scriptures and a misuse in the application of doctrines and traditions of Islamic law in the contemporary age'. (p. 61). Sadly she is absolutely right. However, as Dawoud el-Alami points out in his chapter on 'Jihad', more fundamentalist readings of the Qu'ran and Hadith are possible: 'It would be dishonest, however, to deny that by using the same methods of textual exegesis and Islamic jurisprudence, alternative arguments can be constructed by selecting evidence and opinion to comply with a different agenda. It is entirely possible to put together a case for an aggressive or military *jihad* using many of the same verses and opinions used by those who oppose violence, alongside interpretations of the early history of Islam and the biography of the Prophet'. (p. 73) This is precisely the problem that the centre ground faces.

The complexity of holding fast to the centre comes out in many parts of the book. For instance Michael Lerner says of the God of the Jewish Scriptures: ' ... Yahweh, actually is not a name at all but a concept, the concept of The Force in the Universe that Makes Possible the Transformation From 'that which is' to 'That Which Ought to Be''. (p. 22). Yet for too many people God is an old man with a white beard – rightly to be derided by atheists and serious religionists alike. Such a caricature position will be dismissed by anyone with intelligence who reads Torah in a reflective way and the same can be said for readings of the other religious Scriptures, but the simplistic and naïve reading is preferred by many.

Dawoud el-Alami argues that 'There is no notion in Islam as there is in Christianity of experiencing doubt in order to come to faith. Any expression of doubt, even as an intellectual or spiritual exercise, may be deemed to be the spreading of corruption on the Earth'. (p. 74). Yet without doubt, without critical engagement, fundamentalism is bound to prevail – doubt is the road to wisdom and if it is excluded simplistic and very non-sensible religion is bound to prevail.

These issues matter. There is a truth at stake although the issue of truth in any ultimate sense is not often addressed in the book. One writer who does so is Anantanand Rambachan who explores the problem of the extent to which scripture can be a valid form of knowledge. His chapter seeks to develop criteria by which Hinduism can be seen as sensible religion. 'Valid knowledge, according to Advaita, has the characteristic of corresponding to the nature of reality. It must be in accord with the nature of the object that we seek to know and not be subject to the whims of human preferences. Valid knowledge is object-centred. The source of such valid knowledge is known as a *pramāṇa* and it is a fundamental tenet of Advaita that valid knowledge, religious or secular, can be generated only by a valid source of knowledge. Advaita would concur enthusiastically with Christopher Lewis that religious claims must 'correspond to what is seen as reality'.(p.123). Of course the phrase 'what is seen as reality' can be interpreted in different ways – it can be seen as correspondence to a 'form of life' (as Wittgenstein expressed it) with no reference beyond its own language game or, as I believe Rambachan intends, to correspondence with ultimate reality. If the latter, then one aim of any discussion of religious differences must be to seek to determine to what extent, if at all, different religions do successfully reveal this reality.

Dharmachari Subhuti helpfully identifies the chief failing in Buddhism as laziness (although this could also be applied to all religions) and turns the word 'sensible' round to focus on the use of sense to obscure or even obliterate the struggle that good religion should involve. There is also refreshing honesty about the gap between the ideal of Buddhism and the way it has become practised. Indeed refreshing honesty is, by and large, a feature of this volume. Subhuti concludes: 'There is too much in modern Buddhism that is foolish superstition, harmful to the individual, and of no benefit to humanity as a whole – and in some cases, is actively inhuman'.(p. 148). The same could be said, sadly, for all the major religions as, beneath the dogma and the diversity, may lie what is profound and enduring, but uncovering this and discussing which religions, if any, best manifest that activity of 'uncovering' is not a simple exercise.

It is refreshing to have a contribution from Nokuzola Mndende regarding the perspective of African Traditional Religions (ATR). She says: 'At its best ATR is a profound and sensible response to the divine, to the world around us and to each other'.(p. 191). This might be a worthy sub-title for the book but the key issue is the phrase 'at its best' and providing criteria to determine where the best is to be found is a central challenge.

Finally Dan Cohn-Sherbok provides an excellent summary of the book which emphasises both the importance of the contributions and the difficulty of discovering unity in giving an account of what makes religion sensible. The ethics of religion must be one key element, which he rightly recognises and emphasises.

This book is an important contribution to a debate that is only just beginning but which has never been more important. There is too much bad religion about, too much fundamentalism and intolerance. The voice of moderation and reason has never been more important. Yeats was wrong – the centre can hold and the contributors to the volume are part of this centre. The next stage is to seek to coalesce around a shared vision which can be used to refute the sceptics and atheists and also those who use religion as a weapon of power and oppression. The task is great, the grounds for hope are small but nothing is more important.

Preface

Religion is under attack. Atheists and humanists see believers as deluded or at least misguided. They would like a world clear of religion. Surveying the history of human conflict through the centuries, they maintain that the faithful have been responsible for misery, suffering and bloodshed, outweighing religious learning, culture, beauty and goodness. They see religion as anti-science, in spite of the long involvement of religious people with scientific discovery. This book seeks to challenge these censures. Each of the contributors is a member of a faith tradition, and in different ways they contend that it is possible and vital to distinguish between good and bad religion.

Bad religion, they argue, is narrow and prejudiced, incoherent and insufficiently related to reality. It is fearful of human discovery. Bad religion discourages and restricts human development and fosters conflict and violence. It is too much involved in political struggles and nationalism.

Good religion, however is reasonable and sensitive. It is porous, allowing new influences and discoveries to condition beliefs and activity. Throughout history men and women have, by different routes, responded to the divine. The religious quest is a fundamental dimension of human life and has given people meaning and sustained them through good times and bad. In the modern world good religion is to be fostered, cherished and sustained.

Our intention is not to rate religions against each other, but rather to demonstrate that within each tradition there are thoughtful people, leading ordinary lives in the modern world, lives made richer by reaching out to the divine.

Dan Cohn-Sherbok and Christopher Lewis

Acknowledgements

We are grateful to Peggy Morgan who helped in planning this book. Also to the staff of Ashgate for their patience with its complexities: Sarah Lloyd, David Shervington and Bethan Dixon. Particular thanks are due to Rachel Perham who has worked closely with the authors.

Chapter 1

The Religious Quest

Christopher Lewis

Sensible religion might be seen as dull and revisionist. This book demonstrates that the opposite is true. The courageous and original are, for example, the Muslim woman who works for women's rights, the Jew who campaigns for justice for Palestinians, the Hindu who reckons that 'karma' does not justify a caste system, the Buddhist who opposes violence in Burma. Religion today is often reduced to mere personal experience; sensible religion addresses all that is for it involves both belief and morality.

Religions matter. They matter to the millions of people everywhere who believe in a transcendent realm which reaches out to us and which we can approach in hope and love. Religions also impinge on those who are not believers, for here is a phenomenon, present in every community, that is not going to vanish away. Indeed, as Peter Berger (1999) has pointed out, those who once thought that religions would gradually be swept aside by a tide of secularization have had to revise their views in the face of evidence to the contrary. Some religions have indeed disappeared without much trace (whatever happened to the great organizations set up around worship of Baal and Osiris?), but new ones appear and develop. How and why religions persist is a matter of debate (Hinde, 1999; Newberg et al., 2001), to which should be added an investigation into the reasons behind the phenomenon of secularism. If anything, the spiritual quest seems to have become more pervasive while at the same time being more diverse and eclectic; some societies appear to have become less secular, others more so; all have changed.

This book is not, however, primarily concerned with rise or decline. Instead, its focus is on some of the principal world religions as believed in and practised. It is written by people who are committed believers within particular religions and who also apply critical judgment to traditions to which they belong. This is an age, in the West but also elsewhere in the world, when religious belief and practice are sometimes viewed as at least eccentric or irrational and perhaps as worse than that. The contention in this book is that to follow the religious path is a sensible response to the fact of life in our world, and that the vast majority of religious people are leading ordinary loving lives. The concerns addressed here are therefore related to the philosophical question of whether religious belief, or at least religious belief in some of its forms, is intellectually acceptable: reasonable, justifiable and therefore what Alvin Plantinga (2000), after lengthy and thorough examination, calls 'warranted'.

'Sensible' has a number of connotations. The most common refers to reasonableness in people and beliefs: having beliefs and practices which are both consistent with what is considered to be true and which also correspond to what is seen as reality. Yet there is another meaning, not unrelated to the first, which refers to sensitivity, awareness, being mindful of the views of others and responsive to the world around us, both individually and collectively. It follows, of course, that some beliefs and practices are excluded, but the bracket is wide and contains people who see themselves as radicals and traditionalists, liberals and conservatives. So the aim of this project is to examine the religious quest in some of its principal forms, in order to demonstrate two main features. First that each tradition takes into account the insights both of theology and of other disciplines, together with criticisms made of the particular tradition itself; in other words, that it is a viable, self-critical body of belief and practice, rather than being a self-justifying closed world. Secondly, that the religions can be, and are, followed by rounded and loving people in the modern world, indeed that the traditions enable people to be altruistic as well as fulfilled.

All the authors are well aware that there are aberrations in religious belief and practice as there are in all human activity; in other words, that that there is 'Good and Bad Religion', the title of a book by Peter Vardy (2010). A question worth considering is whether the religious are more prone than others to destructive and deviant behaviour. In favour of that view is the manner in which beliefs and actions gain legitimation and strength by being, as it were, attached to and blessed by supernatural powers. If it is believed that God wills a particular action or conviction, it takes on a new significance, whether it be for good or ill. Religions are ashamed of the evil things which have been done in the name of God.

Evidence against the view that the religious are more prone to destructive behaviour are the wonderful consequences which have flowed from religious belief: compassionate and original people and organizations, art, culture, initiatives for peace. Also, that many of the acts for which religion gets the blame are in fact primarily political and economic with a thin cover of religious justification. Yet nothing can excuse the Crusades or other violence perpetrated in the name of religion.

Aspects of Religion

This book claims that the religious quest, as manifested in different religions, is a reasonable path, as embarked on by millions of people all over the world. Yet when speaking of religion, we are not referring to a uniform system, but to something with a number of dimensions, some more prominent than others, but all shared to a lesser or greater degree by different religions. Ninian Smart (1969) starts his seminal work *The Religious Experience of Mankind* with an examination of the dimensions or aspects of religion. Not surprisingly, religion is hard to define. For example, Buddhism shares in the various aspects and is treated as a religion, yet most strands of Buddhism do not speak of God.

Moreover, people have speculated as to whether communism is a religion, or indeed whether football is. Communism certainly shares some of the features of a religion, for example in having its systems of belief in which people put their faith, its manifestoes, and its founding and heroic figures. Football has its heroes, its rituals involving chants and other singing, and its local clubs. Neither, however, has as its aim communication from and to the divine. Such secular organizations, being rooted in the same world, are bound to share some of the same characteristics as religions.

Basic to religion is an experience or awareness of the divine. If a 'sense of God' (experiences that point to a transcendent realm) did not occur in every society and throughout recorded history, then there would be no religion. Of course, experience may mislead; people claiming to have been abducted by aliens are generally not believed. Yet experience of the divine may call for supporting evidence, for example the corroborating witness of other people (Bowker, 2002: 20–21) and so the transcendent, even when believed to be beyond knowing, may become part of shared understanding.

Beyond experience, what are the main features of religion? The first is prayer, something which many people practise: some perhaps only in desperate straits, but others as a central part of religious observance both alone and together with fellow believers.

> Loose me from sin as from a bond that binds me ... Let not my thread, while I weave song, be severed, nor my work's sum before the time be shattered. Far from me Varuna, remove all danger: accept me graciously, thou holy sovereign ... O mighty Varuna, now and hereafter, even as of old, will we speak forth our worship. (Eliade: 1977. Rig Veda II, 28)

That is a prayer from Hindu writings, showing a mystical longing to reach out to the transcendent and, in this case, for Varuna to forgive and to care for the believer. Mysticism and prayer are natural and universal dimensions of human life; to the believer, the practice of prayer gives assurance of communication with the divine.

A related dimension is ritual and worship in all its different forms. If God is the creator, infinite, loving and perfect, then the hearts of believers go out to God in worship. Prayer and praise go together with music, chant and actions; they are central to the manner in which the religious may experience the transcendent. Indeed it is worship and prayer which define and identify religions, and also which offer something which different religions can do together. Gandhi said that 'More than all, people of all religions should learn to worship together' (Parrinder, 1977: 86).

A consequence of the centrality of worship and prayer are places set apart: temples, synagogues, churches, mosques. The buildings themselves are an important aspect of a religion, expressing the part played by beauty and place in understanding and approaching the divine. Great love and expense are poured into religious buildings although there is, of course, a variety of ways to provide a context in which people may come near to God and at the same time express something of God's nature in the building itself: great soaring temples on the one hand and meeting rooms in converted shops on the other.

More diverse and less open to agreement are the beliefs of the different religions about the nature of the divine and its dealings with human beings and with the world. Religious language is language of a particular kind, trying to express systematically what may be seen as almost impossible to put into words. Religions use myth, stories and narratives, yet also shape beliefs into doctrinal systems. If there are scriptures, then they may be seen as immune to historical and literary criticism on the grounds that they are revealed and therefore sacred. The understanding of scriptures can, however, alter without any change in the authority of those scriptures, so doctrines develop. This doctrinal area is the most problematic both between and within religions, for whereas experience, prayer, worship and ethics may have their similarities, doctrines and the methods by which they are arrived at, often diverge and appear intractable.

A further dimension is that of human behaviour or ethics. I have mentioned violence, but not that evil deeds done in the name of God imply a particular understanding of the divine: only a vicious God could justify many of the things done in God's name. Human behaviour is challenged by an understanding of gods and of the transcendent as essentially benevolent and loving. People running to God to justify their actions collide with love. Religions could be more energetic in disowning some of the actions done and words spoken and written in their name. Having said that, one of the best pieces of evidence in support of the religious quest is the wonderful and self-sacrificial work done, often-unnoticed, by religious people. People are known by their actions, and judgment as to whether a religion is sensible must look with care at actual deeds.

The last, and perhaps the least, of the dimensions or aspects of religion are the representative people, the leaders, the preachers, the administration. A degree of institutional expression of religion is necessary in order for there to be continuity and some sense of order, but there is naturally debate as to quite what significance to give to that expression. Some religious bodies seem to spend an inordinate amount of time and effort on their internal structures, while the rest of the world looks on with a mixture of fascination and horror. Such arrangements are certainly secondary to the essential core of religions, namely the mystical quest, the prayer, the worship, the experience of the infinite and the consequential loving lives.

Aberrations

Sweeping evaluations of a particular religion are always faulty. That is because within each religion, as believed and practised, there is good and bad. So it is necessary with Peter Vardy (2010) to try to spell out the criteria for telling bad from good. Some of the criteria will be ethical such as care for the poor, attitudes to women or the practice of justice. Good religion respects the value and dignity of each human being and has the hope that each person will flourish, becoming transformed, loving and truthful.

Yet religion stretches beyond the individual; the pursuit of peace and justice is an example. Good religion seeks peace and considers that the times when religious people have taken up arms in the name of religion to be betrayals. Of course, like all such matters, to say that is to oversimplify and it is a feature of true religions that they must live among politics and pay what has been called 'the price of existence in the world' (Parrinder, 1977: 63). Books are written on the need, on occasion, to engage in the defense of civilians and of what is seen to be right and true. Suffice it to say that over against the views of some religious extremists, the mainstream of true religion is peace-loving and bent on peace-building, at each level from personal relationships to the world scale. Religions have their violent wings, justified by selective material from their traditions and a sense of grievance and injustice, to the horror of most believers.

A related matter, much discussed in this book, is that of politics in general and nationalism in particular. A religion which grows up endorsing a particular nation against all others may eventually develop and gain maturity, but if it remains nationalistic to the core, then it will not be able to perform a main function of any religion, namely to give meaning and direction to the whole of life both for individuals and for groups. Again, this is a vast subject, but there is a distinction between reasonable national pride on the one hand and aggressive nationalism on the other. In Christian circles there is an essay question which is sometimes set in seminaries: 'Was the conversion of the emperor Constantine of benefit to Christianity?' It is a deliberately challenging question to answer, but at least religions need to be conscious of the arguments which can be marshaled on each side. Those arguing for Constantine's adoption of Christianity as the official religion of the Roman Empire would cite the added influence and opportunities which may come from an understanding of (and involvement in) the ways of politics; the chance to spread a beneficial religious message in a way which would otherwise be impossible; the support gained for glorious art, music, literature and buildings, all of which may have transcendent value; the belief that religions have to make do with life in the 'real world' and that escape is unrealistic.

Those who argue against a Constantinian religion would say that although religions should indeed engage with the world as it is, they should have enough distance to be able to be critical; that the interests of the poor are central to religions and that the world of politics is too much bound up with the rich and powerful; that the temptations of power are too great and should be avoided by those who wish to follow a religious path; that the lessons of history – from Judaism, Hinduism, Christianity, Buddhism, Islam and Sikhism (to name but six!) – lead to the conclusion that direct rule in the name of religion rarely brings justice and good government. The appropriate conclusion is one of balance in the relationship between religion and politics: religion is in the world, but not so bound up with it that it cannot maintain a critical distance.

That raises a question about the religious diaspora. Is a religion likely to be less compromised by powerful political involvement, for example by nationalism, when it is in a minority position in a country other than the one in which it originated? As with many generalizations of this kind, it is hard to come to a clear conclusion. What can be said is that religious groups transposed into an entirely new cultural context and which are not merely vehicles for looking back to the homeland, can and do find new ways of expressing their faith. The debate within Islam about what it means to be a Muslim in a country not ruled by Muslims is an example. Some Jews argue that you can be more truly (and sensibly) a Jew in the diaspora.

Discussion of politics and nationalism leads on to the next factor, which is that good religion lives in the world and, to some degree, affirms it. If a religious group gains its energy and identity from railing against society and living separately from it with a closed membership, it is unlikely to be healthy. To say that may seem to exclude the monastic life, but the evidence does not support such a view. Buddhist monasticism, for example, usually has close contact with its social context through education and prayer; the concerns of the society in which the monasteries are set are known and often energetically expressed. The point here is one which can be put in the language of the sociology of knowledge. Religion exists in a particular social and psychological context. If that context is one of minimum social contact with ideas which challenge those of the group, or indeed of little dialogue with people who do not belong to it, then the group will maintain a view of reality which is generated within it. Study of millenarian and other sects has shown that in a closed world, whether secular or religious, a distinctive and often destructive world-view can be constructed and maintained; what will seem completely implausible outside the closed group will seem plausible within. The situation can be more serious within a religious context as the ideological and physical isolation may be given legitimacy by religious means. Those who have escaped from such groups speak of the immense power used in order to impose meaning on the members. For example, the world may be seen as damned and non-members as corrupt and evil. Good religion abhors indoctrination and respects human freedom.

That point brings us to the set of beliefs held by religions and the criteria whereby they may be held to be reasonable. Many religions have stories and myths which sound strange, but which are seen as helpful guides to being human and as means to an understanding of the basic questions of life: the transitions experienced in human life and death and the 'What am I here for?', 'Who am I?', 'Why me?', 'Why now?' and 'What next?' questions met along the way. This is the point at which the insights of disciplines other than religion/ theology are essential. Theology has always had 'dancing partners', the principal one being philosophy which has tested coherence and checked correspondence with reality, but philosophy has rightly been joined by many others. I will give an example from my own Christian tradition. Back in the 1960s, a book was produced by Christians with the startling title *Objections to Christian Belief*. In it there is a description (MacKinnon et al., 1963: 70–71) of a somewhat medieval scheme of Christian salvation which is worth quoting in full:

It began with an alleged rebellion of Satan against God in which angels fell. By direct acts of God, Adam and Eve were created, apparently as adults, not only innocent but fully righteous. Their descendants were intended to restore the number of the angels depleted by the heavenly revolt. Moved by envy, Satan persuaded our first parents to disobey one absolute command of God, that they were not to obtain knowledge, and so brought about their fall from original righteousness, in consequence of which they transmitted to all their offspring, by natural generation, a corrupted nature wholly inclined to evil, an enfeebled will, and also the guilt of their sin. Thus all mankind lay under the curse of sin both original and actual, justly the object of Divine wrath and destined to damnation. In order to restore his thwarted purpose God sent his Son who, assuming human nature, was born on earth, whereon was wrought the drama of his death and resurrection. Jesus, pure from all defect of original and actual sin, alone fulfilled the conditions of a perfect sacrifice for human sin. By this God's legitimate anger with guilty mankind was appeased and his honour satisfied; he was graciously pleased to accept his Son's sacrifice, enabled to forgive sin, and man was potentially redeemed. The Christian church, a Divine corporation came into being; those baptized into it who by grace persevered in the fulfillment of its commands would be secure in the life to come. From the supernatural life of the church, the world and history derived their meaning and without it would at a last day perish by fire ... The saved were predestined to their salvation by an inscrutable decree of God, not for any merits of their own, but solely for those of Christ. As to the fate of the rest, there were differences of opinion, but it was generally held that they would suffer endless torment in the flames of hell.

It may seem unfair on Christianity to recite such an outline, especially as most of its elements would now be refuted or expressed differently, but all of what is quoted above has at some stage been taught as orthodox, and some is still taught today. Without arguing about every detail, the simple question to ask is: what factors have changed the scheme, so that is now appears embarrassing and inaccurate and why? The answer is that gradually over time, the perception of what it is that Christians believe has altered, not in the essentials of a Christian faith in God seen as he is in Jesus Christ, a faith guided by the Holy Spirit, but rather in the serious matter of the manner in which that faith is worked out and expressed.

The point of quoting the passage is to indicate that numerous insights and disciplines have made the scheme untenable. It is hard to know where to start, but the list of academic disciplines would certainly contain geology, biology, anthropology, psychology, philosophy, the literary-critical and historical study both of the Bible and of the Christian tradition, the study of religions, and then a return to a theological understanding of the teaching of Jesus and, last but not least, our natural informed sense of what is moral and just. To say that does not destroy the Christian faith, but it does show that elements of the faith have to be understood anew: in the light of criticism, the insights of scientific and other disciplines, and a frequent return to the life and teachings of Jesus. Beliefs develop; that does not mean that they have necessarily been compromised or diluted, merely that they have been differently understood and expressed. Textual fundamentalism is a sign of bad religion.

Every religion has a similar intellectual challenge, which it has to face if it is to make its way in the world. For example, in the light of a literary critical reading of the Hebrew and Christian Scriptures, some mythological stories need to be seen in context and interpreted, for if taken literally they cannot be squared with our educated understanding of the world and of human beings: in other words, with what we have discovered (to the best of our ability) to be the case. It follows that good religion is marked by some humility about its doctrinal and other claims.

Meeting 'Other' Religions

When discussing sensible religion, it is crucial to ask what attitude is appropriate in relationships between religions. In this book we are working together to a common brief. That does not mean, however, that 'we are all going the same way', to quote a common saying about religions. Religions have similarities in the sense that they are reaching out to the supernatural and attempting to discover life's meaning in the same world. So they can be compared, for each shares the aspects or dimensions mentioned above and each is likely to have beliefs about the creation of the universe, about birth and death, or about how we should behave to each other and to the natural world. Yet anyone engaged in the study of religions will soon conclude that religions are performing their task quite differently; their methods and routes are distinctive and not susceptible to being put on a route-map, or even less, despite the efforts of William Hocking (1940), to being built into some great composite structure for all. The study of religions will also make us conscious of the fact that no religion is a unitary whole: all have their diversities and divisions, some of which are bitter and have long and complex histories. What then are the options for relations between the religions and between the different parts of them?

In the past, there was the possibility of isolation for religions and therefore of ignorance of each other. That was often accompanied by the belief that 'other' religions were primitive and misguided whereas one's own religion (and particularly the missionary religions of Christianity and Islam) was superior and possessed the absolute truth. Of course, there were two kinds of exceptions to isolation: conflict and cooperation. There are too many examples of religious conflict both within and between religions, often allied to attempted or actual conquest and to religious persecution. Political and religious confidence marched hand in hand and left scars which are long-remembered and which mean that relations between religions will never be easy. The conflicts also explain much of the religious map of the world today. There is no such thing as a religion free of historical and contemporary context: that is the glory and the sorrow of religion: to be not of this world but nevertheless firmly immersed in it.

Yet intolerance and conflict have not been by any means the only rule in the past. The coexistence and cooperation between Muslims, Jews and Christians in Moorish Spain shows that other ways are possible; the inhabitants of Andalucia in the twelfth century would not have agreed that religions are necessarily set against each other. What is more, in the twentieth and twenty-first century major efforts have been made to initiate dialogue between religions.

Today, conflicts and persecution continue, but isolation is no longer a choice in most countries of the world; migration and communications have made the world a different place. Religions confront each other, raising social and cultural questions and also ones of truth: how should they treat each other? Some religions appear to be at ease with such a question, but others have a major theological task to tackle: what precisely do they believe about other religious people or, put in another way, what is one religion's theology of another and therefore of itself in relation to the other? To say 'we are saved and they are damned' or 'there is no truth to be found outside my faith' may have seemed a possible answer in the past, but it is not a plausible response when said living next to deeply spiritual neighbors of another faith.

Indeed proximity may lead to new insights, for it means that ordinary everyday religious practice can be understood and learned from. It was Charles de Foucauld who experienced the devotion of Moroccan Muslims; it was their example which enabled him to see his own Christian faith in a new light. If he had started with an attitude of intolerance, those lessons would never have been taken to heart. Mahatma Gandhi was a faithful Hindu and yet learned much from Jainism and from Christianity, especially about non-violence (Bowker, 2002: 139).

It is significant that most of us are born into the faith to which we adhere: an 'accident' of birth. This fact, that we are where we are, is banal in a sense, but crucial for relations between religions. Arnold Toynbee (1979: 296) puts the point in an extreme form:

> An effective judgment is impossible when one is comparing a religion which has been familiar to one in one's home since one's childhood with a religion which one has learnt to know from outside in later years. One's ancestral religion is

bound to have so much the stronger hold upon one's feelings that one's judgment between this and any other religion cannot be objective.

I would comment that it is not so much 'impossible' as hard to make an effective judgment about another religion. Also that, over against the relativism implied by Toynbee, real dialogue does take place, with significant consequences for mutual understanding and correction. After all, some religions may be 'better' than others when it comes to giving meaning to human existence and they may lead to more admirable and loving consequences.

Yet a modification of Toynbee's view must be taken seriously, especially now that religions are better known and more thoroughly studied than ever before. The extreme position that one religion has every ounce of the truth and that all other religions are sinful, being the work of godless people, is untenable. That should not come as a shock to the religious but rather as a cause for joy: there are other religious people in the world leading exemplary lives in the light of beliefs which have been tried and tested by countless believers and sometimes over thousands of years. To learn that others are not damned should be a reason for rejoicing. These indeed are potential allies in the religious quest over against secular materialism and atheistic humanism.

It does not follow that all religions are equally valid or that one's own faith should be held less faithfully. For a religion may be seen as true (rather than just 'true for me') while recognizing some truths to be found in other religions also. Each religion has its distinguishing marks and there is no reason to lose that distinctiveness although, as has been pointed out above, religions do change and develop, often more than they are prepared to admit. What is implied is a change of direction: away from denigration of the religions and towards dialogue with them (which, if successful, can include criticism) and attention to the incompleteness of the secular world. Good relations between religions require courage and mutual respect.

It follows that it is problematic when missions to religious believers are set up, something in which not all religions are engaged. The true missionaries have always been those who learn the culture, the language and the beliefs of the people among whom they live, treating those beliefs with respect while at the same time wishing to show something of the truths of their own religion. If beliefs are deeply and passionately held and practiced, then it is natural to wish others to be able to share them. In a free society, there is freedom to change one's religion, although conversion will have social and cultural consequences which can be hard for converts and their families.

Relations between different religions, like relations between nations, are often complex and fraught. Yet religions share much and they have the most noble of purposes.

In this first chapter, I have tried to survey the elements of religion and the manner in which (and criteria by which) a claim may be made that religion is 'sensible,' understood in more than one sense. I have also raised the matter of how a religion may relate to 'other' religions, that being one of the important criteria by which a religion may be judged to be sensible. The field is vast and complicated, yet the ever-developing fact of religion deserves serious consideration and an effort at empathy both by those who see themselves as religious and those who do not. What we have gathered here is a committed and thoughtful group of people who see the religious quest as sensible indeed.

Reference List

Berger, P. (1999) *The Desecularisation of the World*, Grand Rapids, MI: Eerdmans.
Bowker, J. (2002) *God: A Brief History*, London: DK Publishing.
Eliade, M. (1977) *From Primitives to Zen*, London: Fount.
Hinde, R. (1999) *Why Gods Persist*, London: Routledge.
Hocking, W. (1940) *Living Religions and a World Faith*, London: Allen & Unwin.
MacKinnon, D., Vidler, A., Williams, H., and Bezzant, J. (1963) *Objections to Christian Belief*, Harmondsworth: Penguin.
Newberg A., D'Aquili, M., and Rause V. (2001) *Why God Won't Go Away*, New York: Ballantine.
Parrinder, G. (1977) *Comparative Religion*, London: Sheldon Press.
Plantinga, A. (2000) *Warranted Christian Belief*, Oxford: Oxford University Press.
Smart, N. (1969) *The Religious Experience of Mankind*, New York: Scribner.
Toynbee, A. (1979) *An Historian's Approach to Religion*, 2nd edition, Oxford: Oxford University Press.
Vardy, P. (2010) *Good and Bad Religion*, London: SCM Press.

Chapter 2

A Sensible Judaism of Love

Michael Lerner

Christopher Lewis invites us to question whether our religious commitments are sensible. In the case of Judaism (and my suspicion is that this may apply to Christianity and Islam as well), there are so many competing strands of the religion that one can only say, 'sometimes yes, sometimes no', depending on which interpretive stream one chooses to identify as 'authentic Judaism' or, more appropriately, the interpretive tradition to which one adheres). Let me explain.

Judaism is the 3,200-year old argument about what Judaism is. At least for the past 2,000 years there have been a multiplicity of answers, reflecting the self-reflective and self-critical tendencies within the Jewish world (sometimes masked as competing interpretations of holy texts). These in turn reflect a larger split in all religions, between a theology of domination (in Judaism I call this Settler Judaism) and a theology of love and generosity (in Judaism I call this An Emancipatory Judaism of Love). The battle between these two is now being fought out in Israel and in the Jewish Diaspora, and in every other religion (and many secular worldviews as well).

It might be comforting to imagine ourselves in a religion where people could bring issues to Moses who could then consult directly with God and give us a definitive statement on what Judaism had to say about subject x, y or z. But Moses, or whoever we think created or received the Torah, passed on to us a document that seemed to rejoice in a plurality of ways of hearing God's voice, and an even larger number of ways of understanding what was at stake in the various commands he or they wrote down.

What seems to have been the guiding light for the composition of the Torah is the principle of inclusion. We can easily imagine there being a variety of stories that the redactor or editor – we can call that person or group 'Moses' or '*Rabbeynu*' (our teacher) – assembled and then tried to put together in a coherent way. Yet too many passages seem to contradict each other in content or underlying approach. There are two creation accounts placed next to each other (Genesis 1–2:4 and Genesis 2:5–Genesis 3), two different accounts of what was heard and by whom at Mount Sinai, and two different views of how to deal with poverty (abolish it through redistribution or live with and ameliorate it). There are passages that tell us to love the stranger and passages that tell us to obliterate the tribes who live in the land of Canaan.

And I could list many other such conflicting approaches in Torah (does God want human beings to eat animals, for example, or is this just a begrudging acceptance of the limits of human consciousness in the period that the Jews received Torah? Or is worship of God through animal sacrifice and at a sanctuary or Temple something that God desires, or is it, as Medieval Jewish philosopher Moses ben Maimon, Maimonides, tells us in *The Guide to the Perplexed* (Friedlander, 1956), a concession to this limited consciousness?

The Hebrew Bible has so many places where alternative worldviews can be viewed as in contention with each other that the rabbis who developed the Talmud, the classic record of the debates that emerged among the rabbis from roughly 200 BCE to 600 CE, needed an explanatory framework which gave them the legitimacy to try to resolve at least those conflicts that needed resolution in order to carry on a society.

That framework was to claim that on Mt. Sinai there had really been two revelations, one the written Torah, the second the Oral Torah which was taught by God to Moses and then passed on by Moses to Joshua, from Joshua to the Judges, from the Judges to the Prophets, and from the Prophets to the rabbis themselves who were shaping the Talmud. Each decision of the ancient high court, the Sanhedrin, was seen as manifesting this Oral Torah, and so the subsequent decision of the rabbis and sages whose discussions went on to comment on the first set of such decisions written down in the Mishna (circa 200 CE) and then further elaborated and debated in the commentary on the Mishnah known as the Gemara (both of which together became the Talmud). But wait, there were two Talmuds, a Talmud developed by the rabbis who remained in Judea even after the forcible expulsion or enslavement of most of the Jews who lived there after the unsuccessful rebellions against Rome 67–70 CE and 132–135 CE, and the other what became known as the Bavli (the Babylonian Talmud) composed by the rabbis and sages who were shaping the religious life of the large Jewish population that developed in Babylonia and Persia.

How did the rabbis deal with the problem of an Oral Torah that had more than one view expressed? By legitimating plurality of interpretations. There are two famous stories about this in the rabbinic literature (Babylonian Talmud: Eruvin, 13b; Bava Metzia, 59b). One recounts the struggle roughly around the time of Jesus between the Mishnaic school of Hillel and the school of Shamai. On what seemed like a wide variety of legal issues, these two schools clashed repeatedly. So much so, the story goes, that finally they appealed to God directly, asking for guidance about which view was in accord with God's will. Suddenly a voice sounded out from the heavens to 'settle' the dispute. It said, 'This one and this one are both the words of the living God'. And if someone were to have said, 'but they can't both be the words of God', then in the spirit of this vision of God's law, God would probably have responded, 'and you who raises that objection, you are also right'.

Indeed, the Talmud is famous for following debates between different sages, often attempting to reconstruct the logic of previous generations of sages and then assessing those views, and this process going on and on and on, and then finally, the debate ends with the word *Teyku*, which roughly means, 'this difficult issue will be resolved when Elijah the prophet returns to clear up all the conceptual difficulties in this text'. Elijah, of course, was said to be returning when he would have the task of announcing the coming of the Messiah, which was not presumed to be happening in one's own lifetime by the majority of Jews who had had rather unhappy experiences with the many supposed messiahs of ancient Judea, none of whom had produced the world in which nation would no longer lift up sword against nation, the swords would be melted into ploughshares, and the lion would lie down with the goat and peace would prevail and God would reign on earth.

A second story recounts a debate between one of the greatest Mishnaic scholars, Rabbi Eliezer, and his fellow rabbis in the period before the second revolt against Roman rule. Debating an obscure point of whether a certain pot was kosher or not kosher, the rabbis adopted the principle that the decision should go according to the position adopted by the majority of sages. Rabbi Eliezer refused to accept that notion in this case, and invoked 'outside' support. 'If I am right', he claimed, 'let the walls of this room bend in' and sure enough, that's what they did. The rabbis were not impressed. 'If I am right', he went on, 'let the trees begin to dance', and so they did, but the rabbis were not impressed. Finally, in desperation, he said, 'if I am right, let God say so', and a voice came from heaven so all could hear saying, 'the law is according to Rabbi Eliezer', but the rabbis still refused to be moved. 'We do not make judgments on the basis of heavenly voices', they said, and cited a verse in the Torah in which God tells Moses about Torah that someday people may ask who will ascend to heaven after Moses to get God's teachings, but God responds 'It is not in heaven, but in your hands to do it'. It is not in heaven, they said, to find out the message of the Torah. In fact, they were claiming, as Rabbi David Hartman pointed out in the lectures I attended that he gave at Hebrew University in 1984, and discussed throughout his book *A Living Covenant* (1998), the dignity of human beings enabled us to be recipients of the Oral Torah and to be actually receiving Torah in the very process of studying and debating the tradition as it had developed through a hundred generations of scholars.

Commenting on this incredible assertion of human rights to re-understand and reshape the tradition in accord with how the scholars in each generation re-understand it, Hartman goes on to discuss the Gemara's coda to this story: an encounter (possibly in heaven) between one of the rabbis and the Prophet Elijah who is asked about God's reaction, and is told that God said, 'My children have overcome/ transcended/ been-victorious over Me' (Babylonian Talmud, Bava Metzia, 59b).

This openness is a startling rebuke to the tendency in any system of beliefs for the dominant belief to become an orthodoxy which cannot be changed. But it would be mistaken to deny that eventually such orthodoxies did in fact develop in the Jewish world. Though for many hundreds of years, some would argue for at least 2,000 years, this kind of intellectual openness characterized at least part of the Jewish religious world, it is also undeniable that rigidity in Jewish life, as in any belief system, including, if Thomas Kuhn's famous study *The Structure of Scientific Revolutions* (1962) is to be credited, in the world of Western science, has frequently come to the fore and created limits on intellectual, spiritual, aesthetic and/or religious creativity. Yet Judaism has had within it the possibility of openness to rational discussion that has frequently led to new and even revolutionary interpretations and evolutions of the law and the struggle to understand who God is and what we are to do with our sense of awe at the universe that have made for an open-ended possibility that the radicalism of one generation can rather quickly become the orthodoxy of a subsequent generation, which then itself generates new attempts to transcend.

But transcend and include. Very often in Jewish communities the views, prayers, religious practices, and legal decisions are not thrown out but retained, studied, engaged with, and remain part of what can best be described as a conversation among the generations, even if in practice some of the positions of the past have largely been discarded.

It is my contention, however, that there is a subset of debates that take place in the Jewish world that have a very different meaning today than they ever had in the past. The existence of Jewish economic and political power, as manifested first and foremost in the State of Israel, calls for a resolution that is not equally open to both views.

Actually, the debate I have in mind is not one which originated in the Jewish people or confined to it. For thousands of years, probably as long as the emergence of patriarchy and class societies as the last Ice Age receded and human being began to develop agriculture, cities and weapons of war, there has been an active debate about the nature of human beings, and how best to organize societies in accord with that nature.

I describe this debate as having two polar opposite views. On the one hand, let us call it the Right Hand (because in the Hebrew Bible there are references to God's right hand being adorned in power), we have the view that human beings are thrown into this world by ourselves, and quickly find ourselves surrounded by others who seek domination and control over us in order to maximize their power, control and access to the material goodies of the world (land, wealth, food, water, comforts of life, sex, etc.). Human beings, on this account, naturally want to have this power, control and access, and will resort to whatever means they can develop to get these, and in the course of so doing, because all of these are relatively scarce compared to the number of people alive at any given moment, they will seek to dominate or manipulate you to become their agents or at least to subordinate you so that you do not interfere with their quest for these goodies.

The Right Hand view is a view that says people will naturally seek power and domination, and then the world will thus naturally be a struggle of all against all, though later formulations have acknowledged the advantage of creating families, clans, and even nation states that could serve to privilege one group or another over other groups in their attempt to have control and access to the goods they seek. Yet the structure of this struggle continues: some group will seek domination and control, so it is only rational that each individual do as much as s/he can to achieve power and control both as an individual or as part of a group, realizing that if you do not succeed some other person and/or group will and will exercise power over you to achieve their goals.

In short, people will seek to dominate and control you unless you get the jump on them, and use your advantage to maximize your own ability to get power and access to the desired goodies.

I call this the worldview of domination and fear of the other. Domination can be exercised in various ways. In much of human history that dominance has taken the form of violence and wars which continue to this day, sometimes world wars with huge global devastation, sometimes with low-intensity struggles like those that increasingly use drones and cyber-weapons to fight the fight. But in the past few hundred years other forms of domination have emerged which can often be just as powerful: economic domination, whether in the form of colonialism, imperialism, or the more subtle forms of globalization of 'power over' others through corporate shaping of global marketplaces; cultural domination as movies, television, computers, and other forms of communication convey the messages of the dominant powers while effectively silencing or marginalizing those who seek a different kind of world; or even 'diplomacy' when big powers with powerful weapons are able to participate in international institutions, shape political associations and pacts, and otherwise impose their will without the use of force. All these have the same goal: for some 'us' to get its way over some 'them' with the outcome being an inequality of power and access to desired resources or other goodies.

Within this worldview, fear of the other and the striving to ensure 'homeland security' become central determinants of domestic and foreign policy. The others are a threat who almost certainly will take away from you whatever comforts and pleasures you have secured for yourself unless you have the ability to take away from them more than they can get from you. So the worldview of 'domination' and 'power over' is also a worldview of constant fear and agitation.

On the other hand, let us call it the Left Hand, we have a different conception of human beings and life itself. Instead of seeing human beings as thrown into the world by ourselves, it recognizes human beings as coming into the world through a mother, and the first experience of human beings is that of being nurtured prenatally in the womb, and then after birth by the breast or other source of food supplied by a 'mothering other' (could be a man or an adoptive parent) who is caring for the child without having a reasonable expectation of a good recompense for her time and energy put into this child, but rather doing it out of love for this newborn infant.

So for the first few years of life every child receives caring that is 'good enough' to allow that child to physically, emotionally and spiritually thrive. Of course, psychologists often uncover various ways in which even in the early years children have been subjected to various distortions from their parents or from the larger environment. Yet the base line of caring and support is, for most children on the planet, sufficient for them to have a strong experience of being cared for and loved.

It is this experience which provides the foundation for a worldview of love, kindness and generosity. This Left Hand view sees human beings as fundamentally desiring loving connections with others, and thriving the more that their lives are suffused with this love. Human beings can achieve their goals best when they learn how to treat each other with love, compassion, generosity of spirit, and true affirmation of what they find lovable about others.

Eventually, children face another aspect of the world: that there is a need to act upon it to grow food, provide clothing, build shelter, and in other ways meet some of their basic needs. Living in family networks in which their basic needs were first met, they slowly come to recognize that they too must contribute in some way to the larger family and tribe or community enterprises that make it possible for these networks to provide love and caring and support in the first few years of life. So children are taught the necessary skills to be part of that larger enterprise. They are taught to see the world around them as a resource which can be drawn upon to fill their own and their family's or tribe's or community's material needs.

Yet this earlier foundation of love and caring makes it possible for children to respond to the not only in a narrow utilitarian way, but also with an aliveness to the miraculous beauty and mystery of all creation. So even as they must learn the techniques of exercising some degree of mastery over the material world, many children retain and develop their own sense of awe, wonder and radical amazement at the grandeur of nature and the universe. And this combination of love and the experience of awe and wonder that combines to produce a fundamental spiritual experience that, however differently it is languaged and how many different forms it is channeled, is a near universal aspect of early childhood experience, and becomes one of the most precious experiences that adults seek to return to over and over again in their lives. They developed rituals, celebrations, songs, dances, and community rites to celebrate the universe, to find forms and language to explain to themselves how this incredible universe came into being and what they could do to express the joy and pleasure that they had received through the many gifts the universe had given them. They often tied their spiritual celebrations to the regular cycles of nature, including solar and lunar cycles, and they frequently personalized different aspects of nature by imagining 'gods' who either were the forces or managed the forces of nature.

No wonder, then, that when patriarchal and class elites emerged in the past 10,000 years they often sought to appropriate the loving and spiritual life of humanity and associate it with their own project. They appropriated the pre-existing spiritual consciousness and celebrations into forms that were more consistent with the structure of social and economic domination that were developing. Gods were seen as fighting with each other, and seeking power over each other as well as power over the earth and human beings. The Right Hand conception of the world began to develop in ways that challenged the more love-oriented understandings that permeated the spiritual consciousness. And religions emerged which served the interests of the powerful precisely to the extent that they justified social and economic inequalities and patriarchal arrangements.

Over the course of thousands of years, religions were successful in appropriating earlier forms of spiritual experience and the deep loving and generosity foundations of human life and reconceptualizing reality so that the actual inequalities of class and patriarchal societies were seen as 'natural' and even sanctified by existing religious configurations.

And yet, the Left Hand consciousness, the love and generosity understanding of human reality, was still there, still being experienced, and still being expressed even in the context of religious forms which seemed to pull for a Right hand consciousness in which power over other and domination seemed based in reality as well, the reality of class and patriarchal societies with their inevitable conflicts, wars and struggles.

It is my contention that for at least the last several thousand years most people on the planet have heard versions of 'reality' that are based in the Right Hand, domination, fear and power over worldviews as well as versions of 'reality' based in the Left Hand love and generosity world view, and that most people are at any given moment in their lives someplace on a continuum between these two perspectives, always having a part of their understanding that has been shaped by each of these contending perspectives. And to the extent that they approach any given circumstance or human interaction from the standpoint of the Right Hand of fear and domination they will help elicit from others that part of the others' consciousness which believes that the world is basically fearful and that the best way to protect themselves is through domination and control over others, and conversely to the extent that they approach any such reality or relationship with the Left Hand of love and generosity they will help elicit form others that part the others' consciousness which believes in the possibility of a world based on love and generosity. Of course, the deeper someone is into fear and domination, the harder it will be for others who are into love and generosity to '*break on through to the other side*' (in the words of the song by The Doors), but such breakthroughs do happen and can happen for many human beings if the circumstances and the invitation to a higher level of trust and generosity seem real and inviting enough.

Yet for most human beings, most of the time, we have both voices in our own heads, and whichever is predominant at any given moment will shape how we understand our own experience. To the extent, for example, that we are more in fear and more aligned with the voices of 'power over' and domination in our own consciousness, the more we will respond to the teachers, preachers, artists, novelists, political leaders, etc., who preach fear and domination. They will seem the most profound when they base themselves on view of human nature that preach the inevitability of competition and domination and power over as essential to the nature of human beings. Conversely, when the voices in our own consciousness that speak of hope for a more loving world are in the ascendency, we will be more likely to respond to those political leaders, religious leaders, cultural creators, etc., whose message is based on the worldview of love and generosity.

Because every human creation, every piece of art, literature, religion, social science, psychology, social movement reflects the internal oscillation between these two ways of perceiving the world, do not be surprised if each of them has elements or holy texts or revered teachers who seem to reflect more of one side or the other of the continuum between the Left Hand and Right Hand views of human reality. It is rarely the case that any given human being is fully the embodiment of one view or the other; most have moments in which we are closer to fear and the domination worldview, and moments in which we are closer to the love and generosity worldview.

And so it is with Judaism. If we look at our Torah we will see this oscillation within the founding texts and within the Talmud, and sometimes within the same teacher, scholar or prophet. So when the Torah tells us to love our neighbour as ourselves and then repeatedly instructs us to care for the stranger (the Other), the poor, the homeless, the immigrants, the widow, the orphan and through those instructions to care for all the powerless and love them, we get a very sensible religious voice that is a reflection of the spirituality and loving energy that has been central to most of the religious and spiritual traditions of the human race.

This gives rise to what I would call an Emancipatory Judaism of love. When God's voice is received by Moses or the Israelites or by those who composed the story a thousand years later, it is received as a voice challenging existing systems of domination.

Patriarchy and class society has taught that the social world, like the natural world, is based on a kind of natural inevitability, so that existing social arrangements are part of the fabric of the universe in the same way that the sun becoming stronger in the summers and weaker in the winters or the moon in its various phases are part of that same fabric. Just as you wouldn't seek to change the way the sun works or the way the moon works, you would be crazy to think you could change the existing distributions of wealth and power in class and patriarchal societies.

Judaism enters the world with a very different and revolutionary message: that the way things are in the social world are not fixed, and that the spiritual energies of the universe that have been previously understood as manifestations of many gods, often at war with each other, are really part of the One God who is a force of transformation. The cruelty of slavery, and indeed of all other forms of domination, are not the products of nature, but the distorted creations of human beings, and the God of the universe is the Force that makes possible the overcoming of those distortions.

Indeed, that God is named YHVH, where HVH is the Hebrew for the present, and when you put a Y before the root of a Hebrew verb it indicates future tense, so what the King James mistakenly translated as Jehovah and now in polite circles is referred to a Yahweh, actually is not a name at all but a concept, the concept of The Force in the Universe that Makes Possible the Transformation From 'that which is' to 'That Which Ought to Be'. God is that about the universe which makes possible the overcoming of the 'repetition compulsion' (the tendency to pass on from generation to generation the distortions that have been passed on to you), God is the Force that makes it possible to pass on to others the love and generosity that others deserve because they, like you, have been created in God's image and deserve hence to be treated as part of God. The Torah tries to convey that when it has Moses ask God for God's name, and God replies '*ehyeh asher ehyeh*' (Exodus 3: 14) which the King James mistranslates as 'I Am Who I Am' but which actually means 'I Will Be Whom I Will Be', i.e. I am not some part of the furniture of the universe, but rather 'I am the possibility of possibility, the Force that makes possible building a world of love and generosity to replace the slavery and oppression that exists in this world – and which you now will see through My act of inspiring you to liberate yourselves from Egypt is not a fixed reality like the seasons but a constructed reality which can and must be changed'.

This is what it means to be a God of love: to insist that the world can be based on love and that the task of God's followers is to build that world.

Yet it should be no surprise that Moses (or the Moses group or *Rabeynu*) also heard God talking in a very much more fear-oriented, punitive, and non-loving way. At those moments we get what I call Settler Judaism, a way of hearing God's voice which tells the people that they have the right and the obligation to God to dominate and then wipe out the inhabitants of the land which God is promising to them. This is when the Right Hand of fear and 'power over' shapes how God's voice is heard, and results in a murderous consciousness in which everything we do to others is justified.

True, the hearing of this voice of power over comes easiest to those who have been previously brutalized and oppressed. The former slaves will pass on to others the cruelty that has been inflicted upon them. This too is part of the human experience, though it can be combated because everyone also has within them the voice of love and generosity.

And so, Judaism itself has developed with both voices, and with both ways of hearing God's voice, both ways of interpreting Torah, both ways of developing theologies and commentaries, rituals, and observances. It is pointless to claim that the love-oriented voice is 'the true voice of God' and the domination-oriented voice is 'merely a distortion'. How we hear God's voice, and how any religion develops, is always a reflection of the capacities of the human beings who are doing the hearing, writing down what God has taught them as best they can hear it!!

So Judaism is the 3,200-year-old struggle about what Judaism is, and a significant part of that struggle has been shaped by the degree to which the Jewish people, its scholars and sages, its prophets and rabbis, are open to an Emancipatory Judaism of Love or can only hear Judaism through the framework of Settler Judaism, a Judaism of fear and domination.

Needless to say, which view predominates among Jews is not only a product of our internal struggles and our own personal spiritual lives. External reality has played a significant role. To the extent that the Jewish people have experienced some 1,700 years of Christian (and to a lesser but not negligible extent, Muslim) oppression, culminating in the Holocaust in which one out of every three Jews alive on the planet at the time was murdered, the post-traumatic stress disorder, which I explore more fully in my book *Embracing Israel/Palestine* (2012), has predisposed the post-Holocaust majority of Jews to embrace a Right Hand of 'power over' and fear mentality that is embodied in the present policies of the state that calls itself 'the Jewish state'. Synagogues around the world pray for that state, pray for the military victories of its army, and de facto embrace a Settler Judaism. This is a tragic development, not only in marginalizing the voices of love for the other in Judaism, but in creating an identity for Judaism that cannot win over the coming generations of young Jews, and is simultaneously building a deep anger at the Jewish people which may yet explode in horrific ways in the twenty-first century.

Yet there is a growing renewal movement in Judaism which will continue to hear God's voice in a different way, and is de facto, though not yet self-consciously, building a contemporary version of the Emancipatory Judaism of Love that has always been a significant strain in Jewish theology and the actual practice of the Jewish people.

It is this tendency within Judaism that I believe to be the sensible religion this book addresses. And it is my belief that such tendencies exist in all of the major religions, though in almost all of them those tendencies are not yet fully developed and hegemonic. Indeed, I have been involved in creating an interfaith Network of Spiritual Progressives so that the Left Hand love and generosity oriented people in every religious community and every spiritual community (including those that do not embrace a god) could build a movement together that would strengthen the voices and prospects of the emancipatory and love-oriented in each of these communities. This is not an attempt to undermine the uniqueness of each religious or spiritual path, but only to give the love and generosity forces in each community a way to strategize with those same forces in other communities, help each other, and receive love and nurturance from each other. Facing the environmental crises of the twenty-first century, there is little time left for the various struggles between religious communities, and the Network of Spiritual Progressives [www.spiritualprogressives.org] is creating a way for those in each community to not only continue to be the voice of 'sensible religion' within their own spheres, but to align with the sensible religious people in all other spheres so that they can unite to develop love-and-generosity-oriented policies to save the planet from destruction. So, it seems to me appropriate to end this chapter with a plea that all the sensible people in all the religious and spiritual communities unite, not only for mutual support, but to adopt campaigns to end global poverty, to end wars and oppression, and the build a world safe for love and generosity. And I welcome the readers of this book to go to that website and/or to be in direct contact with me as we move this effort forward.

Reference List

The Talmud, The Steinsaltz Edition, Tractate Bava Metzia, New York: Random House.

Hartman, David (1998) *A Living Covenant: The Innovative Spirit in Traditional Judaism*, Woodstock, VT: Jewish Lights.

Kuhn, Thomas (1962) *The Structure of Scientific Revolutions*, Chicago, IL, and London: University of Chicago Press.

Lerner, Michael (1995) *Jewish Renewal: A Path to Healing and Transformation*, New York: Harper Perennial.

Lerner, Michael (1996) *The Left Hand of God*, San Francisco, CA: HarperSanFrancisco.

Lerner, Michael (2012) *Embracing Israel/Palestine*, Berkeley, CA: Tikkun Books.

Maimonides, Moses (1956) *The Guide for the Perplexed*, translated by M. Friedlander, New York: Dover Publications.

Chapter 3

Judaism's Critique of Idolatry and the Beginning of Liberative Religion

Melissa Raphael

For any student of religion influenced, as I have been, by Rudolf Otto, religion is not religion without its numinous, non-rational element that cannot, finally, be subsumed into any other category of experience or knowledge (Otto, 1923: 1–30). Religion is more than the performance or narration of an elaborate ethic. It is more than a set of propositions about the world that can be justified by reference to values, goods or truths more or less external to its own revelation or scheme. Although I readily subscribe to the broad aims of the present volume in defending some ways of being religious and not others, and it seems obvious that some religions are more profound, eirenic and generally satisfactory than others, I am not persuaded that human beings with finite powers of understanding can ultimately decide which religionists' truth claims about supra-mundane realities are warranted and which are not. And even moral arbitration can be difficult: all religionists think their beliefs and practices are benign, even if some of the contributors to this book might think certain sorts of belief and practice are not.

Nonetheless, I have little doubt that Christopher Lewis is right, in Chapter 1 of this book, to correlate sensible religion with benign religion. It is not to reduce religion to something merely reasonable, temperate, and easily believable to claim that sensible religion can be distinguished from toxic or false religion by attending to its historical effects on people and polities. Good religion is indeed sensible of its divinely ordained obligation to secure peace and flourishing in society and the natural environment. Good religion's developed sense of the sacred makes it morally sensible of the need to protect the dignity of all creatures regardless of their difference, and aesthetically sensible to the beauty of the world as a creation that must not be desecrated by moral and material ugliness. Sensible to the dangers of hubris, good religion is also self-critical and knows the limits of its power and knowledge.

This chapter will seek to demonstrate that all Judaism's denominations (other than, perhaps, those more sectarian reaches of the ultra-Orthodox Haredi community, though even these I consider to be at least well-intentioned) are committed contributors to the moral and rational goods outlined by Christopher Lewis at the beginning of this book. Indeed, it would be more than possible to respond to the charge of some of religion's recent 'cultured despisers' (to borrow the subtitle of Friedrich Schleiermacher's *On Religion*) that religion is little more than the surrender of the moral and rational will to pernicious nonsense by offering a broad illustrative ethical and historical defense of both various types of Judaism. The present chapter could readily point out how even illiberal forms of Judaism are conducive to a well-regulated life that is attentive to the needs and interests of the vulnerable, careful to limit the causes and effects of conflict, and universalist in its commitment to the flourishing of human beings, animals and the natural environment. But I will instead focus on something at once narrower and more foundational: Judaism's cross-denominational ban on idolatry. It is this that I suggest provides some of the earliest and most enduring grounds of the struggle for freedom from tyranny of all kinds, including that of absolutist, fanatical religion that has elevated its own conditioned interests to the status of ultimate, unconditioned truths and orders to which all others must submit.

The avoidance and criticism of idolatry (*avodah zarah* – literally, the worship of alien things) is widely considered to be Judaism's defining moment. The rabbinic literature regards the repudiation of idolatry as encapsulating the whole Torah: 'Whosoever denies idols is called a Jew' (BT Megilah 13). While it might be the case that the rabbinic literature has a tendency to make inflated claims for the centrality of a given commandment when one or another pillar of Jewish thought is feared to be under threat, the prohibition of idolatry remains one of only three negative commandments with regard to which a Jew is required to give up her or his life rather than violate.

Modern Judaism, seeking to distance itself from the ancient forms of the Jewish ban on idols that effectively weaken or break Jewish social connections with other cultures, has celebrated the critique of idols as its most important contribution to world culture. As Kenneth Seeskin puts it in his study of the modern struggle against idolatry, 'the litmus test for being a Jew is seeing things in the created order for what they are: natural objects of finite value and duration', (1995: 20). If that is so, then the prohibition of idols ensures that all historical, natural objects, ideas and traditions – including Judaism itself – cannot assume absolute power but remain self-critical and self-revising. That commanded humility is precisely Judaism's inbuilt mechanism for preventing the bigotry and supremacism of which religion has in recent years been, time and again, accused (e.g. Dawkins, 2006: 317–48).

For it is the posture of religious humility – of standing before, and under the judgment of, the *mysterium tremendum* – that, in contrast to secular hubris, constitutes a primary safeguard against absolutist human ideas and systems that pretend to unconditioned power and limitless duration and that concede nothing to the contesting thought and experience of the other.

Michael Lerner begins his contribution to the present volume by noting that Judaism makes no greater claim to knowledge than being 'the 3200 year old argument about what Judaism is.' His observation about Judaism reflects that of Christopher Lewis who, in his Introduction to the present volume, notes of all 'good religion' that it is 'marked by some humility about its doctrinal and other claims.' This chapter argues that Judaism is indicative of 'good religion' in so far as it is a counter-idolatrous religion. Granted, Orthodoxy cannot abrogate the basic terms of biblical revelation, but even Orthodox Jews' interpretation of the Hebrew Bible forms a self-revising discursive tradition that maintains first the freedom of God and consequently that of humanity from a variety of absolutist captivities that would coerce them into a fixed idea or projection controlled by those claiming the sole right to their interpretation and dispensation. Judaism is an instance of 'good religion' precisely because it understands itself as a cross-generational argument: the practical outworking of an intellectual engagement with revelation in history. Judaism's being a heated debate (if, like all other theistic religions, one that is traditionally conducted almost exclusively between men) ensures that it produces student/practitioners from the most liberal to the most orthodox communities who both revere their teachers and refuse to defer to them.

Sensible, then, of the limits of its knowledge, authority and power, it is as an argumentative process that Judaism adheres to its own foundational commandment to worship God alone, not a humanly created idol of God in the image of the human in God's place (Ex. 20:3–6; Dt. 5:7–10). Judaism is anti-authoritarian because it rejects any power that is self-appointing: 'By me kings reign and rulers issue decrees that are just; by me princes govern, and nobles – all who rule on earth' (Pr. 8:15–16). Although it is undoubtedly the case that parts of the contemporary Jewish community make claims for their own normativity and authenticity and too readily dismiss the Jewishness of the rest, it is as an argumentative process that Judaism properly remains open to interruptive revelation rather than being an object defined and owned by those who claim to be its leaders. In other words, to claim that Judaism is a reasonable path is to say that it is spiritually and intellectually committed to the application of critical judgment to its own tradition as much or more than to anyone else's. The tradition is not permitted to compete with God; cannot be 'in-stead' of God, because it cannot invent or make images of any other gods before God.

Of course, it cannot be denied that, at least at first glance, any ban on idols seems to be the very cause and sign of religious intolerance: an at least implicit and sometimes physical attack on objects, ideas, and values that other people hold sacred. The association of religious discourse on idols with antiquated illiberalisms might explain why, according to Seeskin (1995: 9–10), contemporary young Jews from even quite conservative backgrounds are almost oblivious of this 'single most important feature' of their own tradition. 'Idolatry' is an inherently pejorative, derogatory term: a charge that, to contemporary ears, has the ring of defamation of religious character and cultural vandalism and intra or inter-religious hostility to anyone's beliefs but one's own. Any religionist should be wary of proposing that idol-breaking protects religious freedom. After all, Jewish identity, not unlike that of other dispensations, emerged in ways that included the destruction of existing Canaanite space, memory and identity. The biblical narrative seems to legitimate assaults of memory and identity that might be considered genocidal: 'This is what you are to do to them: Break down their altars, smash their sacred stones, cut down their Asherah poles and burn their idols in the fire' (Dt. 7:5; cf. Ex. 34:14 and elsewhere).

But by as early as the third century of the Common Era, the rabbis had recognized that not since the beginning of the Second Temple period had Jews been drawn to offer service (*avodah*) to foreign (*zara*) gods: like the prophets, the rabbis attribute no actual substance or power to idols. The Mishnah does not criticize pagans (Romans) for mistakenly adoring gods that Jews now believed to be merely fictive, but rather certain immoral practices attending or licensed by that worship. Contemporary Jews only rarely invoke the *halakhot* or laws relating to *avodah zarah*, and then only by the most Orthodox, usually to proscribe the use of non-Jewish symbols in Jewish environments and legislate the use of three-dimensional figures of the human form such as dolls for children or mannequins in shop windows. Islam has been spared the charge of idolatry altogether. Christianity has generally been judged to be idolatrous only when embraced by a Jew – though not by a Christian – and although Hinduism was once unanimously regarded as idolatrous, it has more recently been widely recognized that the *devataas* are worshipped as manifestations of the one Supreme Being, not as idols in their own right.

In short, the destruction of idols as an act of conquest of the land and as a means of preserving Jewish ethnic identity in diaspora have, by virtue of historical necessity and ethical evolution, long given way to an insistence, arising in medieval Jewish philosophy, that idolatry is a cognitive, not a cultic problem. Idolatry is a sign and act of alienation from God as creator and redeemer: a denial or forgetting that a human being is the creation of God, not the other way round. If idolatry is captivity to a harmful idea and its political dispensation, then the breaking of idols is not so much the smashing of something that is wrongfully precious to another, but the possibility of liberation: the cracking open of a mind-forged manacle or *kelipah* (the term Jewish mystics use to refer the impure shell or husk that imprisons holiness).

It is this account of idolatry as an originary psychological alienation by which a religio-political regime depletes the will and imagination by replacing God or the self with oppressive fictive creatures (see further Margalit and Halbertal, 1992: 6) that can prevent the promotion of ideas dangerously beyond the proper reach and limit of their power. The Jewish (and other Abrahamic religions') prohibition of idols also, necessarily, prohibits glorifying religious traditions, texts, and leaders that pretend to absolute power and deny their self-inventedness while excluding all non-elite others' experience from the naming of ultimate value.

If idols are the media or forms by which we are taken into the cognitive and political captivity of false ideas, then the prohibition of idolatry is not essentially repressive but liberative. The criticism of persons or ideas that are placed beyond criticism as if they were divine is not an attack on 'heretics' or 'infidels' but begins with any system (including one's own religion) that may have closed its borders to dissent.

Judaism and the Liberation of God

As long ago as the twelfth century, Maimonides, the towering intellect of medieval Jewish thought, knew that the power of an idol resides in the human mind, not in the matter – the gold, silver, stone or wood – it may be formed from. He observed that idols are worshipped not as substantial realities in themselves but as intermediaries between themselves and God, where the medium eventually supplants God by substitution (Maimonides, trans. Pines, 1963, I: 36; Mishneh Torah, Laws on Idolatry 1: 1–2). In particular, Maimonides rejected anthropomorphic verbal images of God – even the metaphors, idioms, and homonyms in the Hebrew Bible – on the grounds that they can become so literal or concrete a medium as to take the place of God as effectively as any visual image. For Maimonides, idolatry is not so much about a man bowing to a fabricated God as his believing in a God whom he has conceived himself, in his own mind. When an idea of God includes the notion that God is subject to any bodily emotions, let alone embodiment, its proponent becomes what Maimonides considers an adversary of God. It is, he argues, so impermissible and, indeed, impossible, to attribute a bounded body and its positive attributes to God that he goes so far as to say that there is no representable likeness between God and humanity. To that extent, we must be enraptured, 'love-sick,' for a God who is wholly other even to the point of non-relation: 'the relation between us and God, may He be exalted, is considered to be non-existent' (Maimonides, 1963, 1: 56).

This is why, even if he mourns idolatry as the forgetting of God (Mishneh Torah, Laws of Idolatry, 1: 2) Maimonides' own counter-idolatrous apophatic or 'negative' theology in *The Guide* also requires that we, in some sense, forget God: forget everything we imagine we know about God (including the Torah's anthropomorphic imagining of God). Instead, he believes that an educated mind will provide sufficient knowledge of the created world and the commandments by which to love God, and that such love is properly a love for nothing but the God before God, and the God after God, the One before whom we must fall silent.

Here, Judaism is prevented a priori from over-reaching its theological authority. To claim to know the mind of God would be to claim oneself to be of the same genus of God – who has no genus. God cannot be subsumed under any wider concept as 'man' is subsumed under 'animal' (Maimonides, 1963, 1: 52). Were God to fall under a genus, there would be something prior to or more inclusive than God, which is impossible. Without a genus, it may be difficult to envisage divine–human relationality, but at least there is no possibility of defining God and thus no possibility of limiting God: subjecting God to the conditions of finitude by the operation of the human mind.

The ontological separation of God and the human may produce as many theological problems as it solves, but, by protecting the holiness of God above the human relationship with God, Maimonides does what good religionists must do, which is to serve the freedom of God – and thereby the freedom of the human – by preserving God from the risk of any human coup against God's being and power. It is, after all, the arrogation and abuse of absolute power over others that destroys the possibility of any relationship at all – whether between people or between people and God.

It is surely in the Maimonidean mode that recent Jewish feminists have, in unison with Christian feminists, challenged the exclusive masculinity of an omnipotent God as an idol: a projection of male power named as the divine Father, King, and Lord set up in the high places to preside over the masculine hierarchy of power and secure its power over animals, children, women, and the (female) earth itself (Raphael, 2013). Jewish feminists (non-Orthodox especially), have wanted to say that 'where a religious tradition makes the masculine body the normative bearer of the divine image of a God imagined in male language and values alone, its anthropology should be considered idolatrous' (Plaskow, 1991: 147–8).

Feminist liberation theology is not a secular idoloclasm. In a monotheistic religion the image of God – what Eliezer Berkovits calls 'the secret' of our humanity (1979: 33) guarantees the dignity of the individual for it is bestowed by a God whose unity renders the divine image the defining attribute of any human being, whether male or female. Graven images are forbidden not because God has no image but because God has every image – that of each and every person (Green, 1992: 28). The spiritual-political anthropology of Genesis 1 is a radical one. Unlike other ancient near eastern anthropologies, it is not only the king who bears God's image or is God's 'idol' on earth. That each and every human being, by virtue of being human, is crowned with the glory of the *tselem elohim* is a foundational guarantor of the human equality that imposes a brake on the exercise of hegemonic religio-political power.

The criticism of idols is also the precondition of relationality. Broadly rejecting the more extreme austerities of Maimonides' supra-personal theology, most Jewish theology combines personalist and non-personalist elements – the one always correcting the theological impulse of the other. For most Jews, in practice, God is historically manifest as an unbounded, many-faced, self-transforming God who can, as such, enter into the conditions of human life to establish a historical relationship with the world without being objectified into a mere idol or fixed idea (Muffs, 2005).

Man-made gods are silent, apathetic objects made of stone, metal and wood onto which ideas about power are projected. These unresponsive divinities are pronounced dead because they are in the deepest sense immobile: they have no *ruach* (spirit): 'Woe to him who says to wood, 'Come to life!' Or to lifeless stone, 'Wake up!' Can it give guidance? It is covered with gold and silver; there is no breath in it' (Hab. 2:19; cf. Jer. 2:27, Ps. 135:15, 17; 1 Kg. 18:26). The uncreated, living, speaking, calling, dialogical Jewish God is the One whose very pathos is the narrative drive or dynamic futurity of existence itself. This God's name is no more or less than 'I am': the one who will be who God will be. The criticism of idolatry underpins all prophetic theology whose elusive object is the God before God and the God after God: for 'God is not the strategist of our particularites or our historical condition' but rather the mystery and hope of our futurity (Cohen, 1981: 97). This is a God whose back alone we see because it is a God who is always going on before; named as the place, Ha Makom, of wherever we are, marked by little more than a pile of stones (Gen. 35:11–12). In being sensible of the limits of what it can know of an unlimited God, Judaism's theological humility is the very condition of human becoming: the freedom of the individual whose being is conditioned and finite in so far is it is under commandment (however liberally or conservatively that might be construed) but who, made in the image of God, will also be whoever she or he will be. Thus when the modern Jewish philosopher Emmanual Levinas writes: 'through the face filters the obscure light coming from beyond the face, from what is not yet, from a future never future enough, more remote than the possible' (1969: 254), he affirms that the human can never be forced to satisfy a normative idea of it.

The Liberation of the Human

The liberation of God and the liberation of the human from hegemonic control are one and the same process. Idoloclastic ideas of God and the human are the beginning of religious humanism because they refuse either to deify the human as the creator of all truth and value or to demote the human by stripping it of its value as a creation of the *summum bonum* that is God. Although religion does not allow that humanity is the random product of competing socio-biological forces, the human qua human is permitted its deficiencies, its partial and provisional knowledge, and the fact of its mortality. By prohibiting the estrangement of natural finite things from their own finitude, the human can be truly in the image of God as the possibility of all that will be who it will be, not what it is told it must be.

One example of the liberation of the human from distortive fantasy must suffice. Jewish law permits Jews to use not only language but also visual art to stabilize the operation of the imagination within the economy of divine–human creation precisely by acts of counter-distortion. Just as the *Mishnah Avodah Zarah* specifies that only broken fragments of idols can be used by Jews for other purposes (ch. 3, Mishnah 2) and that an idol can be nullified by cutting off the tip of its ear, finger or nose (ch. 4: Mishnah 5), the standard codification of Jewish law (Shulchan Aruch ch. 141, 'Laws about Images and Forms') requires artists to deface images with some imperfection or absurdity to prevent the human subject it depicts being mistaken or substituted for the divine and set over us as a god. Images that conform to the Code of Jewish Law might therefore make human figures look ludicrous by adding animal features such as a beak, or introduce even barely perceptible imperfections such as a missing ear (Julius, 2000; Schwartzschild, 1990; Raphael, 2009: 28–9, 61–2 and elsewhere).

The only kind of mockery that is mandated by the rabbis of late antiquity is the mocking of idols (Meg. 25b); it is even permissible to give them derogatory names which distorted their real names (Sif. Deut. 61). Modern Jewish artists (Grisha

Bruskin, Sacha Sosno, Maryan S. Maryan and others) whose work is produced in creative interpretation of the second commandment, rather than in spite of it, make ironical, self-deprecating partial images that are the very reverse of idols: they depict bodies that advert to the crisis and loss that is the mark of finitude by cancelling, breaking, or subtracting some of the power of its form. A snowman, for example, is a halakhically permissible sculpture of a person not only because it is patently not worshipped but because it will melt when the temperature rises: it will not last forever. Such a minor, even amusing, instance of the halakhic aesthetic of imperfection illustrates how it enables the production of uniquely Jewish images that are not merely permissible but actively counter-idolatrous in offering a powerful, if sometimes crude, visual corrective to hubristic idolatries of the human by acknowledging the messianic quality of eschatological waiting or unfinishedness that characterizes the human condition.

This kind of religious iconoclasm is less of an act of violence against the human as a diagnosis of a human malaise. It seeks to prevent any substitution of the image of the divine in the human for an image of the human in the human, for this latter is the means by which the human surpasses the license and limits of its own createdness and arrogates divine power to itself. (We might recall that Pharaoh is likened by Ezekiel (29: 3) to a great, heavy, somnolent crocodile basking in the reeds, who, according to the Midrash (Yechezkel 29: 3), has cast himself as the master and creator of all – roaring and snapping to all who pass by: 'The Nile is mine and I have made it myself.')

The Preservation of an Open Tradition

One of the central preoccupations of the novelist and essayist Cynthia Ozick is her belief that no Jew – not even a Jewish novelist – is permitted to play God. Adhering to the rabbinic view that 'a Jew is someone who shuns idols,' an idol, she claims, is 'obviously not only a little wooden graven image standing in the mud. Nor is an idol merely a false idea' (Ozick, 1983b: 188). In accordance with Jewish philosophical tradition, she argues that an idol is anything that intervenes between human beings and God, anything, in short, that is 'instead of God.' Expressing anxieties about the duplicitousness of the fictions conjured by the literary imagination, she notes that an idol (where 'dead matter will rule the quick' is 'a thing-that-subsists-for-its-own-sake-without-a-history' (Ozick, 1983a: 207; 1983b: 178–99).

What Ozik wants to say about the dangers of a secular literary canon creating a textual fantasy world usurping God by its power over the human mind and its aspirations and by beginning to exist for its own sake in a historical vacuum of its own making could be applied to the Jewish textual canon as a whole, including its sacred literature. If the traditional Jewish notion of Torah as *min Ha Shamayim* (as being of divine origin or literally 'from heaven') may be variously interpreted, and if it is accepted that it is mediated through human beings, then all but the most conservative forms of Judaism would acknowledge that its sacred texts did not originate and do not remain in a historical vacuum, even if its source, meaning and referential object is transcendent and eternal (see, e.g. Heschel, [1962] 2006).

Refusing to make judgments that either include or exclude texts from the category of revelation, there are some religious and secular Jews who prefer not to think of Judaism as a religion at all. Most recently, Amos Oz and his daughter Fania Oz-Salzberger, both secular Israelis, have argued that Judaism's transmissibility is not that of a legal or ceremonial institution or a blood-line, but a 'text-line'. As the sum of its words, Judaism is a library and a cross-generational, not invariably reverent, argument. At the very beginning of the tradition Jacob's name is changed to Israel, 'for you have striven with God'. Jews are those who strive to come into the presence of God; they are not a single entity that normatively and exhaustively embodies Jewish tradition. To this extent, the Jews are *b'nei Yisrael* or *Am Yisrael*, the children or people of Israel, not the proponents of *yahudat* (Judaism). 'Judaism' is a concept that only came into being in the nineteenth century as a means by which emancipated Jews could take their civic place alongside Christianity. If Jews were to distance themselves from normative terms like *yahadut* and use the older term 'children' or 'people' of Israel, the tradition would, they believe, regain some of its original and authentic capaciousness. (Oz and Oz-Salzberger, 2012).

It is not to reductively historicize or poeticize the Talmud, for example, to accept that it is a collected oral tradition: redacted fragments of conversations conducted first under a Roman then a Christian dispensation (this latter sometimes being itself the occasion of, or interlocutor in, its own debates). The often hyperbolical, playfully provocative, disputatious tone of the oral tradition of Talmudic argumentation as it remembers past disputes and anticipates those of the future is one that allows it to extend indefinitely in time as a polyphonic text that facilitates a plurality of authoritative rabbinic opinions, not a single set of diktats from a single institutional body.

Louis Jacobs, an influential twentieth-century Orthodox rabbi and teacher who held a modified view of the divine origin of the Torah, did well to remind us of the little-known Hasidic Master, R. Yaakov of Izbica who insisted that the mitzvot (commandments) are not objects of worship, only God is to be worshipped (1983). The commandments are *'kelim*,' or instruments to a yet higher end. If Jacobs, following R Yaakov of Izbica is right that the prohibition of idols prevents idolizing the mitzvot, then a fortiori it prevents idolizing either the codification of the commandments or their human interpreters.

One of the 613 mitzvot is the commandment not to 'lay down a stone for worship' (Lev. 26:1). More than prohibiting the setting up of high altars and pillars to the gods, the commandment might now be interpreted as a warning not to turn your tradition into a gravestone under whose weight you will bury God, yourselves and the world around you. Unowned by any of its interpreters; not laid down like a stone weighing upon the heart, the Jewish sacred text is rather to be likened to seed thrown on the winds. It is an undetermined dispersive process that knows its own historical context and genre to be as much a part of its message as its medium. The tradition does not subsist as a thing interposed between the Jew and God. To prevent its becoming an idol of itself, all but the most Orthodox of Jews are sensible of the textual tradition as something akin to a work of art, and so must be continually broken or chipped in some small interpretative way to show that it is a finite account of eternal truth; not a thing but an occasion and an event.

Liberation from Authoritarian Leadership

The Mosaic biblical constitution is one in which God alone rules. A Jewish monarchy was established about a thousand years before the Common Era, when Samuel, with some misgivings, anointed Saul as its king. Jews from that period to that of Moses Mendelssohn in the nineteenth century of the Common Era (see Freudenthal, 2012), and on to the present day, have henceforth objected to the imposition of single, unified, concrete political power over that of God alone. I Samuel 8:10–18 warns that a king will take for his own everything that the people has and, having stripped them of all their possessions, will then make them his slaves. When the day comes that they have nothing left, Samuel prophesies 'you will cry out on account of the king you have chosen for yourselves, but on that day God will not answer you (v.18)'. Collective sovereign will and rights are not to be conceded to any single form of earthly power – any kind of Pharaoh – at the expense of the covenant made between God and the whole people Israel on Sinai. The Davidic monarchy was permissible only in so far as David was known to be the servant of Yahweh. Again, and again, the prophets demand the justice that is predicated on the servanthood of all earthly powers. The prophets rail against the hubris of rulers' self-aggrandizing projects and look to the restoration of the polity of covenant. The covenant provides a blueprint not for theocracy that puts the dispensation of divine will into the hands of a religious hegemony claiming to be God's regent on earth, but for a religious democracy where the law is inscribed in the hearts and minds of all of God's people, without intermediaries: 'No longer will they teach their neighbor, or say to one another, 'Know the Lord', because they will all know me, from the least of them to the greatest' (Jeremiah 31:34).

In recent years, even parts of the Orthodox Jewish community have demonstrated a healthy resistance to rabbinic authoritarianism. Contemporary Haredim have been widely condemned for insisting that all the Talmudic sages' pronouncements on matters both secular and religious are factually true. Most Jews do not believe that the only legitimate heirs to the Talmudic rabbis are to be found in the Haredi rabbinate who are prone to make binding rulings that are oblivious to current scientific and sociological research. The vast majority of contemporary Jewry believe that this kind of religious totalitarianism is intellectually and practically injurious.

Lawrence Kaplan has observed that the contemporary authority of the *roshei yeshiva* – the heads of the religious seminaries – has arisen in response to the perceived threat of modernity to authority and tradition. Yet Kaplan regards the institution of a 'papal' rabbinic authority as a distortion of the historical tradition. Rabbis – even the greatest of them (the *gedolim*) have traditionally made no claims to infallibility (Kaplan, 1992). The term 'Daas Torah' (referring to binding Torah-guided judgments made by the *gedolim* on all and any aspects of daily life) should refer to no more than wise guidance given by an experienced and learned religious leader. As Maimonides pointed out centuries earlier, when Jews bow to the scrolls of the Torah they are not worshipping it but paying it the respect that they would to a person held in the highest esteem (Maimonides, 1963, II: ch. 8). So too, when rabbinic authority extends beyond the legal adjudication (*p'sak halakhah*) of what may or may not be permitted by the Torah, it should do so only because superior judgment has been earned by life-long scholarly fluency in the tradition. The traditional hierarchy of Jewish scholarship does not extend to infallibility. The Talmud itself provides evidence that the rabbis whose opinions it records did not regard themselves as infallible. In Pesahim 94b, for example, the Talmud records a controversy between rabbis over the orbital relation of the sun and the earth. The Talmud concludes that the non-Jewish astronomers' opinion of the time was more defensible than their own, suggesting that they knew perfectly well that their pronouncements were open to correction. To assert otherwise would be a form of idolatry, substituting the pride of dictatorial human individuals for the self-revelation of God to the whole Jewish people.

Israel as a People, not an Object of Worship

We turn, finally, to how the Jewish tradition is inherently self-revising because while it sanctifies the Jewish people it never divinizes it. The 'marriage' of God and Israel is a historical not an ontological one. In a political bid to wrest power from Moses and Aaron, the rebel Korah was the first to have asserted the holiness of the entire Jewish people as having God in their midst (Num. 16:3). His ploy ended in the terrifyingly audible spectacle of the ground opening and Korah, with all of his people and their every possession, shrieking as they are buried alive. This story can be read as a warning, expressed in the lurid terms of its day, that the ban on idols must applies to the standing of the Jewish people itself. Yeshayahu Leibowitz, and rather differently, Michael Wyschogrod, have contended that Israel is not to be treated as itself a holy body or as an assembly representing divine presence on earth. Such would be idolatrous since nothing is holy except God and his Torah, whose commandments must be observed, not incarnated (Leibowitz, 1987: 449–9). Israel is rather 'a body of faith' whose task as a kingdom of priests is to make a habitation for divine presence. It is not the divine presence itself (Wyschogrod, 1983).

Israel attains holiness (*kedushah*) in being 'set apart' (a term synonymous in Hebrew with holiness) from the nations as a servant of God. Its holiness consists precisely not in coercive power and glory as preeminence over others but in being a rejected and abjected body. The book of Isaiah writes famously of the body of Israel that he has 'no form or beauty that we should look at him: no charm that we should find him pleasing' (53: 2). The world did not fix him in its adulatory stare. Quite the opposite: 'the many were appalled at him – so marred was his appearance, unlike that of man, his form, beyond human semblance – just so he shall startle many nations' (52:14–15). That the privations of the sacrificial task leave the body of Israel 'beyond human semblance' signals that it will always be a counter-idolatrous body. Its power and its powerlessness are one and the same and consist in love alone. To use the image of Israel as a collective servant of God (but never God's slave) who is patently mortal is to preclude its idolization. As a servant who suffers the abjection of servanthood, Israel can never be an idol since idols, by their nature, are immune to weakness, loss and death.

To conclude, this chapter has suggested that Judaism's idoloclastic dynamic prevents the world – including its own Jewish world – being taken captive to authoritarian, fixed ideas or images of God and the human and to closed interpretations of sacred texts. In the great Russian novel *Dr Zhivago*, Larissa says that she finds it strange that Jews 'who once brought about the liberation of mankind from the yoke of idolatry, and so many of whom now devote themselves to its liberation from injustice' should have succumbed to what she calls 'a kind of inward senility, the fatigue of centuries' that she attributes to the Jews' refusal to assimilate and disappear into the nations its vision founded (Pasternak, [1958], 2002: 272). I hope this chapter would persuade her otherwise. Although classical Judaism is not merely an ancient form of humanism, it has a tireless commitment to the humanity of the human that makes it ever more necessary and alive to the crisis and possibility of its historical moment.

Reference List

Berkovits, E. (1979) *With God in Hell: Judaism in the Ghettos and Death Camps*, New York and London: Sanhedrin.

Cohen, A. (1997 [1981]) *The Tremendum: A Theological Interpretation of the Holocaust*, New York: Continuum.

Dawkins, R. (2006) *The God Delusion*, London: Bantam.

Freudenthal, G. (2012) *No Religion without Idolatry: Mendelssohn's Jewish Enlightenment*, Notre Dame, IN: University of Notre Dame Press.

Green, A. (1992) *Seek My Face, Speak My Name: A Contemporary Jewish Theology*, Northvale, NJ: Jason Aronson.

Heschel, A.J. 2006 [1962] *Heavenly Torah: As Refracted through the Generations*, London: Bloomsbury.

Jacobs, L. (1983) 'The Philosophy of the Mitzvot', The Masorti Association Lecture, January 9, 1983, at the London Business School, London. Available at: The Masorti Association (http://louisjacobs.org/library/articles/the-philosophy-of-the-mitzvot.php accessed 10/21/2013).

Julius, A. (2000) *Idolizing Pictures: Idolatry, Iconoclasm and Jewish Art*, London: Thames and Hudson.

Kaplan, L. (1992) 'Daas Torah: A Modern Conception of Rabbinic Authority', in M.Z. Sokol (ed.), *Rabbinic Authority and Personal Autonomy*, Northvale, NJ: Jason Aronson, 1–60.

Leibowitz, Y. (1987) 'Idolatry', in A. Cohen and P. Mendes Flohr (eds), *Contemporary Jewish Religious Thought: Original Essays on Critical Concepts, Movements and Beliefs*, New York: The Free Press, 445–9.

Levinas, E. (1969), trans. Alphonso Lingis, *Totality and Infinity: An Essay on Exteriority*, Pittsburgh, PA: Duquesne University Press.

Maimonides, M. (1963) trans. S. Pines, *The Guide of the Perplexed*, Chicago, IL, and London: University of Chicago Press.

Margalit, A. and Halbertal, M. (1992) *Idolatry*, Oxford and New York: Oxford University Press.

Muffs, Y. (2005) *The Personhood of God: Biblical Theology, Human Faith and the Divine Image*, Woodstock, VT: Jewish Lights Publishing.

Otto, R. (1923), trans. J.W. Harvey, *The Idea of the Holy: An Enquiry into the Non-Rational Factor in the Idea of the Divine and Its Relation to the Rational*, Oxford: Oxford University Press.

Oz, A. and Oz-Salzberger, T. (2012) *Jews and Words*, New Haven, CT, and London: Yale University Press.

Ozick, C. (1983a) 'Riddle of the Ordinary', reprinted in *Art and Ardor: Essays*, New York: Knopf, 100–109.

Ozick, C. (1983b) 'Literature as Idol', reprinted in *Art and Ardor: Essays*, New York: Knopf, 178–99.

Pasternak, B. (2002 [1958]) *Dr Zhivago*, London: Vintage.

Plaskow, J. (1991) *Standing Again at Sinai: Judaism from a Feminist Perspective*, New York: HarperSanFrancisco.

Raphael, M. (2009) *Judaism and the Visual Image: A Jewish Theology of Art*, London and New York: Continuum.

Raphael, M. (2013) *A Patrimony of Idols: Second Wave Feminism and the Criticism of Religion, Sophia: International Journal of Philosophy and Traditions*, published online, 31 May 2014, link.springer.com/article/10.10 07%2Fs11841-014-0409-1.

Schwartzschild, S. (1990) 'The Legal Foundations of Jewish Aesthetics', in M. Kellner (ed.), *The Pursuit of the Ideal: Jewish Writings of Steven Schwarzschild*, New York: New York University Press, 109–16.

Seeskin, K. (1995) *No Other Gods: The Modern Struggle against Idolatry*, West Orange, NJ: Behrman House.

Wyschogrod, M. (1983) *The Body of Faith: Judaism as Corporeal Election*, New York: Seabury Press.

Chapter 4

Islam

Tim Winter

For many in the secular West, the dominant image of Islam is shaped by news of terrorist atrocities and Islamist political totalitarianism. Hardly a day goes by without some new and shocking disclosure of the willingness of Muslim radicals to violate fundamental rights in their quest for a puritan religious sovereignty. Such movements are familiar and have been extensively researched. This chapter will look beyond these manifestations and seek to discern what the majority of Muslims and their religious leaders take their religion to be. In an age of mounting 'Islamophobia', this seems timely. Many Muslims are concerned that a focus on the radical movements has veiled the mainstream 'orthodoxy' from Western consciousness, conveying the impression of a religion which, although followed by a quarter of the world's population, is the complete antithesis of everything 'sensible'. Such Muslims may be heard complaining that many in the West cannot name a single mainstream Muslim imam or theologian, despite intensive media coverage of Islam-related events. Paradoxically, in an age of communication there exists a knowledge deficit. This chapter seeks to introduce readers to the majoritarian reality of modern Islam, defined, with necessary looseness, as the experience and convictions of most Muslim believers. This exercise in demythologizing will begin by outlining the activities of three mainstream, faithful Muslim leaders whose lives and convictions directly challenge popular media-led stereotypes.

In 2008 the British political review *Prospect* teamed up with leading American journal *Foreign Affairs* in a search for the 'world's leading public intellectual.' True to their democratic ideals, the journals chose to let the people decide, and this was done by means of a worldwide online poll. The result startled few in the Muslim world, but bewildered the journal's editors: the votes came in overwhelmingly for Fethullah Gülen. *Prospect*, hitherto a noted platform for anti-Muslim diatribes, had the grace to admit that it was unfamiliar with Gülen and his movement, and ran a long article to try and familiarize its Western readers with the Gülen phenomenon, as an example of a mainstream Sunni movement far larger than any fundamentalist formation, but still little-known to many non-Muslims.

The *Prospect* article opened with this question: 'Is it possible to be a true religious believer and at the same time enjoy good relations with people of other faiths or none?' and added a related but separate question: 'Can you remain open to new ideas and ways of thinking?' (Masood, 2008). The answer, clearly, was a resounding yes. Through his 60 books and his global network of universities and thousands of schools, Gülen claims, in the words of *Prospect*, that 'you can be at home in the modern world while also embracing traditional values like faith in God and community responsibility.' The mutual enrichment of religion and science stands at the heart of his theology and the curriculum of his worldwide educational empire, and drives the movement's establishment of a global network of hospitals and other health facilities. This conservative Sunni organization committed to a pluralist humanitarian vision 'may well be the largest and the most successful transnational Muslim outreach movement of the contemporary age' (Pandya and Gallagher, 2012: 1).

The second of our contemporary imams is Abdurrahman Wahid (1940–2009), who, like Gülen, was a traditional Sunni 'cleric.' He studied first in conservative madrasas in his native Indonesia and then enrolled at Al-Azhar University in Cairo, the Muslim world's most prestigious religious institution. On his return he worked as a journalist before becoming dean of the Sharia and Doctrine faculty of a major Indonesian university, after which he was elected chairman of Indonesia's largest Islamic organization, Nahdatul Ulema. In this role he campaigned against the Western-backed dictatorship of General Suharto, thus joining the ranks of Muslim scholars around the world who in the 1980s and 1990s were agitating for representative government, risking persecution at the hands of pro-Western secularists. Through his sermons and theological writings Wahid gained immense popularity in the mosques as a democracy and human rights advocate inspired by a traditional Sunni theology, and this ensured his election in 1999 as Indonesia's first democratic president. As often in the Islamic world, religiously driven democratic activism had been locked in a struggle against an American-backed dictatorship with an appalling human rights record. However, on coming to power Wahid did not take revenge on former opponents. Instead he sought to build positive relations with the old elites, and with the Western and other secular powers which had persecuted him and his movement before its final vindication at the polls. His lifelong struggle with the country's secular military establishment continued even after his retirement, when he accused elements in the army of covert involvement in the 2005 Bali bombings. Like Gülen, Wahid advocated a positive relationship between religions, full freedom of expression and belief, and a fully democratic political order, all of which had been suppressed under the former military junta.

All this was enabled by his roots in the Nahdatul Ulema, the world's largest Islamic political movement (Barton, 2002).

The third case is 'Pakistan's Mother Teresa,' the devout 'living saint,' Abdus Sattar Edhi. Born in 1928, his childhood was blighted by his mother's paralysis, mental illness and early death. As a refugee in Karachi following Partition, he worked as a street pedlar. But the destitute Edhi offered his life to God through the service of the country's most needy people. Through begging, he bought a second-hand van which he turned into an impromptu ambulance. Today his Edhi Foundation is Pakistan's largest charity, running the world's largest voluntary ambulance service, and maintaining a network of over 300 clinics, rehabilitation centers, orphanages, homes for the mentally ill, and centres for sick animals. Edhi himself, in the Sufi tradition, draws no salary, takes no holidays, lives in a tiny apartment, and, following the Prophet's example, owns only one change of clothes. His organization is now international, and has contributed to emergency relief efforts around the world, including the 2005 New Orleans hurricane (Price, 2001; Oborne, 2011).

All three of these individuals are regarded as heroes in the Muslim world, and are believed to walk in the footsteps of the Muslim saints of past generations. The first is one of the world's leading educators and promoters of science, the second was a theologian-president of the most populous Muslim country, while the third is a champion of the sick and the marginalized. For most believing Muslims it is people like these who incarnate the reality of Islam. Where secular regimes and civil institutions have failed, the sacrifices of such role-models is giving hope to millions. Their example goes some way to explaining the ongoing popularity and growth of Islam around the world, to which striking fact of our age we must now turn.

A Gallup World Poll published in 2007 indicated the substantial religiosity of Muslim cultures when compared to Europe in particular. For instance, when asked 'Are there traditions and customs that are important to you, or not,' 96 percent of Jordanians agreed, compared to only 36 percent of respondents in the United Kingdom (Esposito and Mogahed, 2007: 7). Attendance rates at mosques, and the observance of the rigorous Ramadan fast, seemed high worldwide, and in many cases were rising. Even in Muslim minority settings where the new generation was exposed to modern secular culture from an early age, the signs are that Muslim observance is resilient. A Cardiff University research study on religious nurture in British Muslim families, completed in February 2012, showed that Muslims are generally successful in transferring their convictions and rituals to the new generation. The study showed that 77 percent of adult Muslims 'actively practise the faith they were brought up in, compared with 29 per cent of Christians, and 65 per cent of other religions' (Scourfield et al., 2012: 34). Converts, too, have continued to join the British Muslim community in significant numbers, with an estimated total of 60,000 new Muslims in 2001 rising to some 100,000 only 10 years later. Again, contrary to popular perceptions, 67 percent of these neo-Muslims were female; overall, educated white women were the most likely Britons to embrace Islam (Brice, 2010).

Although a small number are attracted to radicalism, it is generally the case that Muslims (including new Muslims) see their adherence to Islam as a sensible decision, rooted in perceptions of Islamic reasonableness. Other recent surveys seem to bear out this perception. The 2007 Gallup poll highlighted what two scholars describe as 'Islam's Silenced Majority': the Qur'anically faithful Muslims who are alienated by Islamist radicalism, but are seldom heard by outsiders. The statistics demonstrate that Muslims are 'on average more likely than the American public to unequivocally condemn attacks on civilians'. Three times as many Americans believe that attacks on civilians are 'completely justified,' when compared to Iranians (Esposito and Mogahed, 2007: 94, 95). And in the United Kingdom, in a 2009 Gallup survey, Muslims scored remarkably highly on standard tests: 77 percent of Muslims identified 'very strongly' with the UK, compared to 51 percent of the general population; 76 percent of Muslims were 'confident' in the police, contrasted with a national average of 65 percent. On these and a range of other citizenship indicators, Muslims, a community noted for very high rates of religious observance, scored very highly when compared to the current British norm, despite feeling misunderstood (Gallup/Coexist, 2009). Overall, as *The Economist* entitled its article, British Muslims are 'pious, loyal, and unhappy' (*The Economist*, 2009: 27).

All the signs are that mainstream Islamic affiliation seems to add significant value to citizenship and social cohesion, just as radical Islam supplies its polar opposite. Put differently, some might say that Islam's mainstream is offering adherents a form of religious life that is experienced as eminently 'sensible', while margins constitute a lunatic fringe. However, and in the light of the meditations on 'sensible religion' provided by Christopher Lewis in his initial chapter, a brief pause to interrogate these categories may be helpful, before examining the content of Islamic 'sensibleness.' What is it to be 'sensible', after all? Is it not a matter for the eye of the beholder?

Gülen, Wahid and Edhi, role-models for millions, are not conventionally 'sensible'. In general they have been risk-taking, boundary-breaking heroes of faith. We should admit that as in the stories of Moses tapping the Red Sea with his staff, Jesus choosing the road to Jerusalem, the Buddha renouncing his kingdom, or Muhammad accepting persecution by his own people, they are hardly 'sensible' by any contemporary criteria. To be sensible is, all too often, to be perceived as prudent, moderate, consensual, and cautious about stepping into the unknown. It is, usually, to be uninspiring. It is not much of an exaggeration to claim that few people, historically, have had their lives profoundly changed by this kind of sensible person.

What religion offers, at its most prophetic and authentic, may nonetheless be seen as sensible. Islam's millions of adherents will insist on this: they do not consider themselves foolish or reckless or irrational. The difficulty is that this may not be readily discernable by the consensus of a secular, pragmatic, utilitarian age. 'Be in this world as a stranger or a wayfarer,' as the Prophet of Islam is said to have advised (al-Hanbali, 2007: 653). If the founders and saints of the world religions, who are the archetypes for their devout followers in our times, were seldom conformists to the wisdom of their own societies, but were rather 'strangers in a strange land', this ought to suggest that contemporary generations which claim to follow them should also find a way of being sensible while taking lightly the counsels of the age. Religion cannot be itself and is unlikely to be taken seriously if it plods along dutifully behind a set of social or intellectual agendas determined largely by a secular consumer society. It is likely to have liberative and awkward things to say about those agendas, and it will always seek to lead, to criticize, and to challenge. Some, who wish for the Islamic world, and in fact the whole world, to conform to Western liberal capitalist values, will regret, resent and even fear this dissident instinct in religion. However one need not be Muslim to see Islam's insistence on difference as one of its gifts in a world of increasing ethical and cultural homogeneity: it offers some of the most trenchant, counter-cultural, and difficult critiques, which, when well crafted and taken, can only enhance the world's conversations and improve the chances of change. Consider this view by Ahmet Davutoglu, currently the Turkish Foreign Minister:

> Previous civilizational crises were overcome through the injection of new values from other civilizations. The syncretic atmospheres of the historical junctions between two or more civilizations facilitated solutions to these crises by a cross-fertilization of new and dynamic values. Today, we do not have such an alternative because in contrast to the historical civilizations, authentic culture cannot co-exist and survive under the hegemonistic character of modern Western civilization. (Davutoglu, 1994: 26–7)

Davutoglu is warning against what he sees as an emerging single global culture, which he believes to be at risk of stagnating in the absence of challenges from substantive alternatives. Like many Muslims, he claims that Islam, as the West's most salient counter-narrative, can help save the West from materialism, introspection and intellectual and moral decline, by holding to a distinctive rather than a conformist discourse. The radical Islamists are unlikely to contribute greatly to this, if at all; but mainstream Muslims lay claim to a wealth of alternative perspectives to offer to those Westerners who are prepared to learn from cultures other than their own. Just as contemporary Islamic discourse enriches and invigorates itself with new conceptions drawn from the West, so too thinkers like Davutoglu hope that Westerners will learn from others, and not only from other Westerners, thus challenging the frequent Third World stereotype of Westerners as triumphalist and narcissistic (Buruma and Margalit, 2004).

Setting aside the radical Islamists, whose vehemence is considered by some political scientists to be a consequence as well as a reaction to modernity (Zizek 2002; Euben 1999, Murad 2008), how may we claim dissident 'sensibleness' for mainstream contemporary Islam, as reflected in its striking ongoing popularity? More saliently, is there some way in which its religious sensibleness, marked by a degree of courageous and controversial difference from modern consensus beliefs, can be understood as sensible by a pragmatic liberal culture?

Since diversity has been cited as a value, one might begin by trying to explain Islam's appeal, and its 'sensibleness', to outsiders, by remarking on its probable wisdom in incorporating internal diversity. 'Islam' is hugely diverse, and hence supplies homes for humans of a vastly divergent range of tastes and orientations. It does not have an orthodoxy as Christians, particularly Western Christians, might understand the term. Instead, rather like Hindu religion, or post-exilic Judaism, it is polycentric. There is no high priest, no sacraments to be offered or withheld, and no hierarchy canonically accepted as exerting authority over believers. It is true that Sunni Muslims, in particular, tend to recognize certain centers of educational excellence, such as Al-Azhar University, as sources of authoritative teaching which believers may consult and choose to abide by; however, even the divines of Al-Azhar frequently fail to concur on important matters. Hence the exasperation which with scholars of Islam greet journalistic expressions such as 'Sharia Law'. The Sharia is not a law; it is an ever-evolving tradition of legal, moral and ritual interpretation which, like the Halakha among the Rabbis, is comfortable with and indeed proud of its internal traditions of dissent. For Sunnis there are still four great 'schools' of Sharia, which differ markedly, and each individual school contains significant differences of opinion. For Shi'i Muslims there is a still larger range of doctrinal and jurisprudential diversity. Theologically this is not treated as scandalous, since different Sharia interpretations 'of individual jurists, or of the various schools of law, are different manifestations of the same divine will' (Kamali, 2003: 229). The sheer diversity and fluidity of the Sharia has enabled its incorporation in a historically and geographically vast range of cultures, and is probably one reason for its past and ongoing popularity. The Sharia represents an indigenous resource of moral and legal discussion far more diverse than any Western type of law or ethics; and as such, is sensibly being favoured by many, even a majority, of voters in the aftermath of the recent 'Arab Spring', where Sharia-oriented parties, insistent on a democratic end to pro-Western dictatorship, are consistently outperforming their secular rivals. Most Muslims emphatically hold that a sensible religious code is a diverse and flexible one.

Broadly the same sensible insistence on the divine favoring of difference applies in the case of theology. Because of the famous (or notorious) openness of the Qur'anic and Hadith texts to widely divergent readings (a polyphony reinforced by the absence of a single authoritative hierarchy or magisterium), Islamic formal theology, known as *kalam*, has always existed in the form of different schools. The best-known of these are the Maturidi, the Ash'ari and the Hanbali schools, characterized rather simplistically as rationalizing, rational-traditionalist, and scriptural-literalist. All are seen as acceptable by the major traditional centers of learning. As in the case of Islamic law, contemporary Islamic theology is often profoundly influenced by modern Western philosophy, adding further richness to an already pluriform and lively tradition of metaphysical and ethical reflection. To take only one significant example: Muslim theologians debate widely on the ongoing salvific value of earlier religions, with some major figures affirming, and others denying, the possibility of, say, Christian salvation (Khalil, 2012).

With a radically decentered medieval heritage of debate, and a landscape of mosques which were generally autonomous and answerable to congregations rather than to a censorious hierarchy, classical Sunni Islam furnished a hospitable basis for further ramification and diversity following the impact of modern thought.

Despite the often bewildering variety of modern Islamic views on theology, society and politics, the core beliefs and ritual practices of the religion are notably consistent. The practices of fasting in Ramadan, for instance, or the five-times-daily Muslim prayer, appear not to have changed significantly since the beginnings of the religion, and vary hardly at all over the geographical range of the Islamic world. Despite the absence of a 'church', the Islamic world has generally agreed to maintain its core devotional practices intact. It is in these somewhat demanding practices, which comprise the heart of the faith, that we may, perhaps, seek the reason why so many Muslims continue to experience their way of life as sensible.

Ritual seems to be a 'human universal, the glue that holds social groups together', adding a vital psychological support at times of joy, anxiety, and sorrow (Jones, 2013). In particular, rituals that involve ablutions (baptism would be the most evident Christian example; Jews and Hindus also incorporate forms of ritual ablution) have been shown to be psychologically therapeutic, in a version of the so-called 'Macbeth effect' (Zhong and Liljenquist, 2006). The Sharia requires the ablution known as *wudu* before most ritual observances, particularly the canonical prayers, sensibly providing a feeling of cleansing, thus opening the worshippers' hearts to the mood of purity and serenity delivered by worship. The form of prayer itself is strongly embodied, entailing physical positions of bowing, prostration, and calm meditative sitting. Medical science seems to concur that 'religious people tend to be healthier and live somewhat longer than the nonreligious' (Friedman and Martin, 2011: 149), and it appears that regular, disciplined acts of ritual prayer (as contrasted, for instance, with haphazard moments of impromptu petition), supply one explanation of this, not least when the worship is congregational. In the Islamic case, the medical sensibleness of prayer is enhanced by some other features of the Islamic lifestyle, such as the avoidance of alcohol and other narcotics, and the ban on pre-marital sexual activity: in Muslim Zanzibar, HIV prevalence is 0.6 percent, compared with over 25 percent in mainly non-Muslim South Africa (Becker and Geissler, 2009: 120, 309).

Sensible religion does not treat the mind in isolation; it integrates the body into the mind's activities. The highly embodied nature of Islam's ritual life seems well-suited to maintaining this holistic form of life; and several recent studies have detailed the Sharia's strongly affirmatory attitude to the rhythms and functions of the human body, which are not ignored, stigmatized or denied, but are integrated into the insider's ritual existence. Attitudes to sexuality are particularly positive, with celibacy frowned upon as the denial of a Divine gift (Maghen, 2005).

Islam's characteristic integration of body and soul forms part of its desire that human beings should truly know themselves, thus supplying the basis for their knowledge of other human beings and of God. We are embodied beings, and know on that basis. This entails an essentially benign view of the body, as Maghen has shown, and this connects with the religion's wider view of nature.

The religionless man tends to see nothing in nature but a concatenation of atoms marshalled by physical laws and constants. As the Qur'an sums up this attitude: 'there is only the life of this world, we live and we die, and Time destroys us' (45: 24). The believer, by contrast, looks out upon a world aglow with moral and metaphysical meaning, the outworking of the qualities of an infinite and infinitely adorable Divine agent. This enrichment of our perspective is one of the gifts of religion, and accounts for the love of beauty and light in sacred art, which significantly contrasts with much contemporary art, where beauty and light are not intuited as underpinning the phenomenal world, which is instead a meaningless vortex of blind, amoral forces, in which we briefly look around, before being consigned to a bleak and eternal nothingness.

Sensible religion will therefore celebrate nature, perceiving it as a symphony of signs which point to its unitive and beautiful origin. It is intensely aesthetic. In the Qur'an, the argument for the being and nature of God is entirely focused on the contemplation of His signs (*ayat*) in the world: 'Truly in the way heaven and earth are created, and the succession of night and day, are signs for people of insight' (Qur'an 3: 190). But this 'argument from design' is not to be imprisoned in the brain; although medieval Muslims developed intricate systematic theologies, these were never raised to the status of 'queen of the sciences'. Instead, sensible Muslims agreed that logic and dialectic provide probable, but still conjectural, proofs for God's existence and nature. Theology may help to clear up some misunderstandings and false claims, but sensible religion will always recognise that, in the words of Razi, Islam's most reputable philosophical theologian of medieval times, it ultimately leads to 'bewilderment and perplexity' (Shihadeh, 2006: 193). The Qur'an points to nature, which points to God, but this pointing cannot be decisively encapsulated in mere finite words. Instead, sensible religion humbly insists on the limitations of philosophical theology, and prefers to rely on deeper intuition and Divine gifts and disclosures. This was expressed dramatically in the life-story of the celebrated al-Ghazali (d.1111), who experienced a crisis of faith in the middle of delivering a theology lecture to his best students. He walked out, and spent 10 years communing with nature in the wilderness, before God restored his faith through direct 'tasting' (*dhawq*). Whether or not Sufism, itself a vastly diverse tradition, can be described as 'mysticism', it has been far more widely cultivated in Islamic circles than has theology, and the mainstream leadership today insists on its importance.

It is reasonable to conclude that Islam's global popularity depends to a considerable extent on its appeal as a sensible option. This essay has focused on the religion of mainstream Muslims and their leaders. However grave questions need to be asked about the success of that leadership in countering the growing, and eminently un-sensible radicalism of the hardline Islamists. Embittered by the failure of secular elites, and disillusioned by a moderate democratic opposition thwarted by an 'entrenched American policy of preferring autocrats to elections in the Muslim world' (Feldman, 2003: 11), these movements ignore, oppose or assassinate mainstream Muslim scholars, as part of a new fundamentalist wave which is increasingly influential across the Islamic world. Here, Muslims need to ask serious questions about the failure of the scholarly elite to persuade 'ultras' of the al-Qaeda type that democratic means and the tolerance of diversity offer a better way of ensuring Muslim cultural survival in the face of Western encroachment, than suicide bombing and the imposition of a religious totalitarianism in the Taliban vein. Partly because of Islam's relatively decentred and consultative style of religious leadership, it must be admitted that this message has not been adequately communicated.

Sensible religion, defined as a form of faith that satisfies the human yearning for God and for stable and fulfilling social structures, is unlikely to be well-served by extreme and absolutist interpretations. If al-Qaeda is a mutated strain of a type of religion created by Americans, Saudis and the Pakistani intelligence services to discomfit the Soviets in Afghanistan (Johnson, 2002, xii–xvi), it may go on to generate a 'second blowback' in spreading cynicism and disillusion among many Muslims disgusted by its use of terror and constraint. 'A great majority of Muslims do not believe that Islamic practices should be enforced by the state' (Feldman, 2003, 228). Disregarding this, the 'Islamic Republic' of Iran has become, in private, a very secular place (Etzioni, 2002: 16), warning the new Islamist groupings of the wisdom of the caliph Ali, who counselled: 'Allow hearts some respite, for when they are forced, they grow blind' (Ghazali, 1347AH: IV, 321). Iran has been relatively mild, compared to the still fiercer polity promised by al-Qaeda. The conclusion is surely that the real clash in today's Muslim world is not between Islam and the West, but between classical piety, and the new ultras, who may, while posing as holy heroes, turn into the religion's gravediggers.

Reference List

Anon. (2009) 'Pious, Loyal and Unhappy', *The Economist*, May 7, 2009.

Barton, G. (2002) *Abdurrahman Wahid: Muslim Democrat, Indonesian President: A View from the Inside*, Honolulu, HI: University of Hawa'i Press.

Becker, F. and Geissler, W. (eds.) (2009) *AIDS and Religious Practice in Africa*, Leiden: Brill.

Brice, K. (2010) 'A Minority within a Minority: A Report on Converts to Islam in the UK'. Available at: www.faith-matters.org (accessed April 21, 2013).

Buruma, I., and Margalit, A. (2004) *Occidentalism: A Short History of Anti-Westernism*, London: Atlantic Books.

Davutoglu, A. (1994) *Civilizational Transformation and the Muslim World*, Kuala Lumpur: Mahir.

Etzioni, A. (2002) 'Flirting and Flag-Waving: The Revealing Study of Holidays and Rituals', *Chronicle of Higher Education*, December 11, 15–16.

Euben, R, (1999) *Enemy in the Mirror: Islamic Fundamentalism and the Limits of Modern Rationalism*, Princeton, NJ: Princeton University Press.

Feldman, N. (2003) *After Jihad: America and the Struggle for Islamic Democracy*, New York: Farrar, Straus and Giroux.

Friedman H.S. and Martin, R. (2011) *The Longevity Project: Surprising Discoveries for Health and Long Life from the Landmark Eight-Decade Study*, London: Hay House.

al-Ghazali, A. (1347 AH) *Ihya' 'Ulum al-Din*, Cairo: al-Halabi.

al-Hanbali, I., tr. Clarke, A. (2007) *The Compendium of Knowledge and Wisdom*, London: Turath.

Johnson, C. (2002) *Blowback: The Costs and Consequences of American Empire*, London: Time Warner.

Jones, D. (2013) 'Social Evolution: The Ritual Animal', *Nature*, January 23, 2013.

Kamali, M. (2003) *Principles of Islamic Jurisprudence*, 3rd edition, Cambridge: Islamic Texts Society.

Khalil, M. (2012) *Islam and the Fate of Others: The Salvation Question*, New York: Oxford University Press.

Maghen, Z. (2005) *Virtues of the Flesh: Passion and Purity in Early Islamic Jurisprudence*, Leiden: Brill.

Masood, E. (2008) 'A Modern Ottoman', *Prospect*, July 26.

Murad, A. (2008) *Bombing without Moonlight: The Origins of Suicidal Terrorism*, Bristol: Amal Press.

Oborne, P. (2011) 'The Day I Met Abdul Sattar Edhi, a Living Saint', *Daily Telegraph*, April 10.

Pandya, S. and Gallagher, N. (2012) *The Gulen Hizmet Movement and Its Transnational Activities: Case Studies of Altruistic Activism in Contemporary Islam*, BocaRaton, FL: BrownWalker Press.

Price, S. (2001) 'Pakistan's Saviour of the Desperate'. Available at: http://news.bbc.co.uk/1/hi/world/south_asia/1221986.stm (accessed 21 April 2013).

Scourfield, J., Taylor, C., Moore, G., and Gilliat-Ray, S. (2012) 'The Intergenerational Transmission of Islam in England and Wales: Evidence from the Citizenship Survey', *Sociology* 46/1 (2012), 91–108.

Shihadeh, A. (2006) *The Teleological Ethics of Fakhr al-Din al-Razi*, Leiden: Brill.

Zhong, C. and Liljenquist, K. (2006) 'Washing Away Your Sins: Threatened Morality and Physical Cleansing', *Science*, 8 September, 1451–2.

Zizek, S. (2002) *Welcome to the Desert of the Real*, London: Verso.

Chapter 5

Retrieving the Equilibrium and Restoring Justice: Using Islam's Egalitarian Teachings to Reclaim Women's Rights

Sara Khan

Original Principles

In the introductory chapter, Christopher Lewis describes sensible as reasonableness in beliefs and practices but also to 'sensitivity, awareness, being mindful of the views of others and responsive to the world around us, both individually and collectively'. These religious traditions he affirms, enable people to be altruistic as well as fulfilled and this in essence was the message of the Prophet Muhammad over 1,400 years ago. In the Arabian desert in a town called Mecca, this illiterate but well-respected man began to call people to Islam with a message that would reverberate across the world and which continues to impact humanity today. The Prophet Muhammad's message included belief in the one God and called followers of Islam to demonstrate that belief through action by standing up to Islam's core values of justice, mercy and human dignity. He preached a message of respect and duty: that as human beings, our humanity lies in our social dealings with other.

For a Muslim, belief is not enough in itself, but is connected to proactive action: establishing justice (*adl*) and developing *ihsaan* (*ihsaan* does not have an equivalent word in English but generally means good, selfless, tolerant, forgiving). Prophet Muhammad taught, in our relationships with our spouses: 'the best of you are those who are best to their wives'; our parents: 'and We have enjoined on man to be good to his parents' (Quran 31: 14), in our responsibility to our neighbour whether near or far: 'he is not a believer, who eats his fill while his neighbour is hungry'; and even in slaughtering animals for food, the Prophet instructed the believer to 'sharpen his blade and let him spare suffering to the animal he slaughters'. Although rituals are part of most religions, at its heart

Islam stresses that worshipping God is through service to others and inspires human beings to reach the highest levels of human dignity and compassion.

At a time when slavery was part of the very infrastructure of society and female infanticide was common, in the seventh century the Prophet Muhammad radically called for the freeing of slaves and for women to be granted full and equal autonomy – in contrast to European countries who abolished slavery in the nineteenth century, and where women were granted voting rights only in the twentieth century. In times of war, morality is often considered to be the first victim. Yet, even in these difficult times of conflict, which, according to Islamic teachings should always be conducted as a defensive, proportionate and last resort, the Prophet Muhammad gave clear instructions that civilians (the elderly, the young, women and non-combatants) should not be harmed. Destroying any buildings of worship, the unnecessary harming of animals and even the chopping down of trees was not allowed, centuries before the development of the Geneva Conventions.

The word Islam is often translated to mean peace and submission to God but a far more accurate translation of Islam would be the act of peace-making. In his commentary on verse 33: 35 of the Qur'an, jurist Al-Zamakhshari (d. 528/1137) explained Islam as meaning 'entering into a state of peace after war'. Islam by virtue of being a verb, is a proactive word meaning the act of entering into a state of peace, in contrast to the word salaam which translates into peace. Similar to Jesus' statement, 'blessed are the peace-makers' (New Testament Matthew 5:9) Islam actually means peace-making or achieving a state of peace before it means submission, for which the Arabic is *istislam*. Striving towards achieving peace in daily life or even in war is clear in the Qu'ran, where God instructs Muslims always to incline towards peace rather than war. 'If they [i.e. your enemy in war] incline towards peace, incline also towards peace' (Qur'an 8: 61).

Fadl (2005: 238) elaborates on this, emphasizing that Islam's focus is on protecting life, not destroying it, on building flourishing civilizations, not demolishing them:

> The Islamic historical experience was primarily concerned not with war making, but with civilisation-building. Islamic theology teaches that an integral part of the divine covenant given to human beings is to occupy themselves with building and creating, not with destroying life. The Qur'an teaches that the act of destroying or spreading ruin on this earth is one of the gravest sins possible.

Fadl expands further, that Islam's scriptures make clear that those corrupting the earth by destroying lives and property are guilty of the ultimate form of blasphemy and such people are waging war against God Himself.

Most religions have two components: a private, personal faith and a public, outward manifestation, often described as organized religion. Islam's values as mentioned earlier, enrich the lives of many, inspiring them to live sensible, meaningful and humane lives. As a counter-extremism and women's rights activist, it is Islam's message of justice, equality and dignity which drives me to defend human rights, challenge social injustices and contribute to the well-being of humanity. However, there is enormous debate, diversity and disagreement when Islam's beliefs are put into practice through laws and institutions by Muslims through their human interpretation of Islam's scriptures. The diversity of Islamic thought and practice is incredibly varied, yet at the same time can be problematic and confusing for both Muslims and non-Muslims. Today, many across the world question the benefit of religion and its believers, and there is much scepticism about the merit of Islam in particular. It is not an exaggeration to say that Islam is widely viewed, derided and even feared as an extreme religion of violence, intolerance and oppression. One of the worst blights on the reputation of Islam is how Islam and Muslims perceive, or are judged to perceive, women and the idea of gender equality.

In this chapter I will briefly examine Islam's teachings on women's rights and crucially the purpose of shariah as a dynamic and sophisticated process for establishing equilibrium, securing justice and serving the public interest. However I will also explore the dominance of a literal decontextualized and patriarchal interpretation of Islam's religious texts which has influenced sections of Muslim thought. I will outline the historical and contemporary reality of some Muslims, in manipulating and misusing Islam for their own authority whether political, economic or social to those Muslims who through the combined use of modern day Islamic law and international human rights law have secured the rights of Muslim women. Their struggle is not only for the protection of Muslim women's rights; it is about reclaiming the soul of Islam as a force of good and overcoming the challenges that face humanity when extremists exploit Islam.

Islam and Women's Rights

Muslim women's rights activists often comment on the surprising reality that generally Muslim women had more rights available to them back in the seventh century than they do today in many Muslim majority countries. The Qur'an not only banned female infanticide, it gave women the right to choose their own marriage partner, the right to education, to inherit, to vote, to work, to own property, to contribute on a political and social platform, the right to full sexual fulfilment and it even gave women the right to participate in war including an area of much controversy today, the right to participate on the front line.

Western feminist history continues to remain suspiciously silent about the remarkable rights given to women in seventh-century Arabia. This is largely a result of late nineteenth-century colonial feminism which deliberately focused on Islam's alleged suppression of women, while conveniently ignoring the lack of women's rights in Western countries. As Ahmed claims, the language of feminism was adopted by the colonial discourse to give an 'aura of moral justification to the assault' on Islam, so as 'to render morally justifiable its project of undermining or eradicating the cultures of colonised peoples' (Ahmed, 1992: 167). The legacy of unfair and Orientalist representations about Islam and women continues to impact contemporary thinking. Today, at the extreme end, the 'oppression of Muslim women' narrative is used by the far right and the counterjihad movement to further their Islamophobic agenda. More generally, numerous polls highlight that Britons, in large numbers, believe Islam to be a backward religion which subjugates women.

Far from sanctioning the mistreatment of women, the Qur'an deliberately sought to emphasize the equality accorded to men and women:

> For Muslim men and women, for believing men and women, for devout men and women, for true men and women, for men and women who are patient and constant, for men and women who humble themselves, for men and women who give in charity, for men and women who fast (and deny themselves), for men and women who guard their chastity, and for men and women who engage much in God's praise for them has God prepared forgiveness and great reward.(Quran 33:35)

The idea that a woman's role could only be within the home or the private sphere and a man's responsibilities lay outside the home was rejected by the Qur'an. Explaining the purpose of human life, 'I will create on the earth an agent/trustee' (Qur'an 2: 30) God clearly states that human beings, both men and women, were created to fulfill a vicegerancy role, establishing justice and prohibiting evil. Islam does not advocate gender specific roles per se, or expect women to be confined to the private sphere but instead liberates women and men to focus on their human potential by encouraging both genders to excel in whatever they do and does not restrict one gender to one sphere over another. As trustees of earth, God demands that everyone fully utilize their potential for the betterment of themselves, for others and for society. As Badawi (1995: 4) argues 'nowhere does the Quran state that one gender is superior to the other. Men and women have the same religious and moral duties and responsibilities'. This was best demonstrated by the Prophet Muhammad himself. The Messenger of God and leader of the growing Muslim empire who regularly undertook housework did not expect women to be confined to the private sphere. Exemplifying the practical egalitarian spirit of Islam, he turned the limited traditional male/ female roles on their head by focusing on everyone, regardless of their gender, playing a proactive part in family and community life.

This was also demonstrated by the Muslim women at the time of the Prophet. They were outspoken women who made sure their voices were heard; passive or docile they were not. Their authority and testimonies were not belittled as is too often the case today. Many male scholars would deliberately seek out those women who were known to have great intellect and understanding of the faith. Aisha, the wife of the Prophet, was an outstanding scholar and expert on Islamic legislation and over 2,210 hadith (the sayings of the Prophet) are attributed to her. If her testimonies had been ignored just because of her gender, we would not have had access to many of the statements made by the Prophet today. Aisha was described by Ibn 'Ata as 'among all the people, the one who had the most knowledge of *fiqh* (juristic understanding), the one who was the most educated and compared to those who surrounded her, the one whose judgement was the best' (Ibn Hajar al-Asqalani, in Mernissi, 1991: 66).

Many of the greatest teachers in Islam were in fact women like A'isha bint Sa'd bint ibn Abi Waqqas and Sayyida Nafisa whose pupils included Imam Malik and Imam Shafi'i respectively, the founders of the Maliki and Shafi'i jurisprudence. Nadwi (2007) highlights that, historically, the transmission of hadith , has involved at least 8,000 prominent women. The world's first academic degree granting university, Al-Qarawiyin was founded by Fatima al-Fihri in 859 CE and is still in operation today in Morocco. Rather than suppressing women, Islam inspired and fully encouraged them to seek knowledge and to use their knowledge to benefit humanity.

As soldiers, women also joined Muslim armies and participated in battles. Women like Umm Umara who was praised by the Prophet for her tremendous skill, fought in numerous battles including the Battle of Uhud and there are many examples like her, such as Umm Hakim who single handedly killed seven Byzantine soldiers at the Battle of Marj al–Saffar. Much has been written about Khawlah bint al-Azwar, known as the Black Knight who was a remarkable soldier. Whenever she was not in battle, she took responsibility for organizing medical care to treat the wounded, 13 centuries before Florence Nightingale did the same in Europe. Not only were there Muslim women soldiers, teachers and scholars, but they also held high political office and key leadership roles. Ash Shifa bint Abdullah was not only skilled in medicine but it was her skill in public administration which led to her appointment by Caliph Umar Ibn Al Khattab as chief administrator of the marketplace. Umar would tell shopkeepers that if they were in doubt about the legality of a particular transaction, then they should ask financial expert Al-Shifa.

Throughout the centuries Muslim women also held the reins of power. Shajarat al-Dur, a ruler of Egypt who gained power in Cairo in 648/1250 took political and military power after the death of her husband. She successfully led her army to victory during the crusades and captured King Louis IX. Sultana Radia Begum who governed Delhi with a firm hand in 634/1236 was famed for fair dealing. Asma Bint Shihab al-Sulayhiyya (d. 480/1087) ruled Yemen with her husband. Her daughter in law, Arwa held power for almost half a century from 485/1092 to 532/1138. Both these female heads of state were so respected that the Friday sermon in mosques was proclaimed in their names, a rare honour (Mernissi, 2007). More recently, Indonesia, Pakistan, Bangladesh and Turkey, the four largest contemporary Muslim nations, have all had women leaders.

Purpose of Shariah: Securing Justice and Serving the Public Interest

'A day of [commanding] justice is better than sixty or seventy years' worship' (Saying of The Prophet Muhammad via Abu Hurayrah by Daylami and Abu Nu'aym: Kashf al-Khafa' of 'Ajluni, no. 1721). In Islam, religion is not an end in itself but its purpose is to secure justice through the fulfillment of higher objectives in life: in Islam known as *maqasid al Shariah* (the higher objectives of Islam's ethical, legal and moral rulings). The aim of *maqasid* is to achieve a perfect balance, or equilibrium between tradition and reason, where interpretations and legal opinions can and must be modified according to the time, place, local culture (*urf*) and context.

The human endeavor to interpret the Shariah, or the Divine Will which began in the eighth century, resulted in a great collection of juristic legal opinions known as *fiqh*. Imam Ghazzali stated that 'nine-tenths of juristic understanding (*fiqh*) is understanding your context and one tenth is mastering the texts' (Bayyah, 2011). The Muslim jurists of these early times developed a rich intellectual tradition founded on the understanding that the essential purpose of shariah rulings and the higher objectives of the shariah were to secure justice (*adl*). They recognized that the aim of Islam was to prevent human beings from being deprived of their rights and to serve the public interest (*maslahah*). Key to *maslahah* are the twin principles of the removal of hardship (*raf al-haraj*) and the prevention of harm (*daf al-darar*). Legal rulings, particularly with regard to issues unrelated to fundamental beliefs, are determined by the historical, cultural and moral environment, and are not meant to be fixed for all time, as the process of *ijtihaad* (understanding and deriving rules of shariah on particular issues from Islamic sources), encourages interpretations based on current political, social, economic and cultural contexts.

Imam Ibn al Qayyim (d1351) summarized the purpose of shariah:

> The shariah is all about wisdom and achieving people's welfare in this life and the afterlife. It is all about justice, mercy, wisdom and good. Thus any ruling that replaces justice with injustice, mercy with its opposite, common good with mischief, or wisdom with nonsense, is a ruling that does not belong to the Islamic law (shariah), even if it is claimed to be so according to some interpretation. (Auda, 2008: 21)

A ruling made in the name of religion cannot be part of Islamic law if the end result is wrongdoing or nonsense; at their core they should be sensible. This resonates with Christopher Lewis' definition of sensible as described earlier. The Qur'an is clear on the centrality of justice as an end goal, commanding believers to stand up in the name of justice even if it means standing up against oneself, one's family, or against the rich or the poor (Qur'an 4: 135).

Early traditional shariah principles developed the concepts that people were innocent of a crime until proven guilty, that proof is based on unequivocal evidence and that capital/corporal punishments must be waived if there is even the slightest doubt as to culpability. Long before the language of human rights emerged in twentieth century Western discourse, Muslim jurists in the medieval era established the idea of human rights (*huquq al adamiyyin*) and argued that no ruler had the power to deprive an individual of their rights. Shariah, or the rule of law was not to protect the rich or ruling classes, but was intended to secure the rights of each and every individual. As we are all equal before God, everyone was deemed equal in the eyes of the law.

Justice underpins Islamic legal theory. Adl translates as: 'placing something in its rightful place and also means according equal treatment to others or reaching a state of equilibrium in transactions with them' (Kamali, 2002: 103). As an overriding objective of Islam, Kamali states that justice stands next in order of priority to belief in God and the message of the Prophet. Encouraging humanity constantly to reflect on the precise regularity and equilibrium of the universe, God challenges humans to see if there are any flaws in the order of the universe (Qur'an 67: 1–5). Muslims are expected to practice moderation in all aspects of life, to respect the rights of others in order to live well-balanced lives and to recreate the universe's equilibrium among the human race. Any kind of extremism is discouraged, even in worship. 'O People of Scripture! Do not go to extremes in your religion' (Quran 4: 171).

To deny the rights of another is to transgress against the Balance spoken of in the Quran (55: 7–9). 'He has set up the Balance: in order that you may not transgress the Balance. So establish weight with justice, and fall not short in the Balance'. The sources of Islamic teachings and much of the original Islamic jurisprudence repeatedly make it clear that extremism of any kind upsets the balance of the human condition. Without balance there cannot be justice and without justice there is no Islam. Muslims are obliged to seek equilibrium in all aspects of life and justice for all. How do those Muslims who resent women's participation believe such an equilibrium can be achieved if half of humanity is prevented from fully utilizing their skills and talents?

The Dominance of Literal Decontextualized Readings of Islam's Scriptures

At face value, there seem to be some undeniably unjust and deeply disturbing practices against women, most notably that a Muslim man is allowed four wives, and that a man may beat his wife. Verse 4: 34 appears to condone domestic violence against women. But as Hasan states (2011) not only is a holistic reading of the verse required, but an appreciation of the social-historical context is also needed, where violence against women in the seventh century was socially perceived as normal behaviour. The Prophet himself never hit any woman and despised any form of domestic violence including forced marriage. The verse was a temporary measure which fell in line with the gradualist approach of the Qur'an with the aim of eventually outlawing domestic violence (Hasan, 2011). Other examples of this gradualist approach adopted by the Qur'an included the prohibition of slavery. The Qur'an began a process of encouraging the freeing of slaves based on Islam's belief that freedom was the natural state of affairs for human beings. It did not ban it outright immediately, because of the widely accepted and institutionalized economic and cultural dependence on slaves at the time. But it began a long-term process of freeing slaves with the aim of outlawing slavery altogether and as Sardar (2011) points out, the morality of the Qur'an is not the end point of human thought but rather the beginning of morality. Hence:

the evidence for this interpretation is overwhelming, from the 8th-century AD Mufti of Mecca, 'Ata bin Abi Rabah, who ruled that 'a man may not hit his wife' to the 20th-century Mufti of the Zaytuna in Tunis, Ibn 'Ashur, who ruled that the State may ban domestic violence and punish any man who assaulted his wife. (Hasan, 2011: 3–4)

Sardar (2011) points out that the moral goal of the Qur'an is to move towards a society free from domestic violence. Unfortunately, this is still a far cry today where one in four women in the UK, irrespective of faith are victims of domestic violence.

The practice of polygamy was widespread in pre-Islamic times and was drastically limited by the Qur'an. The relevant verses in the Qur'an are about offering the protection of marriage to those widowed or orphaned after battle, but restricts the number of wives a man can have to a maximum of four (Qur'an 4: 2–3). However, the same verse states that if men cannot treat them equally resulting in injustice, then they should only marry one. A later verse (4: 129) then states, 'you shall never be able to do justice among women, no matter how much you desire to do so'. God is in fact declaring that men will never be able to be just between wives and therefore it is best that men practice monogamy. Some jurists fundamentally rejected the view that the Qur'an advocated polygamy but instead supported monogamy as the Islamic norm. 'The goal of the exercise is a transformation: to move a polygamous society to a monogamous one' (Sardar, 2011: 306). These days, the overwhelming majority of Muslim men only have one wife.

One of the current crises facing Muslims today is the dominance of literal, decontextualized readings of Islam's scriptures and a misuse in the application of doctrines and traditions of Islamic law in the contemporary age. Whilst ignoring the overall spirit of the Qur'an, both Islamo-fascists and Islamophobes, select literal readings of singular verses of the Qur'an in isolation of their historical, cultural and moral contexts. This has led to extreme, puritanical sects first breaking away from, and then bullying, mainstream Islam and Muslims. The Qu'ran, it must be pointed out, was revealed over a period of 23 years and was often speaking directly to the early believers and to their political and social circumstances. A literalist reading fails to distinguish between general rulings that were addressed to all Muslims, and ones that were supposed to be restricted in application to the particular circumstances of the early believers. These extremists justify fierce intolerance, aggressive sexism and even terrible atrocities in the name of religion. As Fadl (2002: 23) wisely observes, 'the text will morally enrich the reader but will only be as moral as the reader. If the reader is intolerant, hateful or oppressive, so will be his interpretation of the text'.

In past centuries, the violent puritanism of extreme offshoots, such as the Khawarij were rejected by mainstream Islam. However, the contemporary supremacist puritanism of Wahabi-Salafi ideology that rejects women's autonomy and promotes the complete marginalization of women in public, has come to hold much sway over Muslim thought. The state sponsored spread of Wahhabism by Saudi Arabia and Qatar and the unprecedented scope of the Internet means this extreme version of Islam now reaches Muslims all over the world. Other ideological strands such as Deobandi and Barelvi thought originated in countries where deep chauvinism is the norm. A fusion of patriarchal culture, pre-modern legal rulings and literal decontextualized readings of Islam's texts has in part resulted in highly conservative interpretations of the position of women in Islam. Due in large part to a stagnation in ijtihaad, and an absence of religious authority and of institutions which were pivotal in rejecting extreme interpretations, together with the modern phenomenon of globalization, Muslims find themselves living in unprecedented times.

Patriarchy: Silencing the Female Voice

From the very beginning, there was widespread resistance to the Prophet's campaign for women's rights, even while he was alive. Patriarchy and chauvinism were ingrained in the cultural attitudes of the time and were hard to change. The Prophet himself had to challenge gender-based inequalities directly. Knowing the tensions that existed around treating women with dignity, he repeatedly warned his followers throughout his life and even at his final sermon to treat women justly. When, for example, men tried to prevent women from attending the mosques or denying them inheritance rights, the Prophet explicitly ordered them not to deny women their rights in these and many other areas. It is inexcusable that today, even in the United Kingdom, male dominated mosque leadership has prevented women from sitting on committees and, in some cases, have even denied them entry into the house of God.

Inheritance rights are an interesting example. In pre-Islamic Arabia, it was the norm for women to be denied any share in inheritance, especially as one of the criteria for qualifying for inheritance was to participate in battle. As more and more women began to participate in battle, they began to demand their share in inheritance, whereas the men in Medina insisted that women should continue to be barred from qualifying for inheritance. However God ruled in women's favour.

After the Prophet's death, many men felt they could revert to previous cultural norms that viewed and treated women as lesser beings. Ibn Umar refers to this move in a remarkable statement: 'When the Prophet was alive we were cautious about speaking and dealing with our women in fear that a revelation would come from God concerning our behaviour. But when the Prophet died we were able to speak and deal with them more freely' (Ibn Hajar al-Asqalani in Fadl, 2008: 223). Since the earliest days of resistance to the development of women's rights, a practice of silencing women and in particular of preventing them from interpreting Islamic law and pushing them out of the public sphere, has been in play. As Tucker writes:

> the process of silencing them in the following centuries represented a historic defeat for women, where the development of the law, and in particular, the interpretation of Islamic law was left in the hand of male interpreters. The impact of this can still be felt today, where 'the Woman as silent' both shaped and was shaped by Islamic legal discourse. (Tucker, 2008: 30)

Some of the thinking of early male jurist's was conditioned by their being male. Their jurisprudence was not influenced by malicious misogyny but rather by patriarchal assumption stemming from the culture norms of the time (Ali, 2008.) Some legal interpretations prevailed because they were more politically, socially and culturally acceptable as opposed to being more authentic.

The establishment of the Abbasid dynasty in 750 and for four centuries thereafter played a crucial role in developing institutions and shaping thought on all matters relating to Islam including gender. As Ahmed (1992) argues, the Abbasid dynasty's 'interpretive and legal legacy has defined Islam ever since, heard only the androcentric voice of Islam and they interpreted the religion as intending to institute androcentric laws and an androcentric vision in all Muslim societies throughout time'. Unlike the early Muslim believers, where women actively participated in the public sphere, whether in the battlefield or in the mosques, 'in Abbasid society women were conspicuous for their absence from all arenas of the community's central affairs', where:

> the most significant differences distinguishing Abbasid society from the first Islamic society in Arabia lay in the view that elite men had of women and the relationship in which they stood to them ... the marketing of people and

particularly women, as commodities and as objects for sexual use was an everyday reality in Abbasid society. (Ahmed 1992: 84)

Islam Empowering Women Strengthening Societies: Today's Gender Jihad

Religion is not the only factor impacting on our ability to live sensibly. Britain, for example, has fallen from thirty-third to sixtieth place out of 190 countries in global league tables in relation to women's access to power and representation in politics (Centre for Women and Democracy 2013). It is well known that a lack of education, employment and other socioeconomic indicators acts as a barrier to anyone living a free and independent life and fully realizing their human potential. A recent report (Gallup 2012) suggested that one of the greatest challenges facing women in the Arab world is not religion, but a lack of economic and social development and security. The same report also highlighted that the more men are thriving, are in employment and are educated, the more they support women's rights. This is not just a problem in the developing world; having worked with British Muslim women for the last 20 years, I have witnessed the socioeconomic obstacles affecting both men and women here.

For women to be free to live as they choose, to participate in the public sphere and to be on an equal footing with men, as prescribed in Islam, is not just right or fair, it is beneficial for society as a whole. Development studies have repeatedly proved that proactive women play a critical role in economic progress, good governance and healthy civil society. Educated women in social, political and economic roles are essential to reducing poverty, improving health (including decreasing the transmission of HIV/AIDS), and improving a country's long-term economic growth rate. Women's empowerment, through education and participation in society, is widely recognized as a powerful development objective in its own right and as Coleman highlights, among the Millennium Development Goals, women's empowerment is considered so essential that it underpins all of the other goals. Coleman notes:

> societies that invest in and empower women are on a virtuous cycle. They become richer, more stable, better governed, and less prone to fanaticism. Countries that limit women's educational and employment opportunities and their political voice get stuck in a downward spiral. They are poorer, more fragile, have higher levels of corruption and are more prone to extremism. (Coleman, 2010: 8)

Kristof and WuDunn (2012: introduction xxi) suggest that empowering girls is key to disempowering terrorists and that 'the countries that nurture terrorists are disproportionally those where women are marginalised'. The skills of women as mediators and decision-makers who can effectively come together to form networks and settle disputes has also been highlighted. Their efforts are 'frequently dismissed as irrelevant or are not sufficiently value' (Cardona et al., 2012: 6). 'But research demonstrates that at the local level, women continue to build peace within their homes and communities and come together collectively to create change'.

The message is clear and contrary to the assertions of the chauvinist, Muslim or otherwise: it is not women's active participation in public life but the lack of educated, employed women and the marginalization and silencing of women's voices which contributes to the weakening of families and societies. As we have seen, Islam respects the full independence and autonomy of women and encourages both men and women to make use of their full potential for the betterment of humanity.

Tariq Ramadan (2009: 62) aptly wrote that 'Islam has no problem with women, but Muslims themselves do clearly appear to have serious problems with them'. It is important to note that not all Muslims, men in particular, deny women their rights. Many Muslim men and women true to their faith are engaging in a 'gender jihad', a struggle to reclaim women's rights guaranteed by Islam. Using the egalitarian teachings of Islam, a number of individuals and organizations across the world from Morocco to Indonesia, from Pakistan to Egypt, as well as here in the UK, are working to reclaim Islam's spirit of justice for all. For such change to take place, it is essential for Muslim women and men not to reject Islam, but to master and then arm themselves with Islamic teachings. A genuine understanding of Shariah law and how it has developed provides the tools for undermining patriarchal practices that are usually, ironically, protected and strengthened in the name of Shariah law.

A good example of how Shariah law and women's rights have been proved not to be mutually exclusive is the reform of the family code (*mudawana*) in Morocco. In 2004, with backing from the king and in response both to a civil society campaign led by grassroots activists and to the collection of 1 million signatures from ordinary Moroccans, a new family code was passed by Parliament. The reformed *mudawana* restricted polygamy, raised the permitted marriage age for girls from 15 to 18, gave women further guarantees in marriage, prevented divorces from taking place outside court and granted women greater financial autonomy.

Musawah is a global movement that calls for equality and justice in the Muslim family by challenging dominant decontextualized interpretations of Islamic law. The Musawah approach involves a critical feminist perspective while working within the tradition of Islamic legal thought, fully utilizing Islam's scriptures to help secure justice for women and families. This powerful combination of feminism and Islam can help combat patriarchy effectively in Muslim majority countries and communities.

Not only are Muslim women campaigning against violence, there have been numerous initiatives set up by Muslim men, such as the Muslim Men against Domestic Violence initiative and the Muslims for White Ribbon Campaign. Through reference to the Qur'an and to the example of the Prophet, Islam is used as a tool to help tackle domestic violence in Muslim communities. My own organization, Inspire, is a human rights organization which works to re-liberate Muslim women from injustices experienced not only by those who distort Islam's teachings but also within wider society, where Muslim women are significantly disadvantaged. Inspire campaign for the rights of Muslim women, using both British equality legislation and the egalitarian Islamic tradition. The empowerment of Muslim women is a key focus of our work. Having not been provided with a good Islamic education, many British Muslim women struggle to provide contextualized religious guidance to their children who often dismiss their parents as weak or ignorant of Islam. Some of these children have been shown to be vulnerable to extremist ideologies found on the Internet, or to hateful propaganda taught by intolerant Muslim preachers. Inspire runs workshops all over Britain to equip women not only with an understanding of their rights and how to secure them, but also, crucially, a sound knowledge of Islam is also imparted to them to help them to keep their children within mainstream Islam and to reject extreme ideas.

The success or failure of this gender jihad is one of the main challenges facing Muslims in the twenty-first century, particularly since the 'Arab Spring'. It remains to be seen whether ruling Islamist parties appreciate that the empowerment and full representation of women in all areas of life is a prerequisite to strengthening their countries, politically, economically and socially. As God says (Qur'an 9: 71) 'men and women are protectors and supporters (*awliya*) of one another: They enjoin what is just, and forbid what is evil'. This Qur'anic verse suggests mutuality, interdependence and equality between men and women who should rely on, support and respect one another in order to cooperate in all aspects of life whether private or public.

Both faith-based and non-faith feminists know that despite the achievements made over time the road to full gender equality is a long one. However, the gender equality movement is an influential one; the fear of being accused of discrimination against women is significant in the twenty-first century. This politically correct practice is used effectively by many Muslim women's rights activists and cautiously by the international community in order to apply pressure on communities and countries. The language of gender equality will continue to become customary among Muslims, as is evident among so many ordinary believers. This movement, fused with an egalitarian Islam, should be embraced by all those who believe in justice and should be fully supported by Muslims so as to bring effective change for women. While being faithful to Islamic tradition it is imperative to recognize and filter out patriarchal interpretations in order to meet the higher objectives of shariah that Islam calls for: to retrieve the equilibrium that is lost whenever women's rights are repressed.

Christopher Lewis asserts that following the religious path is a sensible response for many in the world, and that 'the vast majority of religious people are leading ordinary loving lives'. This is true for Islam, but many Muslims, and Muslim women in particular face tremendous challenges. Help can be found within Islam. Societies as a whole would benefit hugely from the genuine empowerment of Muslim women. The climate is ripe. The time is now. We can, through a combined struggle of religious, scholarly and activist endeavour fulfil Islam's promise to women and to humanity.

Reference List

Ahmed, L. (1992) *Women and Gender in Islam*, New Haven, CT: Yale University Press.

Ali, K. (2008) 'Progressive Muslims and Islamic Jurisprudence: The Necessity for Critical Engagement with Marriage and Divorce Law' in O. Safi (ed.), *Progressive Muslims on Justice, Gender and Pluralism*, Oxford: One World.

Auda, J. (2008) *Maqasid al Shari'ah: A Beginner's Guide*, London: International Institute of Islamic Thought.

Badawi, J. (1995) *Gender Equity in Islam*, Plainfield, IN: American Trust Publications.

Bayyah (2011) *A Juristic Reasoning in Regard to the Verification of Case Rationale as Applied to Minority Jurisprudence*, GCRG Seminar, UK.

Cardona, I., Justino, P., Mitchell, B., and Müller, C. (2012) *From the Ground Up: Women's Roles in Local Peacebuilding in Afghanistan, Liberia, Nepal, Pakistan and Sierra Leone,* Institute of Development Studies.

Available at: http://www.womankind.org.uk/wp-content/uploads/downloads/2012/09/From-The-Ground-Up-FINAL.pdf.

Centre for Women and Democracy (2013) *Sex and Power 2013: Who Runs Britain?* Available at: http://www.countingwomenin.org/wp-content/uploads/2013/02/Sex-and-Power-2013-FINALv2.-pdf.pdf.

Coleman, I. (2010) *Paradise beneath Her Feet: How Women are Transforming the Middle East*, New York, Random House.

Fadl, K. (2002) *The Place of Tolerance in Islam*, Boston, MA: Beacon Press.

Fadl, K. (2005) *The Grand Theft: Wrestling Islam from the Extremists*, New York: Harper Collins.

Fadl, K. (2008) *Speaking in God's Name: Islamic Law, Authority and Women*, Oxford: One World.

Gallup (2012) *After the Arab Uprisings: Women on Rights, Religion and Rebuilding*. Available at: http://www.gallup.com/file/poll/155306/MSG_Gender_Report_en-US_062212.pdf.

Hasan, U. (2011) *Have You Stopped Beating Your Wife? The Plain Truth about Domestic Violence and the 'Wife Beating' Verse of the Qur'an Including a Holistic Study of Important but Rarely Quoted Hadiths on the Subject*, published at the author's blog http://unity1.wordpress.com.

Ibn Hajar al-Asqalani (n.d.) *Al-Isaba fi tamyiz al-sahaba*, Cairo: Maktaba al-Dirasa al-Islamiya Dar al-Nahda.

Kamali, M. (2002) *Freedom, Equality and Justice in Islam*, Cambridge: Islamic Texts Society.

Kamali, H. (2010) *Shariah Law: An Introduction*, Oxford: One World.

Kristof, N. and WuDunn, S. (2012) *Half the Sky Turning Oppression into Opportunity for Women Worldwide*, New York: Knopf.

Mernissi, F. (1991) *The Veil and the Male Elite: A Feminist Interpretation of Women's Rights in Islam*, New York: Perseus Books Group.

Mernissi, F. (2007) *The Forgotten Queens of Islam*, Cambridge: Polity Press.

Nadwi, M. (2007) *Al-Muhaddithat: The Women Scholars in Islam*, London: Interface Publications.

Ramadan, T. (2009) *Radical Reform Islamic Ethics and Liberation*, New York: Oxford University Press.

Sardar, Z. (2011) *Reading the Qur'an*, London: Hurst and Company.

Tucker, Judith (2008) *Women, Family and Gender in Islamic Law*, New York: Cambridge University Press.

Zamakhshari Al-Kashshaf (n.d.) *Dar al-Kutub al-'Arabi*, Volume 3, Beirut: Dar al-Ma'rifa.

Chapter 6
Reclaiming *Jihad*

Dawoud el-Alami

Definitions of Jihad

The Arabic word *Jihad* has become familiar to the West and has come to be understood as meaning a form of religiously inspired violence, often manifesting itself in atrocities perpetrated by fanatics against innocent people and civilian populations. This is the only meaning that many people are aware of, and while the definition of the word does include armed struggle against the enemies of Islam, there are many including prominent Muslim scholars in both the past and the present who argue that such acts are a distortion of its true meaning which is more peaceful and constructive.

The word is used by the media often loosely and without any real understanding of its meaning, along with other words such as *fatwa* that have been taken out of context and have become a kind of media shorthand for the actions of extremists. Some dictionaries and reference works simply describe *jihad* as Holy War in the name of Islam. In most of the Western media it is used in an almost exclusively negative sense. Militants and terrorists are often referred to as '*jihadis*' and the term has come to suggest ruthless, brainwashed religious zealots bent on waging war against non-Muslims or those Muslim leaders they see as corrupt and not upholding Islamic values. While this description may be accurate with regard to individuals, it bears no relationship to the core meaning of *jihad* and it may be argued that the use by the media of this term, and in fact the claiming of the name by the groups or individuals themselves is illegitimate.

The word *jihad* and words etymologically linked to it first came into Western consciousness on a significant scale in the 1970s, although it has always been a fundamental concept in Islam.

Jihad is an Arabic word with the basic meaning of 'struggle'. In the context of Islam and Islamic law it means a struggle in the way of God and one who undertakes this struggle is a *mujahid* (pl. *mujahidun* or *mujahidin* depending on the grammar of the sentence.) In modern usage the word *mujahidin* first came into currency in the late 1970s and early 1980s in relation to the Afghan rebels who fought the Soviet backed Afghan government and the Soviet forces in Afghanistan. At that time, for the West the term did not have the connotations that it does now. In these final years of the Cold War, the *mujahidin* were, in the eyes of the West, a brave resistance movement valiantly challenging the might of the Soviets, and in this position in the front line they were supported by the USA and Saudi Arabia amongst others. Their prolonged defiance of the Soviet forces was perhaps even significant in undermining the morale of the Soviet Union in its final decline. The *mujahidin* were rallied by religious fervour to defend their homeland and their culture from what was perceived to be foreign control and at the time the West was happy to encourage this.

At the same time, however, the seeds of a radical form of Islam were being sown by the *madrasas* or religious schools that produced the *Taliban* (literally 'students') who became the hardline faction in which fundamentalist Deobandi Islam and tribal culture came together in their grievance at foreign interference and influence in the region and produced a force that has dominated Afghan and Pakistani politics since then.

In the years since, there have been numerous calls to an armed *jihad* in all parts of the Muslim world and beyond. The Islamic revival that has occurred over the last three decades or so has brought with it a global phenomenon of Islamic militancy manifesting itself in networks which have planned and executed horrific attacks on Western targets both in the West and in Muslim countries, and on Muslim targets where they are deemed to be in league with the West, corrupt or failing to stand up for Islamic values. The most devastating and most iconic single event to date of course is the attack on the World Trade Centre and the Pentagon on September 11, 2001 in which almost 3,000 people of all nationalities, races and religions were killed and another 6,000 or so were injured. There have, however, been countless other acts of apparently senseless violence, many against civilians, each of which is no less devastating to those involved and their families. Many if not most of these have been suicide missions, and we have become accustomed to seeing video clips of earnest and obviously committed young men, and sometimes women, expressing their profound conviction that what they are planning to do is God's will. There is something terrifying in the notion that there are people who are willing to sacrifice their lives, not in an altruistic sense in the protection of others or the achievement of a specific strategic aim such as in the defence of freedom in Europe during the Second World War, but in indiscriminate acts of suicide terrorism for an ideological cause with the absolute belief in divine reward. How can we even begin to counter a threat which knows no deterrent and with which we cannot reason? It seems as if almost every day we hear in the media reports of Islamic terrorism to the extent that the words Islam and terrorism have become linked in the minds of many people. To most ordinary Muslims leading what Christopher Lewis calls 'ordinary loving lives', however, the expression Islamic terrorism is an oxymoron and there are many Muslim voices speaking out against violence, terrorism and aggression.

An Islamic Argument against Terrorism

Ten years on from the September 2001 attacks, Shaykh-ul-Islam Dr Muhammad Tahir-ul-Qadri (2011) produced a *fatwa* (a formal opinion in jurisprudence by a qualified scholar) extending to more than 500 pages in which he completely dismantles the arguments in favour of acts of terrorism and suicide bombing. This *fatwa* was certified and approved by Al-Azhar University, one of the highest internationally recognized sources of opinion on Islamic doctrine. Shaykh al-Qadri is unequivocal in his assertion that terrorism and suicide bombing are criminal acts and can never be justified. In many public lectures and speeches he has put forward a detailed legal opinion in which he sets out what he claims to be the true meaning of *jihad*. According to the Shaykh, acts of terror and suicide bombing can never be called *jihad*. He describes *jihad* as being of five kinds: the first kind of *jihad* is *jihad ul-nafs* (*jihad* of the soul) which is the struggle for purification of the self and against the inclinations towards wrongdoing. This is the daily struggle of every Muslim to be a better person, to listen to their conscience – to resist greed, deception, immorality, prejudice and hatred and to cultivate in themselves faith, moral virtue, honesty, integrity, compassion and understanding. The second form is *jihad bi'l-'ilm* (*jihad* by knowledge) which is the struggle to spread knowledge, to promote education and understanding. The third form is *jihad bi'l-'amal* (*jihad* by works), the struggle in working for the benefit of society, peacefully working against corruption, discrimination, abuses of human rights and other social ills and for democracy and social reform. The fourth form is *jihad bi'l-maal* (*jihad* by money), which includes charitable giving, alleviating poverty and improving life for the poor. This may include direct giving or the endowment or support of schools, hospitals, mosques, food-banks or organizations that work amongst the less privileged. Last of all amongst the forms of *jihad* is *jihad bi'l-qitaal*, the armed *jihad*, which is a form of just warfare. This is only permissible if a number of conditions are fulfilled and it can only ever be defensive, never offensive. If an action does not fulfil all of the conditions then it becomes an offensive action which does not qualify as just war and cannot therefore be considered to be *jihad*. This is then a criminal act.

The conditions for military *jihad* are clearly defined. First of all, no individual or group can initiate the *jihad*; only the legitimate state can declare a defensive *jihad*.

Secondly, there should be no killing of non-combatants, which means that any attacks on civilian populations such as suicide bombings are unlawful and are therefore purely criminal acts which can never be considered to be *jihad*. He adds that the logistical support systems to enemy forces may not be targeted, including medical staff, caterers and suppliers of provisions.

The third condition is that any act of warfare must have a just cause, which is strictly defined as being defensive action. The Shaykh tells us that the Qur'an describes one type of 'just' cause as being of self-defence:

> *And fight in the cause of Allah against those who impose war on you. (Yes,) but do not exceed limits. Surely, Allah does not like those who exceed limits.*
> (Sura al-Baqara, 2: 190)

A further just cause, however, may be the struggle against *'fitna'* described as violence, brutality and terrorism that threatens the peace and safety of society:

> *And keep fighting against them until the disruption and mischief is totally eliminated and Din practically becomes subservient to Allah alone (i.e. peace, security and human rights are completely restored). But if they desist, then offensive action is not permissible except against the wrongdoers (transgressors).* (Sura al-Baqara, 2: 193)

A third just cause would be to help the oppressed where there is violation of human rights:

> *What has happened to you (Muslims) that you do not fight in the cause of Allah (to eliminate violence and aggression), whereas those helpless (oppressed and tyrannized) men, women and children who, (depressed by plunder and carnage) call out (for their freedom): 'O our Lord! Rescue us from this town whose (affluent and influential) people are oppressors, and appoint for us some guardian from Your Presence, and make someone our helper from Your Presence'.* (Sura al-Nisa', 4: 75)

Dr Qadri compares this type of action to UN Security Council resolutions (1199 to 1244) regarding Iraq in 1990/92 and in Kosovo in 1998. In these cases collective action was initiated to put an end to human rights abuses.

A fourth condition for *jihad* would be the case of a breach by one of the parties to a peace treaty between two states and the resumption of war:

> *And, (O people of Truth,) continue your fight against these (chieftains of oppression and terrorism for the establishment of enduring peace), until there does not (remain) any disruption and Din (the system of compliance with law and promoting the phenomena of life) is devoted to Allah alone. And if they desist, then Allah is surely seeing well (the action) that they are accomplishing.* (Sura al-Anfal, 8: 39)

The fifth condition for *jihad* is that it should be proportional. There should be no killing of civilians, no attacks on women, children, the sick, clergy or religious scholars, farmers or traders, or envoys and messengers, no burning of houses, destruction of trees or crops, desecration or destruction of places of worship. Animals belonging to the enemy should not be killed except for the immediate food requirements of the Muslim armies. There should be no desecration or disrespect of the bodies of the dead.

Shaykh al-Qadri is adamant that there can be no such thing as Islamic terrorism, or a Muslim terrorist because by definition there can be no terrorism in Islam. A person who commits an act of terrorism puts himself outside Islam and if he commits an act of suicide bombing then he is doubly guilty both of the terrorist offence and of the suicide which is a grave sin.

This *fatwa* condemning terrorism and suicide bombing is an extensive work that explores the question in the tradition of the Islamic scholars and jurists, examining the texts of the Qur'an and Hadith and the context of Islamic history, and using the tools of jurisprudence. The Shaykh is a very active speaker who travels widely to spread his message about a peaceful Islam. He is the founder of the Minhaj ul-Qur'an organization which works to promote peace and understanding between people of all faiths, and in particular aims to divert young Muslims from radicalization and involvement in terrorism and, it might be said, towards a 'sensible religion'.

The Challenge

It would be dishonest, however, to deny that by using the same methods of textual exegesis and Islamic jurisprudence, alternative arguments can be constructed by selecting evidence and opinion to comply with a different agenda. It is entirely possible to put together a case for an aggressive or military *jihad* using many of the same verses and opinions used by those who oppose violence, alongside interpretations of the early history of Islam and the biography of the Prophet. The proponents of this kind of argument exploit the obligation felt by Muslims to show loyalty to Islam and to other Muslims before everything else. There is then, it could be said, a struggle going on for the heart and soul of Islam. There are those who would, by campaigns of indoctrination, convince others that anyone who argues against them is not a true believer. They are organized and well-armed with an array of pre-prepared arguments and answers to every question that to the unprepared are almost impossible to challenge. While their mantras and programmed responses may be selective and simplistic, they offer the kind of certainty that many people seek particularly when they face uncertainty in other aspects of their lives. For 'sensible religion' to prevail, there has to be a greater degree of religious literacy, particularly amongst the young. Young Muslims who have a deeper understanding of the faith and who are able to question what they are told and challenge dangerous opinions will be less vulnerable to being drawn in by radicals and those who prey on the lost and confused. Muslims need to understand their own faith, as well as that of others, and to have a better understanding and appreciation of the history and heritage of Islamic culture and its interaction with other cultures over the course of fourteen centuries.

The understanding of Islam and Islamic scholarship and ultimately any attempts at reform and agendas for progress have to be framed in Islam's own terms. Christopher Lewis refers to a philosophical question of whether religious belief is intellectually acceptable: reasonable, justifiable and therefore 'warranted'. Throughout most of the Islamic world and Muslim communities worldwide, however, this question is not asked. While there is a rich heritage of Islamic scholarship across a range of disciplines, including philosophy and theology, Islam has not gone through the Enlightenment that has shaped the Judeo-Christian world as we see it today. In Islam perhaps more than in any other religion there are absolutes that are never challenged, for even the questions are considered unacceptable. There is no notion in Islam as there is in Christianity of experiencing doubt in order to come to faith. Any expression of doubt, even as an intellectual or spiritual exercise, may be deemed to be the spreading of corruption on the Earth. In Islam the founding text, the Qur'an, is believed to be the literal word of God, preserved unchanged for fourteen centuries. Acceptance of this is a fundamental tenet of Islam and to challenge this is tantamount to apostasy, the most serious crime in Islam. Critical examination of the text is, therefore, somewhat limited. There is no realistic prospect of this changing as it is the underpinning of the faith, and to attempt to do so would be at best futile and at worst counter-productive. What is important, however, is the way we look at it and understand the text.

Muslims believe that the guidance of the Qur'an is complete and valid for all time. In the first centuries of Islam, religious scholars developed methods of exegesis that while leaving the Qur'an untouched sought ways of applying it to their understanding of the world and to the establishment of law

The Qur'an is not a book of law and although it contains a significant number of clear and explicit provisions in certain areas it does not present a codified or comprehensive body of legislation; it is, for the greater part, a collection of narratives and injunctions to belief and right behaviour framed mostly in general or rhetorical terms. The second main source is the *Sunna* or practice of the Prophet Muhammad, being his words, deeds and tacit acceptance of certain actions as reported in the collections of hadith (individual reports) which were collected, collated, assessed for authenticity and categorized by hadith scholars in the eighth and ninth centuries C.E., resulting in six main authoritative collections. The categories of hadith cover all aspects of human activity both public and private. At the time of the Prophet, the law would have been limited to these elements. Following his death, however, and with the rapid spread of Islam and the need to provide for the infinitely varied needs of an expanding civilization it was necessary to establish methods of regulation and adjudication. The religious scholars developed tools and methods for deriving rulings in specific cases using a set of principles of jurisprudence, the most important of which is *ijtihad* (independent reasoning), a word derived from the same root *j-h-d* as the word *jihad* and closely related to it, and meaning the effort or striving to find the correct or appropriate legal ruling in a given situation. *Ijtihad* was an essential element in the development of Islamic jurisprudence in the first three centuries of Islam but in the tenth century CE the so-called 'gate of *ijtihad*' was declared closed within Sunni Islam, meaning that henceforth all legal rulings would have to be derived by *taqlid* (imitation) from what was deemed to be the comprehensive body of existing legal rulings (although Shi'i Islam retained this as an essential juristic tool). There have been many calls over the centuries for the reopening of the gate of *ijtihad* and there have been examples of *ijtihad* in many parts of the Islamic world. In the last century or so in particular there has been a call by numerous prominent Islamic scholars who insist that Islam has the resources and the flexibility to allow reinterpretation and reform without sacrificing its essential tenets.

The scholar Fazlur Rahman (1982) calls *ijtihad* an intellectual and moral *jihad*, or 'the effort to understand the meaning of a relevant text or precedent in the past, containing a rule, and to alter that rule by extending or restricting or otherwise modifying it in such a manner that a new situation can be subsumed under it by a new solution'.

The Sensible Response

The Prophet Muhammad is reported to have said: The best Jihad is a word of justice to an unjust ruler.

There are examples of this all around us. In her interview with Christiane Amanpour in October 2013, the Pakistani schoolgirl, Malala Yousufzai, who only a year or so before was the victim of an attempted assassination by the Taliban for her campaigning for education for girls in the Swat valley, spoke of her stand and her campaigning as her *jihad*. She made the point that *jihad* need not be by the sword, and, although she is not the first to say it of course, that the pen might be more powerful and create more fear in those who would oppress others. The Taliban who had no fear of Russian tanks or American forces, were afraid of a girl, a child with a book. 'The Taliban' she said 'say that we are going to fight for Islam ... So I think we also must think about them ... and that's why I want to tell Taliban [to] be peaceful', she said, 'and the real *jihad* is to fight through pens and to fight through your words. Do that *jihad*. And that's the *jihad* that I am doing. I am fighting for my rights, for the rights of every girl'.

In the United States a very visible campaign was launched in 2012. Calling itself MyJihad, and with the slogan 'Taking Islam back from Muslim and non-Muslim Extremists alike', it promotes a positive definition of *jihad* in the same non-violent terms as Shaykh ul-Qadri. The key message of the MyJihad organization is that Muslims 'are taught to put forth a concerted and noble effort [*jihad*] against injustice, hate, misunderstanding, war, violence, poverty, hunger, abuse or whatever challenge big or small we face in daily life, with the purpose of getting to a better place'.

The founders of this campaign say that the concept of *jihad* has been misrepresented and misused by people on all sides, by the actions of Muslim extremists who try to use it to justify their indefensible goals, by the opponents of Islam and those who would spread Islamophobia claiming that Islamic extremists represent the real *jihad* and the real face of Islam, and by those parts of the media whose stock in trade is sensationalism. The mission statement for the campaign states:

> For Muslim and anti-Muslim extremists (who ironically are in perfect agreement), Jihad is synonymous with terrorism, blowing up things, and spilling innocent blood. This campaign is about reclaiming our faith and its concepts from these extremists, both Muslims and anti-Muslim, as well as their cheerleaders and clap-trappers, all of whom have for too long now effectively hijacked and dumbed-down the conversation about Islam and Muslims.

MyJihad has organized a public information campaign, asking Muslims to state what their own personal *jihad* is; this may be struggles in the most ordinary aspects of their lives, in caring for their families and in their in their relationships with others, or they may be in finding a place for themselves as Muslims in society, resisting both Islamic extremism and Islamophobia.

It also promotes and publicizes the work of a range of charitable organizations, support groups and educational programs. In Chicago alone, where the campaign started, these include organizations carrying on what it defines as *jihad* against urban and inner-city problems including unemployment, drugs, gang culture and criminal activity, against expensive and inaccessible health care in the form of a clinic offering free treatment, against poverty and hunger, domestic violence, lack of opportunity for disadvantaged women, misunderstanding and the faith divide, discrimination and human rights violations.

It is not the only organization working for a moderate, sensible Islam wholeheartedly integrated in mainstream society.

Nihad Awad of the Council on American-Islamic Relations states:

> extremist Muslims who commit crimes should be called criminals or, in cases where the definition fits, terrorists. We should not legitimize their actions by calling them jihadists, even if they attempt to call themselves by that label and seek a false religious connection or justification. These criminals should not be honored with a religious label.

In the UK, the Islamic Society of Britain promotes a synthesis of thoughtful 'sensible' Islamic faith and committed 'Britishness' and numerous other organizations nationally and locally work for the same aims.

Although Muslims share the key elements of the faith and a sense of a shared received history, and while certain elements of a shared Islamic culture have permeated Muslim communities worldwide, Islam is by no means monolithic. There is enormous diversity of nationality, ethnicity and culture across the countries in which Islam is indigenous including (but not limited to) the countries of North Africa, the Middle East, Turkey, Central Asia, the Balkans and some former Soviet states, the Asian subcontinent, China, Malaysia and Indonesia. There are estimated to be something in the region of one and a half billion Muslims in the world, and it is, therefore, impossible to attempt to define or describe them as a single group. Many live in poor and developing countries with limited opportunities for education and improvement of their situations. Many have lived under oppressive regimes. Some live in highly developed countries with good standards of living but often with limited access to democracy, and some live in countries that were until recently stable and relatively prosperous but which have in the last few years been torn apart by war and civil conflict which has left them dislocated and without any immediately conceivable prospect of any kind of normal life.

According to John Esposito (2003):

> Muslims today face critical choices. If Western powers need to rethink, reassess their policies, mainstream Muslims worldwide will need to more aggressively address the threat to Islam from religious extremists. Governments that rely upon authoritarian rule, security forces and repression will have to open up their political systems, build and strengthen civil society, discriminate between free speech and mainstream opposition and a violent extremism that must be crushed and contained. Societies that limit freedom of thought and expression produce a sense of alienation and powerlessness that often results in radicalisation and extremism. Formidable religious obstacles must be overcome: the ultra-conservatism of many (though not all) *ulama*; the more puritanical militant exclusivist brands of Islam; the curriculum and training in those madrasas and universities that perpetuate a 'theology of hate', the beliefs of militants who reject not only non-Muslims but also other Muslims who do not believe as they do. The *jihad* (struggle) will be religious, intellectual, spiritual and moral. But it must be a more rapid and widespread program of Islamic renewal that not only builds on past reformers but also follows the lead of enlightened religious leaders and intellectuals today who more forcefully and more effectively engage in a wide ranging process of reinterpretation (*ijtihad*) and reform (*islah*).

Whatever a few academics and theologians may say and however the scholars may present a moderate, sane, humane or 'sensible' theoretical picture of what Islam should be, ultimately Islam is and will be whatever a billion Muslims say it is, even if this does not conform to the idealized model that we imagine. All we can do then is to put our faith in the essential qualities in most people of goodness, empathy and humanity.

John Esposito and Dalia Mogahed (2008) published an analysis of a survey carried out over several years amongst Muslims in 35 countries. The fact that it appears from the results that Muslims and Americans want the same things, prosperity, justice and freedom, that they are equally likely to condemn attacks on civilians as morally unjustified, and that those who condone terrorism are no more religious than the rest of the population is a cause for optimism.

Reference List

Esposito, J. (2003) *Unholy War, Terror in the Name of Islam*, Oxford: Oxford University Press.

Esposito, J. and Mogahed, D. (2008) *Who Speaks for Islam? What a Billion Muslims Really Think*, New York: Gallup Press.

Rahman, F. (1982) *Islam and Modernity: Transformation of an Intellectual Tradition*, Chicago, IL: University of Chicago Press.

Tahir-ul-Qadri, M. (2011) *Fatwa on Terrorism and Suicide Bombings*, London: Minhaj ul-Qur'an Publications.

Chapter 7

The Reasonableness of Christianity

Keith Ward

This chapter is in two parts. The first deals with a general definition of 'reason', and the second with the reasonableness of three major Christian beliefs. Humans are, of course, prone to accepting many irrational beliefs, but it is peculiarly difficult to give an account of what it is to be reasonable or sensible. In Part 1 I give many examples that undermine the idea that a belief is reasonable only if it is based on publicly agreed evidence. In Part 2, I show that some basic Christian beliefs can be deemed reasonable or sensible if they formulate ways in which a rational God could communicate the divine nature and purpose to humans through the person of Jesus, and if they are liberating and life-transforming. I think that a number of interpretations of religious beliefs, among them some Christian ones, will conform to all acceptable canons of rationality.

Part 1

Reason and God

There is a stereotype that has become popular in modern British culture. It is that atheism is reasonable whereas religious faith is unreasonable. Thus the 'Rationalist association' is explicitly anti-religious, and it is commonplace to speak of religion as irrational because it is based on nothing more than a 'leap of faith' without any evidence. However, the truth is that this stereotype is itself irrational and not based on evidence. Even a cursory knowledge of the history of ideas would reveal that almost all major philosophers in the European tradition have believed in God for what they took to be good reasons. Indeed, they have usually argued that a fully rational view of the world would inevitably lead to belief in God. Plato and Aristotle, Augustine and Aquinas, Descartes and Leibniz, Kant and Hegel, all produced rational arguments for belief in God (Cf. Ward, 2009).

If you examine the work of two of the most famous skeptics about God, David Hume and Friedrich Nietzsche, you find that they also doubted the efficacy of reason and the ability of reason to understand the world at all. Hume said that 'reason is the slave of the passions' (Hume, 1739, Book 2: Part 3, Section 3), and denied that reason could even show that the laws of nature, the external world itself, and the human self, existed. Nietzsche denigrated reason as a self-deceiving set of rationalizations of the will to power, and set little store by the grandiose claims of most philosophers, whose petty thoughts, he said, were hardly capable of discovering the nature of the universe from their comfortable armchairs. 'The irrationality of a thing is no argument against its existence, rather a condition of it', he says (Nietzsche, 1878: 515).

The history of philosophy testifies that most philosophers who believe in the power of human reason to understand reality do so because they think reality is rational. That, in their view, is because reality is the product of a supremely rational intellect, namely, God. Of course this is 'the God of the philosophers', as Pascal put it, and it may seem to have little to do with the God of Abraham, Isaac, and Jacob, the God of religion. But the plain fact is that most Christian theologians have thought that these two Gods are identical. It is precisely the supreme intellect of God, the *Logos*, as it is described in the first verse of the Gospel of John, which is the God who 'became flesh' in Jesus, and who spoke through the prophets. The God who is supreme wisdom and goodness is one who is capable of appearing in finite form for the sake of creatures, so that they might understand enough of the divine purposes for the world to grow in understanding and goodness. The rationality and supreme perfection of God is the basis and the inspiration for the gradually developing wisdom and goodness of human beings, who were created in the image of God, so that they might grow to be like God, rational and compassionate.

If, on the other hand, human reason is a byproduct or spandrel of a blind evolutionary process which cares only about adaptation and survival, but has no particular concern with truth, there is little reason to trust its deliverances. We are likely to believe what has, by chance, proved adaptive and has helped our species to survive in the far past. Apart from some simple degree of conformity to the immediate environment, there need be little correlation between what has been adaptive and what is abstractly true or reasonable. (This argument is fully set out in Plantinga, 2011.) Nietzsche may be right – power is what drives human survival, and reason, with its preference for impartiality, may actually weaken our chances of survival.

Reason, Science and Evidence

Thus from a history of ideas perspective it is false to say that religious faith has been irrational and atheism has been rational. On the contrary, most Christian theologians have held that God is rational and reason is trustworthy, whereas some atheists have called reason itself in question. The atheist agenda is a different one – to re-define rationality in terms of having overwhelming sensory evidence for all beliefs. This was stated succinctly by W.K. Clifford: 'It is wrong always, everywhere, and for anyone, to believe anything on insufficient evidence' (Clifford, 1879: 240). Far from being a good definition of rationality, I take this to be an irrational, unworkable, and wholly misleading definition. It would make human life impossible. To take a simple example, for various reasons I do not possess a birth certificate, and there is no written record of where I was born. My mother told me where I was born, and I believe her, even though there is now not even a building remaining at that place. Is it wrong for me to believe I was born there, on such flimsy evidence (the word of one woman, who may have had good reason for lying)? Surely it would be wrong for me to say that I do not know where I was born, to distrust my own mother. That would not only be irrational; it would also be immoral. We take thousands of such simple things on trust, especially when we are young, and I think it is absurd to say that we should wait for 'sufficient evidence' before we believe them.

Ah, you may say, but there must *be* some evidence, even if I do not myself possess it. But this plunges us into all the problems that torpedoed the Verification Principle in the early twentieth century. A.J. Ayer, the best-known propounder of that principle, admitted that 'even in its weaker form ... the verification principle runs into difficulties', and gave up the attempt to defend it (Ayer, 1973: 26). If last night I dreamed that I was on Mars, no one else, and certainly no electro-encephalograph, can have any evidence of what the content of my dream was. Even worse, neither can I have any evidence, since I cannot get back into my dream. My memory is all there is to go on. There is no sensory evidence at all. Yet it would be irrational to refuse to believe me. In a rather similar way, many historical claims are not based on any written traces, but on the testimony of someone's memory. Even where there are written accounts, they involve someone's personal interpretation and memory. That is hearsay, not evidence. Does that mean we are never to believe any of them? Much will depend on the reliability and expertise of the testifier, and on corroboration by others. But it is almost inevitable that we will also take more general considerations into account – like whether the alleged occurrences are intrinsically probable, whether there is a good explanation for the testifier being mistaken, and whether the occurrences cohere with our general view of the world. Richard Swinburne defends 'the principle of credulity' (which I prefer to call the 'principle of trust') as essential to building up a rational view of the world, and I think succeeds in showing that, contrary to what Clifford says, we could not build up a rational view without a great deal of trust (Swinburne, 1979: 254–76).

Now an irreducible element of subjectivity enters in. We must judge the reliability and expertise of our informants; we must ask what sort of occurrences are intrinsically probable; and we must even finally resort to a general worldview. Do we have 'sufficient evidence' for any of these judgments? There is evidence, of course. That is, there are facts we can appeal to in support of our beliefs. But if we have any degree of self-awareness, we know that many of these facts are disputed by others, and that there are different interpretations of the facts that cannot be resolved just by appeal to the facts themselves. Perhaps, many philosophers suggest, there are few totally value-free facts.

Consider an example: Einstein said that 'God does not play dice with the universe'. He believed there would always be a deterministic explanation for sub-atomic processes. Most quantum physicists disagree with Einstein, and believe some such processes (for instance, the decay of radioactive nuclei) have no deterministic interpretation. For Einstein, this was too 'improbable' to be believed. For Niels Bohr, on the other hand, we just have to adjust our thinking about what is probable in nature. There is no disagreement here about what is observed. There is a deep disagreement, which may have further important consequences, about the nature of causality. Was Einstein irrational in continuing to hold his belief when the evidence seemed to be against it? Surely not; we should applaud him for sticking to his guns, hoping he would be proved right one day. Was the dispute resolvable by appeal to sensory evidence? Obviously not. Such evidence left various options open, though it certainly undermined common-sense beliefs about causality. The best way to account for this situation is to say that such beliefs are not *based on* sensory evidence. They hope such evidence may come up one day. But they are based on trust in mathematical beauty and on certain deep assumptions about how nature works.

Most of us have some basic beliefs about what is likely to happen in the world, and how to interpret it adequately. One example is the belief, held very strongly by some, that we have libertarian free will, and should be held responsible for our actions, other things being equal. There is no sufficient evidence for this view, except that we seem to experience doing things responsibly. But we know that others disagree with us, and they have no sufficient evidence either – just an assumption that deterministic causality must always obtain. Here is an unresolvable dispute with important practical consequences that no appeal to evidence will decide – though, of course, empirical evidence is always relevant, and we might hope that one day we might find out the truth, even though we have no idea of how this might come about.

Another example is the belief that the natural sciences can answer every meaningful question of fact. This is also a belief that cannot be established by evidence. All evidence could show is that every question so far has been answered by science, or that there are some questions that have not been so answered (actually, the latter claim is obviously true). After all such evidence is in, we have to think about whether there are logical limits to the sort of questions natural sciences ask. I think most people who have considered the question rationally would say that natural science, as we have it, deals with data that are publicly observable, controllable, quantifiable, repeatable, regular and predictable. Good science requires us to devise controlled experiments, where various properties can be measured, put in as values to relevant mathematical equations, which are then used to make predictions that can be tested repeatedly. If that is the case, there are many sorts of data that do not seem to be amenable to this sort of procedure. They would include virtually all subjective experiences – feelings, sensations, thoughts, and intentions, none of which can be precisely measured, repeated exactly, or made subject to controlled experiment. I agree with Richard Swinburne in distinguishing 'personal explanations' (explanations of actions as performed for the sake of achieving an envisaged goal) from 'scientific explanations' (in terms of general causal laws), and in holding that neither is reducible to the other (Swinburne, 1977: 131–8). This seems to point to another area with which natural sciences like physics, for example, are not concerned. Moreover, moral beliefs are real beliefs which many would hold to be truth-valued (it is either true or false that treating women as inferior is wrong), but which cannot be shown to be true by appeal to evidence. In general, beliefs about subjective experiences, creative purposive actions, philosophical beliefs, mathematical beliefs, moral beliefs, and beliefs about historical events, simply do not fall into the class of data which are measurable, repeatable and experimentally controllable. This counts against the view that all proper beliefs can be settled by scientific evidence.

A Broader Definition of Reason

All in all, it seems an unduly restrictive definition of 'rationality' to say that it consists in having sufficient sensory evidence to settle all our beliefs. We need a much broader and more supple definition of what a reasonable belief is. Fortunately, we possess such a broader conception of reason, and we use it most of the time. It is not helpful to think of 'reason' as a faculty which tells us truths. We learn truths through experience, either personal or the publicly tested sort of experience upon which the natural sciences rely, and through interpretations of experience that may exist on various levels of abstraction. Whatever beliefs we have, we can hold them reasonably or unreasonably. So reasonableness is more a matter of the way in which we hold our beliefs rather than a way of deciding which beliefs are true. Reasoning is a procedure rather than a source of truth.

In Chapter 1 of this volume, Christopher Lewis presents a number of criteria in accordance with which sensible religion can be distinguished from irrational religion. The contributors to the volume show how these criteria can be applied to their own traditions. The criteria provide a good account of what reasonableness is, a much more adequate account than one which seeks to confine reasonableness to having good public evidence. If I may rehearse them in my own way, I would say that a reasonable view will be aware of its basic first principles, will be consistent, and will know what relevant alternative views exist. It will try to understand such alternative views as sympathetically as possible – for instance, stating them only in ways that would be acceptable to people who actually hold them. It will be self-critical, always being open to reasoned objections and seeking to see what strength they have. It will be aware of the historical origin and development of various views, and seek to see them in a fully global context. It will be aware of relevant facts and arguments, and the strength and limits of expert opinion. It will not pretend to be a 'view from nowhere', without any prejudice or partiality. But it will seek to develop a view which is internally consistent, coherent with other well-established knowledge, comprehensive in covering as wide a range of experience as possible, elegant in relating different areas of experience as simply and clearly as possible, and fruitful in forming the basis of a life-stance which is both morally acceptable and personally fulfilling. Thus a reasonable view will seek to be open, empathetic, critical, and engaged – a delicate matter of balance and judgment, for achieving which there is no algorithmic formula. It follows that there will not usually be just one reasonable view on a topic. There will be a number of reasonable views. It will be sensible to see one's own view as a defensible one, and indeed as the most comprehensive and adequate one of which one is aware, but not necessarily as an overwhelmingly obvious one.

Some atheists and some believers fail these tests – not realizing the fragility and contestability of their basic axioms, failing to take other views seriously or state them accurately, failing to be self-critical, not realizing how beliefs have developed over time and now much they are stated in historically conditioned forms, or failing to take expert opinion in relevant disciplines seriously. Thus scientifically informed atheists sometimes do not bother to read works of classical theology, while theologically trained Christians are sometimes ignorant of the strength of scientific claims. All these failures render beliefs less reasonable than they should be. But such failures can be remedied, and both atheism and theism can be stated in more or less reasonable ways. It is highly doubtful that only one of them is reasonable, just as such, and that the other is irrational, however carefully and subtly stated.

It is also false to say that there are no considerations that count for or against belief in God. The existence of suffering and randomness in nature count against belief in a good creator. The elegance of physical laws, the fine-tuning of the fundamental laws and constants of nature, the appearance of directionality (of increasing integrated complexity) in cosmic evolution, the existence of consciousness, with the emergence of freedom, purpose and value, and the frequency of religious and moral experiences, count in favor of a spiritual basis to reality. There are, however, no conclusive or compelling evidences, and these all seem to be matters of general and partly subjective interpretation.

The most fundamental dispute between theism and atheism is the dispute about whether all that exists is physical or dependent upon physical entities and causal laws, or whether mind, purpose, and value are the ultimate realities, and the physical cosmos is their expression or product. Both views can be reasonably stated, in consistent ways that are coherent with all well-established empirical knowledge. You could say that both are matters of 'faith', if you mean that both are generalizations that go well beyond the evidence of the senses alone. Or you could say that both are matters of 'reason', if you mean that coherent and plausible interpretations can be given of available data that appear to make sense of those data, and that can be developed through critical and informed discussion. It is not a matter of 'reason' versus 'faith', but of whether these general philosophical world-views can be developed reasonably. Since they not only can be, but have been and still are developed reasonably by philosophers of many different persuasions, the stereotype of atheistic reason verses religious non-rationality is itself an unreasonable and misleading duality which should be given up by all reasonable people.

Part 2

The Nature of Revelation

It might be said, however, that this sort of faith is not 'religious faith', and that is true. It is more of a philosophical commitment for or against the mind-like or spiritual nature of reality. I therefore want to move on to consider some specific Christian beliefs which some might consider especially unreasonable. I will select three fundamental and distinctive Christian beliefs – that God is one but is also three (a Trinity); that the infinite God is identical with a finite man (the Incarnation); and that the indestructible God died to take away sin (the Atonement). Some would argue that these beliefs are unintelligible or even self-contradictory, and I have intentionally stated them in a way which makes them sound self-contradictory, to make my case as hard as possible to argue.

I will begin by re-stating the basic theistic claim that there is a mind-like reality of supreme perfection which is the basis of all reality, and that the physical cosmos depends wholly upon it, and was brought about by it for a specific purpose. That is the basic philosophical postulate of theism. If it is true, it would be very odd if that mind (let us call it God) did not communicate its purpose in any way to beings who were supposed to help in realizing it. Further, if that purpose involves knowledge of God as creator, as it probably does, it would also be very odd if God did not make the divine presence and nature known to at least some finite beings. In other words, philosophical theism naturally leads to the expectation that some human experiences, whether public or private, will communicate the presence, nature, and purpose of God to human beings. This is how philosophical faith leads to religious faith. Religious faith is, partly anyway, a belief that God has communicated the divine presence, nature, and purpose, a response of trust that God will realize that purpose, and a commitment of loyalty and devotion to God as the revealer and enabler of that purpose. Religious faith is more than philosophical faith, but it naturally and reasonably arises from it.

Christianity belongs in the Abrahamic set of religious traditions, and as such it shares the Abrahamic view that the prophets of ancient Israel and Judah were genuine recipients of divine revelation. Like Muslims, Christians generally hold that the prophetic writings of the Hebrew Bible were genuine but partial revelations from God. The Christian way of putting this is to say that the prophets point, though they did not explicitly know it, to Christ. The books of the Hebrew Bible consist of a number of writings from different periods of history, expressing a number of different points of view, and recording how the writers or editors saw the revealing activity of God in ancient Jewish history.

Understandings of God develop over the centuries, moving, for instance, from passages which seem to see God as one God (albeit the greatest) among others, who was only concerned with Abraham and his descendants, to passages in the book of Isaiah which explicitly see God as the only God, who is concerned for all the people of the earth, even though the Israelites still have a special part to play in the religious history of humankind. It seems reasonable, though it is not overwhelmingly obvious, to think that God would reveal the divine purpose gradually, in ways that humans could understand, and in the cultural forms and language of their time. God might lead people towards a fuller understanding of the divine as they came to greater understandings of the nature of the world and of morality. If so, we would expect a growth from cruder ideas of God towards more systematically thought out and morally developed views of God. In other words, God might inspire human minds to new insights, but would not simply over-rule the natural capacities of humans by planting unexpected and quite novel information in their minds (Cf. Ward, 2010).

For most Christian theologians, the Hebrew Bible is naturally seen as a diverse and developing set of records of human, though inspired (spiritually influenced), understandings of a God who has been encountered in the history of one people. They see this development as culminating in the hope for a Messiah, a ruler who will liberate the people of God from tyranny and oppression, and usher in a society of peace and human flourishing, the kingdom of God. They then see Jesus as this Messiah, though the hope is spiritualized, in that the Messiah (the Christ, in Greek) is not a political leader, but a spiritual leader who liberates humans from their own pride, greed, and hatred, and ushers in an 'inner' rule of God in the hearts of men and women. This rule is opened to the whole Gentile world through a new set of communities, the Church, which mediates (though rather ambiguously, it must be said) the rule of God as a real spiritual force, and makes Jesus not just the King of the Jews, but the inaugurator of the rule of the divine Spirit for the whole world. This again seems a reasonable though unpredictable possibility. It obviously never convinced everyone, but it is a way of realizing a spiritual purpose of transforming human hearts and lives so that they might achieve an inner unity with the divine life.

The Incarnation

The central claim of the Incarnation is that God reveals the divine presence, nature, and purpose in the life and teachings of Jesus. The purpose is claimed to be that human and divine should be so intertwined that they actually become one. Human beings find their true fulfilment in being filled with the divine

Spirit of love, joy, wisdom, and compassion. God realizes the divine nature as love in particular ways by uniting human lives to the divine in an intimate and inseparable communion of love. Jesus is seen as the origin and paradigm in human history of this divine-human unity. He is fully human, but his humanity is filled and transfigured from its beginning with the Spirit of God to such an extent that he can be said to be the perfected image of God in human life who, by divine inspiration, knew God fully and mediated the divine wisdom and power in a unique way. As such, he can be called 'Son of God'.

Christians believe that Jesus also expresses, in human form and as fully as a human person can, the eternal *Logos* or wisdom of God, through which all things were created, in whom all things subsist, and in whom all things will ultimately be united (see the first chapter of the New Testament books of John, Ephesians, and Colossians). What Jesus shows is God's ideal for human nature, God's unlimited wisdom and compassion, and the final destiny of humans to be united fully to God. Jesus' death as a tortured victim of the state shows God's sharing in the suffering and estrangement of the human world. Jesus' resurrection (his appearances to the disciples after his bodily death) shows the purpose of God to liberate human lives from pride, hatred, and greed, and raise them to union with God.

That Jesus lived, died and was raised from death in these ways is a matter of faith, of trusting the testimony of the first followers of Jesus. We have seen that trust is an essential element in forming reasonable beliefs, and if we think the first disciples were admirable figures who experienced spiritual transformation and were prepared to endure persecution for their beliefs, we will think that an initial trust in their testimony is not unreasonable. If we are convinced there is no God, we will of course think that they were mistaken, and there is no conclusive proof that they were honest and reliable witnesses. But if we think there is a God, and that God would probably reveal the divine purpose through the medium of unusual (even amazing) and spiritually meaningful events, there is reason to take their testimony seriously. At the least, the probability is that Jesus was a charismatic healer and teacher of great spiritual and moral insight. That is enough to make it reasonable to see whether we might achieve a degree of psychological healing and spiritual awakening by reflecting on the recorded life and teaching of Jesus.

That teaching has already been reflected on over 2,000 years and passed on to us through the Bible and the teachings of the Christian churches. It would be unreasonable to neglect these resources. If we attend to them, we will learn of doctrines of God, of creation, of the soul, of the human condition, and of salvation (liberation from evil), that have developed over the centuries in various ways as a result of continued reflection and debate. We will see that there are a number of traditions of interpretation of the God who is believed to have been revealed and to have acted to liberate humans from evil in and through Jesus.

With regard to the Incarnation, for instance, there is not just one clear and agreed definition of what that is. On the contrary, the Incarnation is usually said to be a 'mystery' – not something that is completely beyond human reason, but something that human minds cannot fully understand with the rather general and inadequate concepts that we have available. We can see enough, however, to realize that the contradictory way in which I described Incarnation earlier – as an infinite God being identical with a finite person – is almost wholly inadequate and misleading. For Christian theology, God is indeed infinite, not limited in time and space, or by anything beyond the divine being itself. But when Christians say that Jesus is 'identical with' God, they do not mean that Jesus is beyond time and space. 'Identity' is here being used in a special, extended, sense, and the Christian claim is that this is not an incoherent claim, even though the concepts we have are not adequate to enable us to understand it with full adequacy. Many philosophers say similar things about the basic concepts of quantum physics. Those concepts, or the interpretation of them, cannot at present be fully understood, but they are not taken to be self-contradictory.

It seems quite possible that a God beyond space-time could appear in space-time, simply by creating something which in some way images or represents the nature of God. It also seems possible that God could shape a human life to be such an image, and a human life of compassion, wisdom, forgiveness, mercy, and life-giving power might be a good finite image of an infinite God. The Incarnation could be seen as a perfect human image of a God who transcends every finite image, but who calls every human being to image and mediate the divine presence and power in their own unique way. Jesus would be both an image of the divine nature and a foreshadowing of God's purpose for all human lives – that they should all become 'sons of God' in this sense. For them, however, this is a task yet to be accomplished by divine help, whereas in Jesus' case God ensured that he would be such an image from the beginning of his life.

This is just one way of thinking about Incarnation, and perhaps all our models emphasize some aspects and neglect others. I should perhaps say that the recent theologians who have most influenced me have been John Macquarrie (Macquarrie, 1966), Paul Tillich (Tillich, 1951–63), and Karl Rahner (Rahner, 1978). They belonged to different Christian churches, so their views are not especially sectarian. They were all concerned to restate Christian beliefs in the light of modern European thought. While there are other interpretations of the Incarnation than theirs, they do express a broad spectrum of Christian thought that shows that thinking of 'God becoming human' does not have to be self-contradictory, and is not a matter of God turning into something finite. It is a way of speaking of the purpose of the transcendent God as forming a unity of human and divine, and shaping a paradigm of this unity in the particular human person of Jesus.

The Trinity and the Atonement

From such a thought the doctrine of God as Trinity arises quite naturally, as we are led to think of God in a threefold way, as the transcendent and infinite supreme being, as the divine wisdom which enfolds the archetype of perfected humanity and is manifested in the human person of Jesus, and as the creative and inspiring Spirit which molds other human lives in the image of Jesus, and so unites human lives to the divine life. It is not a matter of God being somehow both three things and one thing of the same sort at the same time. It is rather that Christians think of the one God as existing in a threefold way, as transcendent ('the Father'), as objectively expressed in space-time ('the Son'), and as an inner presence in human minds and hearts, uniting them to the divine life ('the Holy Spirit').

In a similar way, the Christian mystery of the Atonement is not the contradictory statement that a God who cannot die suffers death. We can better think of it, as the Oxford theologian Paul Fiddes does (Fiddes, 1988) as God entering, in Christ, into and experiencing the sufferings of human existence, in order that estranged human lives can be united to the imperishable life of God. The eternal God is not destroyed, but can suffer the experience of human death, and show how the power of love can conquer even the death of the physical body, and bring humans to 'eternal life', a new and higher form of life in conscious unity with the eternal.

What I have tried to do, ridiculously briefly, is to show how even the most paradoxical sounding Christian beliefs can be shown to be reasonable, in the light of the existence of an eternal God whose purpose is to unite human lives to the divine life. That does not show that such beliefs are true, much less prove them beyond reasonable doubt. It is meant to show that Christian beliefs are plausible candidates for rational belief, not just irrational absurdities. If it seems that God comes to someone in the form of Jesus Christ, convicts them of sin (of moral and spiritual failure), yet begins to liberate them from sin and give them an intense awareness of an empowering spiritual presence, then they might commit their lives to following this God. I have simply tried to show that this would be a wholly reasonable thing for them to do.

Reference List

Ayer, A.J. (1973) *The Central Questions of Philosophy*, London: Weidenfeld and Nicolson.

Clifford, W.K. (1879) 'The Ethics of Belief', in *Lectures and Essays*, London: Macmillan.

Fiddes, Paul (1988) *The Creative Suffering of God*, Oxford: Clarendon Press.

Hume, David (1739) *A Treatise of Human Nature*.

Macquarrie, John (1966) *Principles of Christian Theology*, London: SCM.

Nietzsche, Friedrich (1878) 'Human, All Too Human', in Oscar Levy (ed.), (1964) *The Complete Works*, New York: Russell and Russell.

Plantinga, Alvin (2011) *Where the Conflict Really Lies: Science, Religion, and Naturalism*, Oxford: Oxford University Press.

Rahner, Karl (1978) *Foundations of Christian Faith*, New York: Sheed and Ward.

Swinburne, Richard (1977) *The Coherence of Theism*, Oxford: Clarendon Press.

Swinburne, Richard (1979) *The Existence of God*, Oxford: Clarendon Press.

Tillich, Paul (3 volumes: 1951, 1957, 1963) *Systematic Theology*, Chicago, IL: University of Chicago Press.

Ward, Keith (2009) *The God Conclusion*, London: Darton, Longman and Todd,

Ward, Keith (2010) *The Word of God?* London: SPCK.

Chapter 8

Christianity and Sensible Religion: A Feminist Approach

Mary Grey

Introduction

Jesus of Nazareth during his lifetime introduced to his followers the idea of 'sensible' religion in its broadest meaning, by proclaiming a way of life that appealed to peoples' deepest longings: 'You have the words of eternal life', said Peter (John 6:68). He also offered an experience of the fullness of life (John 10:10) that addressed the whole personality. Despite the fact that the position of women in Jesus' time according to Jewish law was subordinate to that of men, it was not until Christianity encountered Greek culture and certain interpretations of philosophy that women became considered deficient with regard to reasoning powers. Even though the Christian Church has consistently defended the rationality of its faith, the restriction of this rationality to men has had serious repercussions for the position of women within Christianity and Church, while at the same time a narrower version of this very reasonableness has been developed.

Contemporary feminist thinking, both philosophical and theological – as well as post-colonial theologies – has challenged not only the exclusion from the tradition of women as rational beings, but explored and discovered richer meanings of rational knowledge. But it could be said that what has been attacked by sceptics and atheists has been a diminished notion of the rational in Christianity and that the historical tension and dualism between reason and emotion did scant justice to either. The word 'sensible' is open to diverse interpretations, as Christopher Lewis has said (Chapter 1), including sensitivity, awareness, and a more relational, intuitive notion of 'logos'. This chapter argues that by opening up these richer meanings of rationality, Christianity can be shown to contribute to human happiness and well-being in the contemporary world in both a profound and at the same time reasonable way. (In speaking of happiness I am aware of the contemporary discussion and wish to distance myself from any shallow, materialistic approach.)

Encountering Greek Culture

Christianity faced the challenge of defending its rational basis from its very beginnings: it could be said that St. Paul, proclaiming the Christian faith against pagan idolatry in the Court of the Areopagus in Athens, (Acts 17:22–31) was its first exponent and defender. What was important was, not only the argument that a living God could not be worshipped in the form of idols of gold or silver, but that Paul engaged with many types of public discourse – with Jews and Gentiles, with Epicureans and Stoic philosophers, and with 'casual passers-by'. The reasonableness of faith was crucial and had to be credibly demonstrated, even if its message – sometimes paradoxical – was to prove a stumbling-block.

The problem became, as Christianity spread throughout the Greek world in the first three centuries of the Common Era, that reason became understood through a dualistic lens that opposed mind over matter, male over female, and reason over passion. This hierarchical schema had been widely held since its classic expression in Aristotle's *Politics*, where the philosopher understood it to be *ordered in nature*, that men were to dominate women and slaves, and the human would be superior to the animal:

> It is clear that the rule of the soul over the body, and of the mind and the rational element over the passionate, is natural and expedient; whereas the equality of the two or the rule of the inferior is always hurtful. The same holds good of animals in relation to men ... Again, the male is by nature superior, and the female inferior; and the one rules, and the other is ruled; this principle of necessity extends to all mankind ... And indeed the use made of slaves and often animals is not very different; for both with their bodies minister to the needs of life ... (Aristotle, *Politics*, book 1, chs 4–5, cited in Plumwood, 1993: 46)

This dualistic view was absorbed by Christianity very early – and not only from Greek influences. For example, the Jewish writer, Philo (a contemporary of Paul), wrote an allegory of the Fall, in which the mind, (representing Adam), was tempted by the pleasure (the serpent), through the senses (Eve). Adam's sin was in allowing his sense to overwhelm his self-control. Thus Philo thought that the sense (or passions) should be under the control of reason – and ordered in society through marriage (Boring, 1996: 236). Already it is possible to see the consequences of this line of reasoning in, for example, a text generally thought to be written after Paul's lifetime:

> A woman must be a learner, listening quietly, and with due submission. I do not permit a woman to be a teacher, nor must woman domineer over man; she should be quiet. For Adam was created first, and Eve afterwards; and it was not Adam who was deceived; it was the woman who, yielding to deception, fell into sin., Yet she will be saved through motherhood ... (1Tim 2:11–16)

Reason/Emotion Tensions

St. Augustine (who died in 430 CE) held similar views, with a stronger reason/emotion opposition, clearly linking men to being created in the image of God, because of being (presumed) more rational, and women rational only when taken together with her husband (Augustine: *De Trinitate* 7.7). But it was the views of St. Thomas Aquinas (1225–1274) which have had the most lasting influence on Christian thought, although the reason/faith tension had already been given famous expression in the earlier text of St. Anselm (1033–1109), 'Faith seeking understanding'. In Anselm's *Proslogion* (Prologue) he sets out an understanding of Atonement similar to the excerpt cited by Christopher Lewis in Chapter 1 – which he described as generally recognized as outdated. (I have critiqued this form of atonement in Grey, 1989.)

Because Thomas Aquinas followed Aristotle's understanding of biology, namely, that the male was the norm for humanity and woman a defective – or misbegotten – form of human being, he developed a dual anthropology: 'Males naturally excel at the higher faculty of reason; females have less rational capacity and are less capable of moral self-control. Good order requires that the naturally superior rule the naturally inferior' (cited in Ruether, 1983: 96).

Apart from his distorted, inherited views on women, Aquinas held a tightly – integrated, theocentric view of the relationship between faith and reason, one from which the Catholic Church has never swerved. Because God – who can neither deceive nor be deceived – has revealed these truths, then they are in accordance with our human reason (*Catechism of the Catholic Church*, 1994: 39 – a paraphrase of paragraph 156). Christianity has equally always affirmed that human intelligence is capable of discovering the truth of its origins and discovering the existence of God by reflecting on his works (*Catechism* 67, para. 286).

It should be kept in mind that it was not only the dualistic polarity of mind over emotion that is at issue in this discussion of the 'reasonableness of Christianity' but the negative associations of emotion with concupiscence (Augustine), chaos, nature, sexuality and the body. Above all, the fear of being out of control of sexual feelings was a dominating motif.

Although this situation was revisited at the Reformation with its notable tenet '*sola fides*' (faith alone), there was no change in the dualistic anthropology which reinforced the social subjugation of women. The Romantic Movement did bring a different view of emotion – somewhat idealized – but failed to change the dominant thinking about women and reason (Massey, 1985). René Descartes (1596–1650) in his search for certainty, privileged reason over the body, which he distanced from his thinking self, and set the Enlightenment's path for dispassionate reasoning and many subsequent atheistic debates. It has been said ironically that philosophy is less a series of footnotes on Plato than a series of footnotes to Descartes, whom Mary Daly called modern philosophy's 'severed head' (Griffiths and Whitford, 1988: 139)! It is certainly true that he set the terms in which the discussion would become conducted.

At the same time another current was emerging. Blaise Pascal (1623–1662), like Descartes a brilliant mathematician as well as engineer, also inherited the same dualistic tension between mind and body; yet at the same time he discovered through his experiential method, the importance of sentiment or emotion. (It should be noted at this point that the distorted understanding of reason affects not only the exclusion of women but produces un-reasonable patterns of thinking in general for both men and women. Women have frequently colluded with these distorted patterns.) Pascal did not oppose rationality in itself, but thought that the two should be combined: he considered both reason and emotion to have their limits:

> Those who are accustomed to judge by feeling have no understanding of matters involving reasoning. For they want to go to the bottom of things at a glance and are not accustomed to look for principles. The others, on the contrary, who are accustomed to reasoning from principles, have no understanding of matters involving feeling, because they look for principles and are unable to see things at a glance. (Cited from *Pensées* in Kung, 1980: 49)

The word Pascal uses for 'feeling' is 'sentiment' which should not be understood as 'sentimentality': rather, the word 'heart' sums up better what he means:

> The heart- of which the bodily organ is a symbol- means the personal, spiritual
> centre of man, his innermost operating centre, the starting point of his dynamic
> personal relationship with other people, the precision instrument by which he
> grasps reality in its wholeness. (Kung, 1980: 49)

Thus did Pascal develop his most influential aphorism, which greatly inspired
future thinking: '*Le coeur a ses raisons, que la raison ne connait point. On le sait
en mille choses*'. Or, 'The heart has its reasons of which reason knows nothing: we
know this in countless ways' (Translated by Hans Kung, 1980: 50 from Pascal,
Pensées B282, K11).

Towards a More Inclusive Understanding of Reason

It should now be clearly manifest that what is at stake is not merely the supremacy
of rationality but the narrowness of its definition. Because the Enlightenment
paradigm of knowledge dominated public life, it had the effect of sidelining
religion, forcing it into defensive, apologetic mode – which long influenced the
way religion was taught to young people. My early education in religion was
dominated by apologetic defenses for the existence of God – we called them proofs,
though were told they were not 100 percent watertight! These were accompanied
by various devotions which did not pretend to be open to any empirical challenge.
Scientific developments – unarguably of crucial importance – also privileged this
over-rationalized kind of knowing, emphasizing detachment, objectivity, and the
importance of empirical evidence. In fact this became the norm for the method of
knowing. My own experience of Oxford philosophy in the early sixties was one of
misery, where the supremacy of logical positivism derided theological statements
as outside both verification and falsification, and therefore to be discarded as
nonsensical. This kind of approach was led by the late Professor A.J. Ayer, whose
text, *Language, Truth and Logic* (1936) was regarded as a classic at the time. To be
a philosopher – the distinct impression was given – was to be either a non-believer
or a fool, incapable of respectable reasoning.

Christopher Lewis has described philosophy as one of theology's 'dancing
partners' – but it is critically necessary to be discerning as to which dance! In
response to this narrow understanding of reason, theology argues that:

> there is another form of knowing, an equally valid kind of knowledge, based on
> the personal participation, engagement and involvement of the individual in the
> subject matter under review that applies to the Arts, Humanities and Religion.

Further, theology questions this division of knowledge into such watertight compartments pointing out that the dividing line between the objective and subjective, between the detached and engaged, between the neutral and participative knowing is far from neutral. (Lane, 2011: 47–8)

Once the principle is conceded that 'there is no view from nowhere', that all knowledge involves some degree of interpretation, and may – while *appearing* to be objective – conceal vested power interests, the field is opened up to more diverse forms of knowing and indeed to challenging the reason/emotion dichotomy itself.

One of the most significant philosophical developments has been suggested by Martha Nussbaum, in her explorations into emotional intelligence (Nussbaum, 2001). Emotions, she declares 'are appraisals or value judgments, which ascribe to things and persons outside the person's own control great importance for that person's own flourishing' (Nussbaum, 2001: 4). Emotions contain three salient elements, Nussbaum argues: – the idea of a cognitive appraisal or evaluation, the idea of one's own flourishing and the idea of the salience of external objects as elements in one's own scheme of goals. This is a complex view, combining cognitive choices, an individual's personal histories and values, as well as external circumstances – involving more dimensions than are usually evoked by the words 'feeling' or even 'emotion'. (The emotions discussed are grief, compassion and love.) What is significant for the argument this chapter is developing is that a critique is presented of the 'motif of Ascent' of both Dante and St. Augustine. This is the traditional assumption that the path of faith and virtue reaches its ultimate perfection only in Heaven and the afterlife. Following a narrow notion of rationality – opposed to emotion, intuition, the body, the materiality of earth, as discussed earlier – this can be the only logical conclusion. But working within a new paradigm of emotional intelligence, the Ascent motif can be challenged from a *this-worldly perspective*. Nussbaum, introducing an imaginatively – stretched horizon, uses as examples, Emily Brontë's novel, *Wuthering Heights*, Mahler's *Second Symphony*, Walt Whitman's poems and James Joyce's *Ulysses*. In each case, the horizons of emotion are expanded in the direction of her ideas on emotional intelligence: in the case of *Wuthering Heights* it is particularly striking that the complex emotions retaining the integrity of self, clash with traditional notions of Heaven/Hell and even of the power of love itself. This is developed in the case of the famous – but doomed – passionate relationship between Catherine Earnshaw and Heathcliff. In her dream Cathy dreamt she was in Heaven:

Heaven did not seem to be my home; and I broke my heart with weeping to come back to earth; and the angels were so angry that they flung me out, into the middle of the heath on the top of Wuthering Heights, where I woke sobbing for joy. (Brontë, 1943: 94)

The tension – that a Christian vision based on a narrow rationality – cannot allow any integrity or honest admission of the love between the two is maintained till the very end. Only Heathcliff, the despised outsider, is true to the authenticity of their love, whereas Catherine has had to bury hers in the bourgeois conventionality of her marriage with Edgar Linton. As Heathcliff cries:

Because misery and degradation, and death, and nothing that God or Satan could inflict would have parted us, *you*, of your own will, did it. I have not broken your heart – *you* have broken it; and in breaking it, you have broken mine ... *Why* did you betray your own heart, Cathy? (Brontë, 1943: 189)

And Nussbaum succinctly concludes, revealing as she does, why a widened understanding of both reason and emotion is crucial for Christian theology today: 'We have already had questions for both Dante and Augustine about anger and intolerance, and about the hierarchies created by them. Christianity will need to become more inclusive of the alien and the stranger than either of these two Ascents has yet been ...' (Nussbaum, 2001: 608).

Towards a Listening Logic

But there is still another step in this quest to broaden and diversify the understanding of reason. I have been exploring a way of knowing called 'connected knowing' that comprehends a diversity of factors (Grey, 1993: 89–91). It is based on Alfred North Whitehead's Process thought that opens up the complexity of the way we perceive the world (rather similar to Nussbaum's expansion of the language of emotion). Whitehead called this 'prehension', describing this as a 'flow of feeling from one subject to another'(Suchocki, 1989: 203). But 'feeling the world', 'letting the world in' is a thoroughly embodied process. In all the acts of perception that ground the process of knowing, we are composed of feeling/experiencing/hearing/touching and knowing processes of our many selves. As Catherine Keller wrote: 'Through my bodiliness I come to the animating knowledge that the energy of matter and the energy of soul are at base indistinguishable. Soul *matters*' (Keller, 1986: 236):

> 'Connected knowing' recognises the indistinguishability of the energy of bodiliness and soulfulness. Jung understood the psyche as inseparable from 'world'. He describes the symbols of the self as arising in the depths of the body: they express the self's materiality as much as the perceiving consciousness: 'At bottom the psyche is simply 'world.' (Cited in Keller, 1986: 237)

Thus there is an ecological element included in the process of knowing – now acknowledged and integrated as a dimension into the pastoral therapeutic process: *damage to the environment is also damage to the psyche at its most vulnerable level*. In addition there is a dimension of care. The ethics of care spring from a knowing which is 'tending' and 'attending', cherishing and nourishing the many interconnections between all living things.

In this way, 'connected knowing' not only invokes a wider basis of knowledge, less adversarial and confrontational than the Cartesian paradigm; not only does it hold together perceptions, feelings, sensations, images and ideas, but it also recalls a more ancient meaning for *logos*, logic. This has been explored by the Italian scholar Gemma Corradi Fiumara in her book, *The Other Side of Language: A Philosophy of Listening* (Fiumara, 1990).She appeals to the Greek root of logos – from the verb, *legein*, λεγειν, which means far more than simply 'speech'. As Heidegger wrote, clarifying the non-confrontational roots of *logos*:

> No-one would want to deny that in the language of the Greeks from early on, *'legein'* meant to talk, to say or to tell. However, just as early and even more originally, *legein* means what is expressed in the German word 'legen: to lay down, to lay before'. In legein a bringing-together prevails, the Latin 'legere' understood as 'lesen', in the sense of collecting and bringing together. *Legein* properly means the laying down and laying-before which gathers itself and others. (Cited in Fiumara, 1990: 3)

The second ingredient proposed is the activity of listening, sadly absent from contemporary culture. There can be no genuine relationship or encounter without listening. If we were to *recognize the narrow interpretation of logos in which we are imprisoned*, says Fiumara, and respond to the challenge of becoming a 'listening culture', we might unblock the creative resources which have been immobilized by traditional 'logical' education. Listening will function as part of the effort whereby we seek to establish a relationship between our world and different worlds. This meaning of *legein* leads Fiumara into advocating the Socratic idea of 'maieutic' or midwife thinking, meaning the task of philosophers is to be 'matchmakers, or midwives', committed to the birth of thought, nurturing its becoming, but not owning or controlling its further existence. (These ideas are also expressed in Plato's *Theaetetus* (1953) on whom she draws). Listening logic makes room for other ways of knowing, other ways of interpreting the world and viewing reality. It requires a certain humility and vulnerability, a vulnerability to the other and her way of interpreting reality.

The Reasonableness of Christianity – Revisited

Does this broadened re-interpretation of rationality succeed in Christianity being seen as more or less rational? Lacking the incisiveness of adversarial logic, will it not fail to offer an acceptable *credo* to contemporary challengers? I argue first of all that it should be widely understood that that human existence is enriched, not impoverished, by the discovery of many ways of knowing. Secondly, that there has always been a dimension of reason in the act of faith, even if not universally accepted. The nineteenth-century Catholic theologian John Henry Newman (1801–1890) asserted that 'the act of faith is an act of reason, but of what the world would call weak, bad or insufficient reason; and that, because it rests on presumptions more, and on evidence less' (Lane, 2011: 56–7, citing Burrell 256–7). But Newman recognized that this admission would be perceived as weakness and, 30 years later, went on in *The Grammar of Assent*, to spell out what he calls 'presuppositions' more than evidence. For him they are part of the rationality of faith, without reducing faith to rationality:

> Among the presuppositions attaching to the act of faith as an act of reason there are at least three moments or phases in the journey of faith. These include the call of conscience, the presence of first principles such as the love of truth, justice and respect for others, and thirdly, what he calls antecedent probabilities or instruments of conviction in religious matters. (Lane, 2011: 57)

Newman denied there was any such thing as pure reason since almost every day we act from trust in the words and actions of others.

Thirdly, the opening up of different, more inclusive ways of knowing, frees up what appears to be 'eternal doctrinal truths', frozen in their expression. Once knowledge is recognized as being clothed in time-bound language and images, but also as being linked as with the exercise of power and having vested interests, there is a task of re-interpretation for each successive age. The Orthodox theologian, Elisabeth Behr –Sigel put this beautifully:

> Sometimes tradition seems frozen under a great ice-shell but below this frozen and rigid surface flow ever-fresh springtime waters. It is up to us, with the help of God's grace, to break the ice that is above all the ice of our hearts become cold ... From the ancient spring we will drink water that will give us new force to answer the questions of today. (Behr-Sigel, 1991: 94–5)

Example of the obstacles of time-bound expression of doctrine would be both Anselm's explanation of the Atonement (mentioned earlier), contentious interpretations of the Real Presence of Christ in the Eucharist, and the arguments against the Ordination of Women in the Roman Catholic Church. The former uses the argument of 'the wounded honour of God' to explain why Jesus was sent to his death. 'Wounded honour' was a serious issue for the mediaeval lord: analogously God's honour had been wounded by sin since the Fall – and only the Divine Son could repair this damage by his sacrifice. But the concept of 'wounded honour' does not now mean so much – at least in the Western world – and this mediaeval explanation of the Atonement has currently lost popularity. In the third example, the Ordination of women, the theological arguments prohibiting this are now considered to be deficient: what the ban rests on is a combination of 'frozen tradition', motives of power, and (concealed) misogyny together with a conservative view of the role of women in the Church. But to act on the implications of this, it was necessary to move away from an exclusive way of reasoning –which in some cases still has not happened.

Fourthly, a broadened understanding reason liberates new readings of Scripture. Freed from the Enlightenment paradigm we can recover more holistic understandings – rooted in the Hebraic world, which was of course, the world in which Jesus operated. The richness of the metaphor of 'connected knowing' is the possibility of resourcing ourselves in the past, overcoming existential aloneness by reconnecting with community memory. We can also reconnect with other dimensions of faith without fear of being repudiated – for example, the mystical way, the Apophatic Way, or Way of silence. This has been a cherished dimension of Christianity, currently seeing a re-emergence in some parts of the world. For example, in France, the popularity is growing of such groups as 'Les Frères et Soeurs de Jerusalem', 'Brothers and Sisters of Jerusalem', a group based on a mystical liturgy and form of prayer, yet whose members have jobs in the society around them.

Mystics have found it almost impossible to express linguistically the content of their visions in their profundity – although they have never stopped trying to communicate, and to be understood, as the late Grace Jantzen so eloquently explained (Jantzen, 1995). But their utterances would never stand the test of empirical reasoning or the challenge of logical positivism. Yet contemporary understanding reveals how mystics like Julian of Norwich did respond to the questions of their contexts, and attempted to explain the visionary knowledge they had been given in ways that inspire the faith journeys of their contemporaries, as well as inspiring new understandings of contemplation in the present day. Since Ludwig Wittgenstein's opening up of the notion of Language games, it has also been possible to view religious language as a 'form of life' which also includes the mystical way as its own distinct form – although Wittgenstein himself is ultimately ambiguous as to the expressibility of religious language, especially the mystical (Kung, 1980: 502–8).

Conclusion

Just as Nietzsche's madman so memorably proclaimed, 'God is dead – and we have killed him – you and I!' (Kung, 1980: 371), ushering in on the one hand, the rise of nihilism, and on the other, a radical questioning of traditional arguments, so the critique of the Enlightenment paradigm of reason encourages the possibility of Christianity offering a more convincing engagement with urgent questions of our times. Since the end of the two World Wars and the dropping of the atomic bombs, the God of classical theism – at least in the way the arguments have been presented – had seemed to have failed humanity. Dostoevsky had already demonstrated the unsatisfying nature of the classic defences concerning God and evil in his novel *The Brothers Karamazov* (Dostoevksy, 1958). As Ivan Karamazov cried:

> And if the sufferings of children go to swell the sum of sufferings which was necessary to pay for the truth, then I protest that the truth is not worth such a price. I don't want HARMONY; and it's beyond our means to pay so much to enter it. And so I hasten to give back my entrance ticket. (287)

It is at least possible that with a widened concept of rationality, including the language of emotion with its links with materiality, that Christian faith may be seen to speak to some of the key issues of our times with a wisdom born of listening and humility (Chapter 1 concluded with an appeal to humility about the extent of a particular religion's doctrinal claims). It was significant in this respect that Pope Benedict XVI chose as title for his Regensburg Lecture in 2006, 'Faith and Reason and the University: Memories and Reflections' (www.vatican.va). Yes, he controversially used a quotation from a fourteenth century Byzantine Emperor's critique of Islam, causing a hostile reaction from the Islamic community. For this he apologized twice, and maintained that this was not his personal view, but an attempt to explain that it was not religion and violence *but religion and reason that go together* (cited in Lane, 2011: 82). Christian faith, along with other faiths, offer dimensions of ultimacy and mystery that cannot always be expressed with self-evident empirical statements. But at their best Christian beliefs invite to a depth of fulfilment – of the self, but with the notion of self that is widened to include the community. The challenge of the work on which we are engaged is to enlarge this notion of community to reach out beyond narrow boundaries.

In this chapter I have highlighted the problems cause by a narrow understanding of rationality in Christianity. I have argued that by excluding the language of the body and the emotions, a distorted understanding of reason has created inadequate forms of faith within Christianity and prevented widened views of compassion, sensitivity, humility and tolerance with regard to other religions. But, 'dancing' with a philosophy of inclusivity and a logic of listening, it is possible to uncover a richness that is ultimately satisfies criteria of reasonableness – and more. So I end, as I began, with the words of St. Paul in his famous discourse on love – they point to a state of being where knowledge is mutual and total: 'At present I know in part: then I shall know fully, as I am fully known' (1 Corinthians 12).

Reference List

Anselm (1), *Proslogion* (PL 153, 225A) *Prayers and Meditations of St Anselm with the Proslogion*, Harmondsworth: Penguin Classics, 1973.

Anselm (2) *Cur Deus Homo?* London: Religious Tracts Society, 2nd revised edn, 1890.

Ayer, A.J. (2002 (1936)) *Language, Truth and Logic*, New York: Dover Publications.

Behr-Sigel, Elisabeth (1991) *The Ministry of Women in the Church*, Redondo Beach, CA : Oakwood.

Benedict XVI, Pope (2006) 'Faith and Reason and the University: Memories and Reflections', Regensburg. Available at: http://www.vatican.va/holy_father/benedict_xvi/speeches/2006/september/documents/hf_ben-xvi_spe_20060912_university-regensburg_en.html (accessed October 25, 2013).

Boring, Wendy Sue (1996) 'Reason/Passion', in Letty M.Russell and J.Shannon Clarkson (eds), *Dictionary of Feminist Theologies*, London: Mowbray/Cassell, 236.

Brontë, Emily (1943) *Wuthering Heights*, New York: Modern Library.

Burrell, David (2009) 'Newman in Retrospect', in Ian Ker and Terrence Merrigan (eds), *Cambridge Companion to Newman*, New York: Cambridge University Press, 256–7.

Catholic Catechism (1994), edited by Geoffrey Chapman, London: Cassell.

Descartes, René (1998) *Meditations and Other Metaphysical Writings*, translated by Desmond Clarke, London: Penguin Classics.

Dostoevksy, Fyodor (1958) *The Brothers Karamazov*, London: Penguin.

Fiumara, Gemma Conradi (1990) *The Other Side of Language: A Philosophy of Listening*, London and New York: Routledge.

Grey, Mary (1989) *Redeeming the Dream: Christianity, Feminism and Redemption*, London: SPCK.

Grey, Mary (1993) *The Wisdom of Fools? Seeking Revelation Today*, London: SPCK.

Griffiths, Morwenna and Whitford, Margaret (eds) (1988) *Feminist Perspectives in Philosophy*, Indianopolis, IN: Indiana University Press.

Jantzen, Grace (1995) *Power, Gender and Christian Mysticism*, Cambridge: Cambridge University Press.

Keller, Catherine (1986) *From a Broken Web: Separation, Sexism and Self*, Boston, MA: Beacon.

Kung, Hans (1980) *Does God Exist?*, London: Collins.

Lane, Dermot (2011) *Stepping Stones to Other Religions*, Dublin: Veritas.

Massey, Marilyn Chapin (1985) *Feminine Soul: The Fate of an Idea*, Boston, MA: Beacon.

Nussbaum, Martha C. (2001) *Upheavals of Thought: The Intelligence of Emotions*, Cambridge: Cambridge University Press.

Plato (1953) *Theaetetus*, Oxford: The Clarendon Press.

Ruether, Rosemary Radford (1983) *Sexism and God-Talk*, London: SCM.

Suchocki, Marjorie (revised edn 1989) *God, Christ and Church: A Practical Guide to Process Theology*, New York: Crossroads.

Plumwood, Val (1993) *Feminism and the Mastery of Nature*, London and New York: Routledge.

Whitehead, Alfred N. (1929) *Process and Reality*, Cambridge: Macmillan.

Chapter 9

The Ecosystem of Religions:
A Hindu Perspective

Rita D. Sherma

Introduction

There are different ways in which we can view the relationship of religion to all that exists. One way is through the perception of religion as a 'closed system' with a linear, unconditioned, historical trajectory like a GPS mechanism with a destination programmed in. Such a perspective encourages an understanding of religion that is based on an unchanging profile and offers unalterable primacy to a specific time, text, location, event, narrative, interpretation, and direction. This approach does not acknowledge the mutual conditioning of religious cultures; nor does it recognize the fact that the history of religions shows a pattern of constant alteration and reinterpretation; it is *not*, therefore, a 'sensible' approach to understanding religious culture. 'Sensible' in this case, denotes both 'reasonableness' and 'sensitivity' as explained in Chapter 1 of this volume by Christopher Lewis.

A very different way to perceive and experience religion – and one that is supported by the history of religions – is that of an 'open system' with permeable boundaries, and a dialogical dynamic where currents of information and insight flow in and out of religious traditions much like that of an ecosystem. I would suggest that what I am referring to as the open system model brings a more 'sensible' awareness to our conception of religion. When religion is perceived as an open ecosystem, we begin to understand that religion is supported and nourished by feed-back loops that move and transform information: (a) from the natural world into religious culture; (b) amongst different religions, and (c) between religion and the rest of society including data from all facets of human experience.

The acknowledgement of this mutual enrichment between a religion and other sources of knowledge challenges the 'closed system' approach, which tends to create brittle and violently defended barriers. An 'open system' approach not only allows for respectful and non-defensive dialogue; it points to the possibility of a teleology where both human and natural flourishing are recognized as increasingly dependent on the acknowledgement of the widespread mutual conditioning of the past and the ever tighter interdependence of the future.

There are significant resources in the Hindu tradition that deeply support the view of religion as an open, interconnected system, which need to be identified and reclaimed. The challenge for Hindu thought and practice lies in (1) positing a religious identity, no matter how fluid; (2) re-envisioning a faith still embedded in geography in a way that is meaningful to a global civilization where culture and ethnicity can no longer be the glue that holds a religious world together, and (3) rejecting customs of inherited injustice, while theologically asserting their irrelevance to Hindu first principles.

This chapter begins by bringing to light the fact that religious worlds as open ecosystems has been normative for India's religious history; the undoing of the open system approach in the modern era; the consequences of schismatic changes to the world of Indian religion in general and Hinduism in particular, and the need for an approach that transcends trauma. I then argue for the necessity of a clear Hindu identity that is based on universally applicable Hindu principles rather than sociological, ethnic, political, and geographic factors and forces. I further suggest that there are certain key orientations that have historically marked Hindu experience which should be kept in mind when moving towards a Hindu identity for a global era that at once preserves the profound insights of the past, but moves Hinduism into constructive conversation with the present. The chapter ends with a caveat that praxis alone is not enough for lasting transformation. Thus, new priorities and interpretations that inform contemporary socially engaged Hindu movements would benefit from systematic integration into the Hindu theological-philosophical traditions.

Open Ecosystems and Closed Identities: Schism and Self-Definition within the Modern Indian Religious World

A history of mimesis, dialogue, and cross-fertilization between the religious traditions of ancient and classical India created a culture of osmosis, of porous boundaries. Ancient polemicists of different schools of thought would argue equally against certain Hindu, Buddhist, and Jain tenets in the same document. Thus a sense of a variety of denominations, guru lineages, and schools of thought existed without the sharp demarcations that are present today. As a result, present day Hindus are particularly prone to conflate all the religious traditions of Indian origin as part of one whole. That 'whole' however, is called 'Hindu' by them, and is identified not with a 'religion' as we understand the word today (that is, exclusive of all other religions) but with a civilization.

However, since the modern era, adherents of minority religious traditions of Indian origin have often resented such a conflation and have demanded the recognition of their distinctiveness. The Sikhs began to seek a separate *religious* identity during the colonial period. As Darshan Singh Tatla (2008: 77) reports:

> Although Sikhs joined hands with Hindus in launching this reformist [Arya Samaj movement], differences arose ... Through various Singh Sabhas, the first of which was established in 1873, the Sikh reformists took up the challenge ... To Aryas' assertion, 'Sikhs are Hindus', Sikh reformers retorted, 'Sikhs are not Hindus', the title of a famous tract by Khan Singh in 1899 ... The new print media at Lahore and Amritsar sharpened group consciousness ... shaping their sense of a religious identity ...

Such sentiments have continued to intensify amongst Sikhs. Meanwhile, Jains, both in India and the Diaspora, have also begun to carve out a distinct identity. Such an effort can be seen in the following tract (Jain 2009: 52):

> If we compare Jainism and Hinduism, we find that the differences between them are great and that their agreement is in respect of a few particulars only [*sic*] concerning the ordinary mode of living. Even the ceremonies which appear to be similar are in reality different in respect of their purport if carefully studied.

The author, a Jain practitioner, goes on to articulate differences based on a highly essentialized presentation of Hinduism which posits, for example, an exclusively monotheistic and monolithic version of Hinduism. But what the essentialism indicates is not necessarily a lack of knowledge about Hinduism as much as a deep desire to distinguish Jain and Hindu identities. Such a desire for a distinct and sometimes schismatic identity is visible in South Asian Buddhism as well. We see this tendency in several movements including those inspired by Sri Lankan Buddhist revivalist Anagarika Dharmapala and others (Levine and Gellner 2005: 9):

> Dharmapala, influenced by Olcott and others, set most of the agenda for Buddhist modernism or what [has been termed] 'Protestant Buddhism' ... A key part of Buddhist modernism is the attempt to mark Buddhism off as clearly distinct from Hinduism; indeed it is sometimes aggressively anti-Hindu. This feature was certainly Dharmapala's contribution ... All tendencies within Buddhism of

which the Buddhist modernist disapproves are labelled as Hindu (or Mahayana) influences. A paradigmatic exponent of this form of Buddhism was Bhimrao ('Babasaheb') Ambedkar (1891–1956), leader of India's Untouchables, who announced in 1935 that he would not die a Hindu.

The centrifugal trajectory of the religious traditions that were born in India indicated by such efforts is not likely to reverse itself. Hindu resistance to these separative efforts have perhaps served to create greater resistance. Hindu nationalism which, in its earlier iterations, claimed all native born Indians as 'sons of the soil' and therefore Hindu, has a history of conflation of 'Hindu' with all other religious cultures born in India. However, beyond politics and the desire to affirm the interwoven nature of India's religious history, there are other reasons that Hindus continue to resist the centrifugal movement of Indian religions. Hindus come from a multitude of backgrounds in terms of theology, praxis, culture, language, denomination, guru lineage, and so forth. The divergences within Hinduism are vast and many Hindus, unable to clearly delineate what it means to be Hindu, often resort to a phrase that has now become a cliché: 'Hinduism is a way of life'. This 'way of life' may seem to have more in common with persons of other faiths from the same ancestral cultural/ linguistic region in India than with Hindus from other regions with different food, languages, customs, and practices of piety.

Many Hindus have not yet made peace with the desire and determination of adherents of other religions born in South Asia to seek alternate and exclusive identities. Paul Dundas (2002: 6–7) describes the fluidity of the Indian religious world from a socio-historical perspective:

> It could be salutary for those who would compartmentalise Indian religions into discrete and mutually incompatible entities to reflect that, at various times and situations in India's past, what might be regarded as exclusive labels such as 'Hinduism' and 'Jainism' have not in fact always been sufficiently adequate indicators of the complex and often shifting nature of religious identity ... [B]roadly speaking, the types of conceptual boundaries that the [Abrahamic] monotheisms have tended to erect against each other have never functioned with the same degree of intensity in South Asia. Religious identity in India has not invariably had a fixed, 'all or nothing' exclusivity attached to it and there can be identified consistently throughout South Asian history a commonality of religious culture which has operated across what are ostensibly sectarian divides. So, for a Jain lay person to worship occasionally or regularly a markedly Hindu deity such as Hanuman ... does not betoken abandonment of

Jainism ... but rather an easy participation within and desire to confirm linkage
to a South Asian religious world richly populated with figures redolent of power,
prosperity, and transcendence who are accessible to all.

Thus, we see why the conflation of 'culture' and 'religion' is comfortable for
Hindus and why even in the Diaspora, and even amongst those who are *not*
Hindu nationalists, there is a lack of acceptance at a psychological level of the
establishment of distinct identities on the part of Jains, Sikhs, and Buddhists of
South Asian origin. This, of course, has led to charges of Hindu chauvinism in
recent years, as Hindu sensibilities have not kept pace with the desire of members
of other Indian traditions to assert a strongly divergent identity.

Religious worlds as open ecosystems has been normative not only for India's
religious history but for other non-Western cultures as well. One clear example
of the attempt to integrate multiple religious cultures is found in the Chinese
concept of *sanjiao heyi*. As explained by Timothy Brook (1994: 68):

This phrase [*sanjiao heyi*] states the proposition that the Three Teachings
(*sanjiao*) of Buddhism, Daoism, and Confucianism could be merged (*he*) into a
unity (*yi*). The expression emerged during the Yuan dynasty, when Chinese found
themselves having to explain to their new Mongol overlords ... the existence of
three competing intellectual and religious traditions within their culture. At the
heart of the concept of unity in the Yuan dynasty was the idea that the Three
Teachings provided three different vocabularies for the same single reality that all
of them sought to approximate. This interpretation fits well with the ecumenical
tolerance that prevailed in the fourteenth century ...

Sanjiao heyi challenges the normative understanding of the word 'religion'
especially in terms of exclusive religious affiliation. The concretization of the
porous boundaries of Indian religions enabled by the introduction of the term
'religion' and the exclusivity that it implies is explained by Arvind Sharma
(Sherma and Sharma, 2010: 23):

[I] shall develop the following six points: (1) that the Western hermeneutics of
the word religion is conceptually foreign to India; (2) that its foreignness consists
in the double implication of the word religion (a) that one may adhere to only
one religion at a time or what may be called singular or unilateral religious
participation and (b) that religion is separate from and separable from culture;
(3) that this foreign concept of religion was institutionalised in India during
the colonial period; (4) that the introduction of this foreign concept met with

both acceptance and resistance in India; (5) that the tension generated by this dual reaction was foundational for the development of Hindutva ideology, which might not have arisen in a purely Indian context and that therefore (6) the hermeneutical approach of the West to the category of religion, and its application to India, is in a large measure responsible for the appearance of Hindu nationalism, specially as denoted by the word *Hindutva*.

If Hindu nationalism is a reaction to trauma as Sharma's analysis suggests, how is Hinduism to move beyond a response that is rooted in the victimization that resulted from colonialism and towards an expansive and healing response? Jeffery D. Long (2007: 49) approaches this problem from the viewpoint of a Hinduism that respects but transcends its geographic origins:

> [If] Hinduism is also to be a truly global tradition, it must put down new roots in new soils – not instead of, but in addition to those of India – from which it will draw yet another kind of sustenance. Its ability to remain relevant to current and future generations of diasporic Hindus growing up in cultural spaces very different from that of India depends on this, as does its ability to be relevant to non-Indians, whose affiliation to the tradition can enrich it even further, just as it has been enriched historically by cultural diversity of the Indian subcontinent.

Long is correct that for non-Indian Hindus and newer generations of persons of Hindu origin who have grown up in the Diaspora, the lack of a clear *religious identity in conversation with the cultures in which they are embedded* can be problematic particularly in Western nations that hold religion as a clear, definable, and recognized category.

Hinduism is no longer solely a regional faith confined to the cultural mores and geographic boundaries of India. Many factors including the international proliferation of the Hindu Diaspora; the influence of the Diaspora on transnational Hindu organizations, and the proliferation of numerous international guru-based movements have created a global Hindu paradigm. In addition, the pervasive impact of Hindu thought on contemporary Western spirituality, literature, consciousness movements, alternative medicine, music, New Age ideology, and New Thought theology for over a century has thrust the Hindu ethos into the global arena. As a result, the future direction of Hindu thought must be necessarily interwoven with concerns of a far more transcultural nature than heretofore envisioned. Without such an interrelationship, generations of Hindus born in the Diaspora, regardless of ethnicity, will struggle with fractured identities. Kim Knott (2000: 97–8) has documented the prevalent attitudes of young Hindus in Britain:

> British Hinduism in the hands of pro-active young people ... is dynamic. There is an increasing demand for English-medium instructional material, for the meaning of belief and practices to be explained, for new leadership opportunities, greater ethical engagement (e.g., on issues of sexuality and environmentalism) and more public responsibilities for women.

Perhaps the most dangerous aspect of politicized Hindu nationalism is the implication that Hinduism without India cannot (or should not) exist. Religious life is about the search for, and embrace of the infinite and the eternal; nation states are, on the other hand, historically unstable and politically unpredictable. There are many dangers to geography-oriented religions. The conflation of Hinduism and the Indian nation state also displays a lack of remembrance of Hindu history: the Hindu ethos, over different periods of time, existed across a vast span of territory and culture from what is now Afghanistan to Indonesia and Malaysia. Hindu civilizations emerged organically without violence against indigenous cultures, through adaptation, and interrelationships.

In a similar fashion, if novel articulations of Hinduism evolved in the global Diaspora, it would likely present as multiple expressions with commonality in regards to the attenuation of gender disparity, caste discrimination, regional dogmatism, and other markers of separation. It is not difficult to envision a way to a more universally approachable religious culture in the Diaspora. Such alternate versions of Hindu worldviews, that retain the soul of the tradition but are evinced in diverse cultural idioms, cannot be fostered anew if geography is identified with eternality in the Hindu mind.

Another roadblock to Hinduism's ability to acculturate is presented by specifications of the word 'Hindu' that prioritize ethnicity or a reified 'Hindu way of life'. Such specifications are neither accurate (since there are non-Indian or mixed race Hindus and as many varieties of the traditional Hindu 'way of life' as there are regions in South Asia), nor just (as it effectively disenfranchises a significant number of heritage Hindus in the Diaspora and non-Asian Hindus). Therefore, alternate definitions and markers of identity must be sought – ones that are based on Hindu first principles that speak to all humanity and are germane to an interdependent world. Such a cultivation of identity will also be helpful in fostering Hindu acknowledgement of the desires of other faiths of Indian origin to assert their own distinctiveness. An acceptable definition must be able to resist the mildew of anachronism as Hindu demographics, interpretations and practices change over time. It must, therefore, be based on worldviews and conceptions of the Divine-human relationship that are *foundational* to Hinduism, welded into the structural integrity of the Hindu tradition(s) and yet are, at the same time, *diachronic* and *transcultural*. With this caveat in mind, the soul of Hinduism will not be lost in transmission.

Towards a Hindu Identity for a Global Era: Seven Orientations for Reflection

For a definition to be true to the multidimensionality of the Hindu tradition, it needs to be multivalent; for it to be useable and meaningful for Hindus, it needs boundaries – however mutable and inclusive. Each Hindu denomination will always have its own theological orientations and particular practices. There are no overarching credal statements that will be accepted by each of the thousands of Hindu denominations and guru lineages (*sampradāyas* and *paramparās*). However, there are certain general guiding principles or orientations that would be acceptable to most Hindus. In the following, I have highlighted seven orientations that have, in general, marked the historical directionality of the Hindu traditions. I feel they may be best expressed through what is non-normative for Hindu traditions in general:

1. Non-exclusive:
- permeable boundaries;
- personal affiliation with more than one religious tradition is possible.
2. Non-static:
- ongoing revelation through new teachers and texts is integral to the tradition;
- insight into the nature of reality is understood as continuous;
- renewal and new expressions of ultimate truth are expected for each period of time.
3. Non-monolithic authority:
- an individual's ultimate quest and personal religious life have primacy over the dictates of any one institution or leader;
- unmediated connection to Divine Reality or Ultimate Truth is possible;
- spiritual masters can be abandoned and students can seek new paths;
- there is no single authoritarian figure, group, scripture, or institution that directs or regulates the religious lives of every Hindu.
4. Non-abandonment:

- no canonical doctrine of apostasy that results in eternal ejection from, or punishment by a community of adherents;
- no canonical doctrine of heresy to halt the emergence of new religious teachers and teachings.

5. Non-homogeneity:
- diversity of thought, teachings, and texts have been the historic norm;
- many paths, philosophies, and practices;
- variegation results in the possibility of always finding one small exception somewhere for every claim staked.

6. Non-disjunction:
- the *general* historical orientation of the Hindu ethos has been against the fragmentation of life into brittle disjunctions such as secular versus sacred; body versus mind; humanity versus nature, etc.;
- union or, at least, communion is possible and expected between the human and the divine;
- the cosmos is reflected in its parts; the microcosm reflects the macrocosm;
- the Human is a reflection of the Divine;
- the highest state of consciousness, variously defined, allows traversal of the conventional level of reality (*vyāvahārika*) to the ultimate level (*pāramārthika*) which is its underlying form;
- conventional reality *is* transcendent reality experienced through the unenlightened consciousness.

7. Non-dogmatic:
- there is, of course, doctrine in Hinduism; but praxis, not dogma, is central to communal coherence;
- lack of knowledge of scripture and doctrine is permissible and common;
- lack of adherence to religiously ordained codes of responsible conduct is discouraged;
- religious practices (rituals of worship; pious ceremonies; sacraments; festivals) bind the Hindu community.

The above are simply some points of departure for conceptualizing the development of a Hindu identity that is both faithful to the tradition and capable of fostering critical-constructive reflection on re-envisioning scriptural principles for contemporary applications.

Towards Critical-Constructive Reflection for a Socially Engaged Hinduism

Today, there are numerous charitable projects, worldwide, established by twentieth- and twenty-first century Hindu religious leaders with international followings, or 'Jagadgurus' (for example, Amritananda Mayi, Sri Sri Ravi Shankar, Athwale and others), who have taken the notion of service to, and care of, humanity and the natural world to a different level altogether than has heretofore been witnessed in Hindu experience.

There are, of course, Hindu resources for benevolent world engagement in text and tradition as well as historical movements, individuals, and denominations that have emphasized self-less service as spiritual practice – starting with the re-envisioning of karma yoga in the *Bhagavad Gītā*. There is also a historical background for social and political engagement (and sometimes environmental as well – e.g. the Bishnoi-s) from the colonial period. Some of the best known colonial era leaders of social engagement include Swami Vivekananda and the Ramakrishna Order of Monks, and Swami Dayananda and his Arya Samaj movement. The nineteenth century Bengali reformers are also notable in their efforts at social engagement. Even earlier, there is, for example, Caitanya Mahāprabhu's fifteenth-century Gaudiya Vaishnava Acintya-bhedābheda movement which was socially inclusive and concerned about the welfare of persons beyond the common expectation of familial care for individuals.

In addition to these historical phenomena, one can reflect on the fact that the modern and post-modern gurus who emphasize self-less service in their teachings and activities, do not posit that they are reformulating the Hindu tradition(s). What they do claim is that their social and/or environmental engagement is ultimately rooted in the doctrines and principles of Vedāntic or Yogic philosophy, and they continue to refer to Hindu texts and traditions as the primary sources for guidance regarding service as praxis.

Placing the amelioration of the human condition on a par with contemplative practice as a legitimate path to enlightenment is no doubt laudable. However, there are structural issues within the edifice of the Hindu ethos that are not critically examined by such efforts. Indeed, the heightened emphasis on *karma yoga* or *seva* (service) may have helped to strip attention from the thought traditions that lie at the heart of Hindu praxis. There are critical concerns that need to be addressed not only in terms of service and practical effort but reimagined and reconstituted in terms of the philosophical traditions – enshrined in new interpretations of scripture (Śabda pramāṇa).

These critical concerns include but are not limited to (1) women's personal rights; institutional religious authority, and acceptance to the priesthood; (2) the reinterpretation of the *Dharmaśāstra* (codes of conduct) for our time; (3) engaging the issue of *varna* and *jāti* (caste) from the viewpoint of Hindu theologies of liberation; (4) cultivation of a Hindu theology of religions that is based on the Hindu value of deep pluralism rather than the more common Hindu universalism; (5) the renewal of constructive systematic theologies (*bhashya*).

These concerns are not often voiced by major leaders but, instead, actions are sometimes undertaken to circumvent the problem by compassionate service, inclusion, and/or empowerment of the disenfranchised. For example, let us consider the case of women's religious leadership: the modern and contemporary guru lineages (*paramparās*) tend to be inclusive of women in leadership roles with many examples such the Ramakrishna Order of Nuns; the Brahma Kumaris; women's empowerment in the Arya Samaj, and the notable list of modern and contemporary era women gurus such as Ananda Mayi Ma; Sri Ma (Pondicherry); Jayshree Talwalkar (Swadhyay Movement); Gurumayi Chidvilasananda (Siddha Yoga) and, of course, the well-known Amritananda Mayi (Amma), among others. It is difficult to predict whether such exemplars of women's religious leadership in Hinduism have permanently cracked what I often call the *sandalwood ceiling* or whether they are trailblazers whose trails will close up after them. Many of these women were or are outside the fold of historically powerful, entrenched denominations. If, however, women's religious authority is carved into the theological manifold of the Hindu tradition(s), one could predict, with a far greater degree of certainty that the *sandalwood ceiling* could indeed be viewed as fractured. Similarly, devotees of modern gurus intermingle with each other without concern for class/caste status or affiliation. But disjunction within Hindu society (as well as discrimination) continues to exist due to the lack of conclusive engagement with these explosive issues by revered religious authorities.

Conclusion

Tomorrow's Hindu ethos will be very different from that of today. This is a certainty; what is uncertain is what form it will take. Will Hindus forget their own history throughout which religion has generally been perceived as an open ecosystem, supported and nourished by feed-back loops that moved and transformed information amongst different religions; between religion and the rest of society, and from the natural world into religious culture? Or will the ecosystem approach to religion which is such a valuable heritage for Indian religions be rediscovered and reformulated for a new era? Will the commendable emphasis on service as spiritual praxis increase the attenuation of the reinterpretive theological tradition and eventually also *contemplative activism* itself? Or will praxis lead theory towards an interpretation that embraces and doctrinally supports increasingly wider circles of compassionate world engagement? If the latter is to become reality, the lack of attention to the Hindu intellectual tradition, to systematic theology, and of reconstructive philosophical ethics, must be reversed. It may be worth contemplating whether gains made through religious activism and advocacy alone, without the support of systematically re-envisioned doctrines and principles, can be more easily overturned.

For religion to be both 'sensible' (appropriate to the conscience and reason of humanity) and 'sensitive' (aware of the need of practitioners to keep ancient spiritual aesthetics and time-honoured traditions from vanishing), religions must engage in self-aware constructive reflection on both principles and practices.

Reference List

Brook, Timothy (1994) *Praying for Power: Buddhism and the Formation of Gentry Society in Late-Ming China*, Boston, MA: Harvard University Asia Center.

Coward, Harold, Hinnells, John R. and Brady, Raymond (eds) (2000) *The South Asian Religious Diaspora in Britain, Canada, and the United States*, Albany, NY: State University of New York Press.

Dundas, Paul (2nd edn 2002) *The Jains*, London: Routledge.

Jain, Arun Kumar (2009) *Faith and Philosophy of Jainism*, New Delhi: Kalpaz Publ., an imprint of Gyan Books.

Levine, Sarah Ethel and Gellner, David N. (2005) *Rebuilding Buddhism: The Theravada Movement in Twentieth Century Nepal*, Boston, MA: Harvard University Press.

Long, Jeffery D. (2007) *A Vision for Hinduism: Beyond Hindu Nationalism*, London: I.B. Tauris.

Sherma, Rita and Sharma, Arvind (eds) (Softcover reprint and e-book version of hardcover 1st edn (2008) 2010) *Hermeneutics and Hindu Thought: Toward a Fusion of Horizons*, New York: Springer.

Tatla, Darshan Singh (2008) *The Sikh Diaspora: The Search for Statehood*, New York: Routledge.

Chapter 10

Hinduism: True (Satyam), Good (Shivam) and Beautiful (Sundaram)

Anantanand Rambachan

In Chapter 1 of this volume, Christopher Lewis speaks of 'sensible' religion as fulfilling a number of significant criteria. First, the claims of such religion must be in accord with what is widely regarded as true and which corresponds with reality. It must engage meaningfully with the insights of other disciplines through debate and mutual interrogation. Second, 'sensible' religion must justify values that promote the flourishing of human beings. Such values include compassion and an affirmation of the dignity and equal worth of human beings. My aim in this chapter is to show that the Hindu Advaita Vedānta tradition has the resources to fulfill these criteria. I will also identify interpretations of the tradition that are unreasonable, unjust and oppressive. It is necessary, however, to begin our discussion by noting that what we speak of today as 'Hinduism' is a remarkably diverse phenomenon.

The Richness of Diversity

The term 'Hindu' has been and is still used to name geographical, religious, cultural and, in recent times, national realities. 'Hindu' is the Iranian variation for the name of a river, that was called the 'Sindhu', 'Indos', and 'Indus'. Those who lived on the territories through which this river flowed were called 'Hindus', and did not share a homogeneous religious culture. Pennington (2005) has documented in detail the interaction between colonial Christian missionaries and Hindu subjects that resulted in the discourse about a homogenized 'Hinduism'. In order to argue against the Hindu tradition, missionaries had to give it uniformity and to think of it in ways structurally similar to Christianity and Islam. The defenders of the tradition, on the opposite end, like Rammohan Roy, also spoke of it in homogeneous terms. Evidence suggests that the term

'Hinduism' was being employed, perhaps for the first time, in missionary circles in the 1780s (Oddie 2006: 70–72). Hindu traditions have always been diverse, reflecting India's rich diversity of geography, culture and language. Hindu traditions, on the whole, do not problematize religious diversity or see it as something to be overcome. It is helpful to think of Hinduism as a family name, recognizable through shared features, but preserving also the uniqueness of its individual members. The traditions comprising this ancient extended family continue to intermingle, influencing and being influenced by each other. If we keep this fact of diversity in mind, our generalizations will not mislead.

The Advaita (Non-dual) Tradition

Our discussion in this chapter, while drawing from diverse Hindu traditions, will be grounded specifically in the tradition of Advaita. Advaita is one of several Hindu theological traditions that look to the four Vedas (Ṛg, Sāma, Yajur and Atharva) as sources of authoritative teachings. More specifically, these traditions look to the dialogues in last sections of the Vedas, the Upaniṣads, as the repository of the highest teachings in the scripture. For this reason, the name 'Vedānta' (literally, 'end of the Veda') is usually appended to Advaita. While regarding the Upaniṣads as the primary authoritative source for its teachings, Advaita looks also to the Bhagavadgītā, and to the Brahmasūtra, an aphoristic summary of the teachings of the Upaniṣads attributed to the ancient teacher Bādarāyaṇa. These sources are regarded as the three pillars of the tradition. Advaita is an exegetical tradition that derives its truths from a reading of the meaning of the Upanisads. It looks to a line of distinguished teachers for the interpretation of these texts and for the transmission of its teachings. The most distinguished among these is Śaṅkara (*c.* eighth century CE), who wrote extensive commentaries on the Upaniṣads, the Bhagavadgītā and the Brahmasūtra and who is credited with the legacy of the finest systematic exposition of Advaita.

Scripture as a Source of Valid Knowledge

Before discussing the specific truth claims of the Advaita tradition, with a view to considering whether these are reasonable, it is helpful to consider the Advaita arguments for the scripture as an authoritative source of knowledge. These arguments are particularly important in the light of Christopher Lewis's argument in Chapter 1 about the dangers of textual fundamentalism. Religions, in their different ways, regard texts, persons, texts and persons, or special experiences, as epistemologically significant and rational arguments must be offered by way of explanation. How a tradition understands the nature of its authoritative source determines the manner in which it regards the content of this source vis à vis other sources.

Advaita regards the Vedas as a revelation from God (*brahman*). According to the Bṛhadāraṇyaka Upaniṣad 2.4.10, 'Those that are called the Ṛg Veda (Yajur Veda, etc.,) are but the exhalation of this great Being'. Advaita arguments for the authority of the Vedas, however, do not centre on the divine origin of the texts. The tradition thinks that such arguments become hopelessly circular since one establishes God's omniscience from the Vedas and then the authority of the Vedas from God's omniscience. The cornerstone of the tradition's argument for the authority of the scripture is that it satisfies the criteria of being a source of valid knowledge. Valid knowledge, according to Advaita, has the characteristic of corresponding to the nature of reality. It must be in accord with the nature of the object that we seek to know and not be subject to the whims of human preferences. Valid knowledge is object-centred. The source of such valid knowledge is known as a *pramāṇa* and it is a fundamental tenet of Advaita that valid knowledge, religious or secular, can be generated only by a valid source of knowledge. Advaita would concur enthusiastically with Christopher Lewis that religious claims must 'correspond to what is seen as reality'.

If the authority of the scripture is connected with its nature as a source of valid knowledge, what criteria must it satisfy to be so regarded? Advaita proposes two conditions (Rambachan, 1991: 15–19). First, in order not to be redundant, scripture must inform us of a subject matter that is not known or knowable through any other valid way of knowing. Scripture, in Advaita, has a very limited sphere of revelation. It is not the function of the scripture to reveal matters within the range of human experience, ascertainable through our ordinary means of knowledge like perception or inference. History, for example, is not within the authoritative sphere of the scripture, and so also are matters that may be known through empirical methods of inquiry. A religion may offer an interpretation of the meaning of history, but the facts of history are not the authoritative concern of religion. The understanding that each source of valid knowledge has a unique and limited field of authority has helped the Hindu tradition to avoid major conflicts with the empirical and behavioural sciences. Advaita affirms that the conclusions of valid ways of knowing ought not to contradict each other. In the case of contradictions, the advocates of religion must make earnest efforts to resolve these through further inquiry. It is necessary, as Christopher Lewis argues, that each should take into account the claims of the other, but religion, contends Advaita, ought not to claim authority in those fields of inquiry where its methods and sources are not appropriate. At the same time, the Advaita tradition calls for a similar acknowledgement of the limits of empirical modes of inquiry. Humility is a virtue for both religion and the empirical sciences and a necessity for sensible religion.

The second criterion that a source of valid knowledge must satisfy is non-contradiction. This criterion, as far as Advaita is concerned, is the crucial test of the validity of knowledge, scriptural or otherwise. In the view of Śaṅkara, the disclosures of one valid source of knowledge should not be contradicted by the disclosures of another valid source, if these are both operating properly within their respective spheres. For Śaṅkara, the teachings of the scripture cannot be opposed to fact. If a scripture statement contradicts a well-established fact of experience, it cannot be considered authoritative, since such a matter will be outside the scope of the scripture. Scriptural teachings cannot be exempt from critical interrogation. Śaṅkara speaks unambiguously on this in commentary on the Bhagavadgītā (18: 66):

> *Sruti* [Veda] is an authority only in matters not perceived by means of ordinary instruments of knowledge such as *pratyaksa* or immediate perception; - i.e., it is an authority as to the mutual relation of things as means to ends, but not in matters lying within the range of *pratyaksa*; indeed, *sruti* is intended as an authority only for knowing what lies beyond the range of human knowledge ... A hundred *srutis* may declare that fire is cold or that it is dark; still they possess no authority in this matter.

If scripture did describe fire as being cold, we would be obliged to construe this meaning figuratively, since the purpose of the scripture is not to reverse the nature of anything. The teachings of the scripture must be understood within the parameters of human reason and experience and contradictions cannot go unaddressed. When contradictions occur, earnest inquiry is necessary for the resolution of these and religious teachers must welcome and be active participants in such discussions.

One of the important consequences of defining the scripture as a source of valid knowledge is that it cannot claim exemption from being subject to the same criteria that are employed to establish the validity of every other source of knowledge. Advaita is opposed to the compartmentalization of human knowledge. Sensible religion cannot claim epistemological privilege and be sheltered from wider engagement with the growing body of knowledge about our universe. The view of scripture as a source of valid knowledge helps to overcome the privatization of religious claims and the exemption of these from rational scrutiny. Religious claims that are refuted by valid sources of knowledge cannot be professed in ways suggesting that such contradictions do not matter. Sensible religion must not be afraid of truth, whatever its source. The Advaita tradition will concur wholeheartedly with Lewis's view in Chapter 1 that the claims of sensible religion must be in accord with what is regarded as true.

The Necessity for Scripture

If we regard the scripture as a source of valid knowledge that must satisfy the criteria of revealing a subject that cannot be known otherwise and of being free from contradictions with other sources, what does it uniquely reveal? What is the rational necessity for the scripture? Why do we need a source of knowledge other than the generally accepted ones such as perception and inference? According to Śaṅkara, *brahman*, the limitless, is the unique subject matter of the scripture. The infinite *brahman* does not have qualities associated with finite objects such as sound, sensation, form, colour, taste and scent, that may be known though the senses. In the absence of data from perception, any inferences that we make about the nature of *brahman* will be tentative and inconclusive.

In addition to the limits of perception and inference as modes of knowing, there is the additional difficulty that arises from the fact that the infinite is not an object, a thing among other things. The process of empirical knowledge involves a distinction between subject and object, the knower and the known. We know things by making them objects of our awareness and, in this way, they are available for scrutiny and analysis. This includes also disciplines such as psychology and psychoanalysis that study the contents of the mind. *Brahman* is described in the Upaniṣads as the non-objectifiable subject that is not available for knowledge through the senses or the mind. Objects of the senses and mind are finite. Speaking about a non-objectifiable reality presents special challenges for language that is constructed principally for the purpose of describing the world of finite objects. In a fascinating comment on Bhagavadgītā 13: 12, Śaṅkara explains the limits of even words such as existent (*sat*) and non-existent (*asat*)) in speaking of *brahman*:

> Being beyond the reach of the senses, it is not an object of consciousness accompanied with the idea of either (existence or non-existence). That thing indeed which can be perceived by the senses, such as a pot, can be an object of consciousness accompanied with the idea of nonexistence.

Science, from the perspective of Advaita, deals with the realm of the objectifiable universe. It is not the appropriate method for inquiring into a reality, like *brahman* that is not the object of perception or inference. Science and religion must be willing to admit the specificity of their subject matter and methods. None is comprehensive.

The Human Problem

If the scripture is a necessary and logically appropriate medium for our knowledge of the limitless, how is this knowledge relevant and useful to us? Sensible religion must make the case for itself by a willingness to speak with more clarity about its fruits and its transformative impact on human life. The fruitfulness of knowing *brahman* can only be discussed in relation to the tradition's identification of what we may speak about as the fundamental human problem (Rambachan 2006: 9–17).

The Advaita approach to the human problem is empirical in orientation. It identifies a problem that is recognizable in human experience and characterizes it as a sense of inadequacy or incompleteness that expresses itself and seeks resolution in a plethora of desires for gains such as wealth, power and fame. Although specific desires are conditioned by culture and history, Advaita teachers describe the desire for self-adequacy as one that obtains across culture and geography.

> Thus, we find that in addition to the basic urge to survive, there seems to be another basic urge that manifests in the mind. It can be expressed by saying, 'I want to be full, complete, adequate, fulfilled, happy, self-possessed', and so on. However one says it, it means the same thing. Unlike all the cultivated desires for a specific thing that one picks up in time, this one seems to come along with birth. No one has to be told that being full happy etc., is desirable. This urge to be full, complete etc., is not a particular trait of some people, but is common to all human beings in all times. (Swami Dayananda 2006: 20)

Human beings are distinguished from other species by a heightened self-consciousness that allows for the experience of inadequacy and the comparison of ourselves with others.

We seek to overcome our persisting sense of self-inadequacy by desiring and acquiring finite things. Every finite gain and experience, however, whether it is sense pleasure, fame, power or wealth, results in a short-lived sense of well-being but the sense of want persists. The reason, according to the Upaniṣads, is simple – finite actions can only produce results that are transient. In addition, finite ends are often sought not for their own sake but for the enhancement of our sense of self. This means that the self-value that we grant to ourselves depends on unfavourable comparisons with others. In the case of wealth, for example, our worth increases when our assets are worth more than those in the group used for comparison and diminishes when these assets decline. The consequence is a sense of anxiety, fear and discomfort. Finite gains, as Bhagavadgita 5: 22 reminds us, have a beginning and end and we must not be attached to these.

The meaning and significance of religion assume new urgency when a reflective and thoughtful person comes to discover that self-inadequacy is not overcome by finite gains. The religious life is then pursued in earnest for the purpose of finding a solution to this most basic of human problems. This must not be construed as implying indifference to wealth and power or any other necessities for decent living in community. The Hindu tradition is not anti-materialistic or opposed to the enjoyment of life in the world. It does not condone or celebrate the life of involuntary poverty. It proposes a scheme of four goals that it understands as necessary for a flourishing human life: wealth (*artha*), pleasure (*kāma*), virtue (*dharma*) and liberation (*mokṣa*). This is an inclusive scheme that identifies the material, aesthetic, ethical and spiritual as vital to human well-being. Recognizing the limits of finite gains in relation to the fundamental human problem ensures that religion is not pursued merely as a system of magical techniques for the gaining finite objects of human desire. Sensible religion offers something that is far more profound in helping us to identify and resolve the problem of an unfulfilled life. At the same time, the Advaita tradition recognizes that people are different and look to religion for a variety of ends. Persons who aspire exclusively after finite things are not condemned but instructed to pursue such goals with attentiveness to basic ethical values such as non-injury, truth, non-stealing, generosity and self-control. Religious teaching can be shared but not imposed. It can be shared only when there is an explicit request from another to receive teaching and must be done with sensitivity to religious needs.

The person, however, who sees clearly the limits of the finite and asks whether life offers any deeper and enduring fulfilment and meaning is advised in the Muṇḍaka Upaniṣad 1.2.12 to approach a teacher (*guru*) who is well-versed in the scripture and who is existentially centred in the limitless (*brahman*). The same Upaniṣad (1.2.13) implores the teacher to instruct the student about *brahman*, that he may come to know the true and imperishable being.

Liberating Teachings

How does the instruction about the nature of *brahman* help the religious seeker overcome inadequacy? The Upaniṣad resolution to the human dilemma, according to Advaita, is the teaching that we are already the full being that we strive to become; the seeker is the sought. The Upaniṣad teaching is articulated in concise form in the four great sentences of the Upaniṣads: 'That Thou Art' is taken from Chāndogya Upaniṣad 6.8.7 of the Sāma Veda; 'This ātmā is *brahma*' is taken from the Māṇḍukya Upaniṣad 2 of the Atharva Veda; 'Awareness is *brahma*' is taken from the Aitareya Upaniṣad 5.3 of the Ṛg Veda; and 'I am *brahma*' is taken from Bṛhadāraṇyaka Upaniṣad 1.4.10 of the Yajur Veda. Each one of the great sentences points out the existing identity between the self and the limitless. If, as Advaita teaches, the self is identical with the limitless and we are already the full and complete being that we yearn to become, the problem is one of ignorance (*avidyā*).

In the Chāndogya Upaniṣad (6.14.2) the human condition is likened to a person forcibly taken away from her beloved home, blindfolded and left in the wilderness. A compassionate person answers her appeal for help, removes her blindfold, and shows her the way back to her home. In a similar way, a teacher liberates the ignorance-bound individual by teaching about her identity with *brahman*. Through the instruction of the scripture and teacher, we discover and understand that the self (ātmā), which we just assumed to be finite and subject to time and spatial limits, is, in fact, identical with the limitless *brahman*. Advaita is a teaching tradition that aims to instruct about the true nature of the self.

In considering Advaita as sensible religion, there is a further question that must be addressed. The fundamental subject of Advaita inquiry is the self (ātmā). How do we know that the self exists? Are there any rational proofs to be offered? Are we speaking about a self that exists only as a possibility? It is a fundamental claim of the Advaita tradition that the existence of the self does not need any form of proof. On the other hand, the existence of the self is the necessary ground for any kind mental process, including attempts to 'prove' the existence of the self. The self is self-revealing. In the introduction to his commentary on the *Brahmasūtra*, Śaṅkara explains that though the self is not an object of perception like a sense object, it is not unknown. 'The Self is not absolutely beyond apprehension, because it is apprehended as the content of the concept 'I', and because the Self, opposed to the non-Self, is well known in the world as an immediately perceived (i.e., self-revealing entity).'

Later in his commentary on the first *sūtra* of the same text, Śaṅkara returns to the question of the self that is identical with *brahman*:

> Besides, the existence of *brahman* is well known from the fact of Its being the Self
> of all; for everyone feels that his Self exists, and he never feels, 'I do not exist'. Had
> there been no general recognition of the existence of the Self, everyone would
> have felt, 'I do not exist'. And that Self is *brahman*.

The denial of the existence of the self is its affirmation; the absurdity of trying to deny one's existence is apparent in the fact that one must exist to deny oneself. This is important for the reason that the kinds of arguments advanced traditionally for establishing God's existence, deductive and inductive, are not necessary in the case of the self-revealing ātmā. The purpose of the scripture is not to establish the existence of the self, but to instruct about its nature since, according to Advaita, there is erroneous understanding. The self-shining ātmā, intrinsically full and free, is regarded as a limited and finite entity, bound by time and space, and subject to birth, growth, change, decline, and death.

One of the important consequences of the fact that Advaita focuses on a self that is immediately and always available is the possibility of employing other sources of valid knowledge in a supplemental role in the inquiry about the nature of *brahman*, This is not possible with other subjects of religious inquiry. There is no way, for example, for using other sources of knowledge to prove or disprove the existence of a heavenly world or the claim that actions performed in this life may have consequences in a future one. Such results are in the future and are not available for immediate inquiry. Since the self, however, is not outside human experiences, Upaniṣad instruction may be supplemented by other sources of knowledge, and there is a greater burden to ensure that scripture does not conflict with experience. Māṇḍūkya Upaniṣad, for example, discusses the nature of the self through an analysis of the waking, dream and sleep states.

The fundamental Advaita truth claim is twofold. The first, discussed above, is the identity of the self with *brahman*. The second is that *brahman* constitutes the truth or reality (*satyam*) of the universe, in a way that is analogically similar to clay constituting the nature of all clay products. Like God in theistic religious traditions, *brahman* is described in the Taittirīya Upaniṣad (3.1.1) as 'that from which these beings are born, that, by which, they live, that into which, when departing, they enter'. The Upaniṣads deny the origin of the world in anything other than *brahman*. There is an explicit refutation of a preexistent matter out of which *brahman* creates, the origination of existence from non-existence or non-being, and the spontaneous evolution of the universe from insentient matter. As Uddalaka, asks in Chāndogya Upaniṣad 6.2.1–2, 'How could being arise from non-being?'

In describing the emergence of the world from God, the Upaniṣads offer many suggestive analogies. The Chandogya Upanishad (6.1.4–5) employs the analogy of the relationship between clay or gold and their various modifications to speak of the God-world relationship:

> Just as, my dear, by one clod of clay all that is made of clay becomes known, the
> modifications being only a name arising from speech while the truth is that it is
> just clay. Just as, my dear, by one nugget of gold, all that is made of gold becomes
> known, the modification being only a name arising from speech, while the truth
> is that it is just gold.

In relation to God, all analogies, like all words, eventually fall short, but these point to *brahman* as the operative or the intelligent cause and also as the 'material' ground of creation. Advaita does not employ the language of *creatio ex nihilo* to describe the emergence of the world from *brahman*. 'Truth (*satyam*)', as Taittirīya Upaniṣad 2.61.1 states it, 'became all this that there is'. At the same time, although *brahman* brings forth the world out of itself, *brahman* is not lost, depleted or ceases to be infinite through self-multiplication. Without any loss of nature, God intentionally brings forth a world of unimaginable diversity and remains as the substantive ontological truth of all that is created. As in the analogy of gold and gold ornaments, there can be manyness without ontological dualism. I have argued elsewhere that Advaita invites us to see the world as a celebrative expression of God's fullness, an overflow of God's limitlessness. Its value is derived from the fact that it exists in, depends upon and derives its reality from God (Rambachan 2006: 78–80). As expressing but never exhausting God's fullness, the world is both good (*shivam*) and beautiful (*sundaram*).

According to Advaita, these two core claims, that the self is identical with *brahman* and *brahman* constitutes the single ontological truth of everything that exists, are not contradicted by any valid source of knowledge. Contradictions with reason and human experience cannot go unaddressed All the possible resources of reason and experience are marshalled to show support for these claims. Advaita welcomes the engagement with science about its teachings, but science must be cognizant of the limits of its own methods of inquiry and proof, dependent as these are on specific assumptions about the nature of reality.

Living Liberation and Human Transformation

One of the significant arguments made for science as a source of valid knowledge is the pragmatic one that it generates results which may be experienced here. Karl Marx criticizes religion for promising results in a life to come and ignoring the human predicament in this one. What kinds of results can we speak about in Advaita and where are these results to be realized? The end of Advaita instruction is liberation (*mokṣa*) but, unlike many other religious goals, liberation is to be attained here and now. The ideal is referred to as living liberation (*jīvanmukti*). This becomes possible because the human problem is characterized as one of ignorance about the nature of self. Liberation is equated with the transformation that follows from right understanding. This is not an end that must await the death of the body. Śaṅkara alludes constantly to the transformed like of the knower of *brahman* as evidence for the validity of the teachings of the scripture. In his commentary on Brahmasūtra 1.1.4, for example, he contends that:

> For one who has realised the state of unity of the Self and *brahman*, it cannot be proved that his mundane life continues just as before; for this contradicts the knowledge of the unity of *brahman* and the Self arising from the Vedas which are a valid means of knowledge.

The most immediate fruit of a new understanding of self is freedom from greed. The root of greed, according to Advaita, is self-ignorance that causes a false sense of incompleteness and inadequacy. Desire-multiplication becomes the path of self-fulfilment. Understanding the identity of the self with *brahman* leads to the discovery of one's fullness and the overcoming of the suffering occasioned by a sense of lack and insignificance. Liberation, however, does not isolate us from the community of beings. Since *brahman* is the self of all, liberation results in the deepest identity that we can have with others. We recognize ourselves in all beings. Īśa Upaniṣad 6 understands this insight to free from hate: 'One who sees all beings in the self alone and self in all beings, feels no hate by virtue of that understanding'. The value and worth that we discover for ourselves must be extended to every other being; none can be excluded – *brahman* exists equally and identically in all. This identification with other beings transcends the boundaries of nationality, religion, race and ethnicity. Hating and oppressing others on the basis of caste, sex or race is unjust and a consequences of blindness to the truth of *brahman's* non-dual nature and identity in all. To hate another is to hate oneself; to hurt another is to hurt oneself. Advaita offers a teaching that enables human beings, in Lewis's terminology, to be both 'altruistic as well as fulfilled'.

We must admit that there are interpretations of the Hindu tradition and practices that do not reflect this vision of human unity and equal worth. Many Hindus continue to define the meaning of Hindu identity in the context of a hierarchical caste order that labels others as impure and denies them dignity and worth. The doctrine of *karma* is interpreted in ways that justify caste inequalities by contending that birth in a lower caste is the deserved consequence of evil actions in past lives and there is no freedom from its indignities without rebirth into a higher caste. Such views justify violence against persons seen as belonging to lower castes and promote passive acceptance of injustice. No incentives or motivation are offered for social reform and change. The Hindu tradition developed in a patriarchal culture with assumptions about male supremacy in which women derived value only through relationships with men. Patriarchal values are reflected in the fact that a disproportionate percentage of the illiterate in India are women, in demands for dowries from the families of brides and in the abortion of female foetuses. The oppression and injustice of caste and patriarchy cannot be justified or condoned by sensible religion and are contrary to core Advaita teachings about human unity and equal value. Caste and patriarchy, when legitimized by religious arguments, are examples of irrationality and non-sensible religion. Sensible religion does not condone inequality and injustice.

Compassionate Engagement in the World

Although the resources of liberation in Advaita have not been explored for all their social implications, these provide a powerful justification and impetus for a life of compassion and engagement in the world. Seeing oneself in all, and freedom from greed are powerful sources of motivation for devoting our energies to the service of others. Bhagavadgītā 3: 25 suggests that liberated persons can bring as much energy and enthusiasm to the work of serving others as the unliberated expend for the achievement of personal goals. If we see the suffering of the other as our own, action for the alleviation of such suffering becomes natural and inevitable. The Bhagavadgītā speaks repeatedly about the liberated as a person who exerts herself for and who delights in the flourishing of others. Love is another way of speaking about the fullness of self and identification with others. Love of self cannot be self-centred, when the self is the self of all. It may indeed be argued that without love for ourselves, we cannot embrace others in love.

Although Advaita is committed to its core truth claims about the nature of *brahman* as the self and as the single ontological truth of the universe, the tradition is well aware of the limits of language and other symbols in articulating anything about the nature of the infinite. Word formulations, though necessary, can never reveal fully the intrinsic nature of *brahman* 'Brahman', as Taittirīya Upaniṣad 2.9.1 reminds us, 'is that from which words turn back with the mind'. Bṛhadāraṇyaka Upaniṣad 2.6.3 cautions us about the limits of language with the famous words 'not this, not this (*neti, neti*)'. This acknowledgement of the limits of our formulations must dispose us always to think critically about these and to be attentive to learning from other ways of speaking. We must not associate truth only with our way of speaking. The wise, as the Bhagavadgītā 6.18 teaches, is rich in knowledge and humility. Although confident about its own twofold claims, Advaita must engage respectfully with other viewpoints, theistic and non-theistic, learning, sharing, clarifying and critically reflecting on its teachings.

Advaita addresses what it regards as the fundamental human problem that it identifies as a persistent sense of lack and insufficiency about ourselves. This resolution of this problem is the understanding of our identity with the limitless *brahman*, revealed in the Upaniṣad teaching that the ātmā is *brahman*. This teaching enables us to embrace our intrinsic fullness and to discern our unity with all beings. It liberates us from greed and the isolation of self-centeredness and liberates us to be compassionate, to practice justice, to desist from oppression, and to devote ourselves to the flourishing of others. These implications for human well-being have not always been specified or practiced in the history of the tradition and Advaita has all too easily accommodated itself to unjust social structures of caste and gender. The realization of its truth, beauty and goodness requires critical examination of its relationship with social structures and a readiness to think anew about all the implications of its unitive vision of reality. There is growing evidence that diaspora Hindus, less constrained by the politics of religious nationalism and the identification of the Hindu tradition with India, living in new social and political contexts influenced by political philosophies of human equality, dignity and justice, are already engaged in the process of rethinking what it means to be Hindu. They are discovering a Hindu identity that is not inextricably bound to caste and patriarchy.

Advaita Criteria for Sensible Religion in Hinduism

I conclude by identifying core constituents for developing the criteria for sensible religion in Advaita.

1. Sensible religion must explain and offer reasonable grounds for looking to an authoritative source or sources of knowledge other than the generally accepted ones such as perception and inference. It must rationally explain the need for such sources, by clarifying why the knowledge gained through such a source is not otherwise available. Without such explanations, claims for the authority of scripture will appear to be irrational and uncritical.

2. Sensible religion requires that the claims of such authoritative texts not be opposed to fact. If a scriptural statement contradicts a well-established fact of experience, it cannot be considered authoritative. Scriptural teachings cannot be exempt from critical interrogation. The teachings of the scripture must be understood within the parameters of human reason. Sensible religion must be especially attentive to the claims of science, be in conversation with these claims and seek earnestly to show how its own truth affirmations relate to these.

3. Sensible religion must justify the need for religion by identifying clearly the human problem or problems that religion uniquely addresses. Such a problem must be one that is universally recognizable by human beings within their experience. If the problem that religion addresses can be resolved by non-religious methods, then religion becomes redundant and has no special role. Sensible religion, therefore, has a responsibility to explain what religion offers that is not available elsewhere and why other solutions to the human predicament may be inadequate. In the absence of such a rationale, religion may be reduced to magical techniques for procuring finite gains.

4. The truth claims of sensible religion must be universally accessible and valid. It is contradictory, in the perspective of Advaita, to define a religious teaching as true, but limit that truth to specific national, racial or cultural groups. There are claims about the nature of Hindu identity articulated by V.S. Savarkar and others that conflate the meaning of being Hindu with Indian national identity, race and culture (Savarkar: 1989). Such interpretations, identifying Hinduism with nationalism, contradict the Advaita understanding of religious truth, negativize others and create conditions for violence.

5. Without ignoring goals that are beyond this life, sensible religion must make the case for itself by a willingness to speak with more clarity about its fruits and its transformative impact on human life in this world. It must demonstrate the ways in which it is conducive to individual well-being by

addressing fundamental human needs and offering an understanding of fulfillment that is not dependent on the multiplication of desire.

6. Sensible religion cannot be content only with the flourishing of the human individual. It must demonstrate also how its teachings foster a deep sense of human community and a unity of humanity that transcends boundaries of nationality, race, ethnicity and culture. Sensible religion promotes the flourishing of human beings in community.

7. Sensible religion must advocate teachings that support the equal worth, value and dignity of all human beings. Sensible religion cannot validate the injustice, inequality and indignity of caste and patriarchy.

8. Sensible religion must offer values that motivate human beings to lives of compassionate engagement, generosity and justice in the world. It must help to identify the sources of human suffering and work for the overcoming of these. Such sources must include poverty, illiteracy and injustice. A central focus of sensible religion must be what the Bhagavadgita 3: 25 speaks of as lokasaṅgraham, that is the flourishing of the universe. This is an inclusive vision that embraces all living beings, as well as the world of nature.

9. Sensible religion, though affirming its own truth claims, must acknowledge the limits of all human symbols in relation to the limitless. It must engage other traditions with humility, respect, self-criticism and in relationships that are conducive to learning and sharing.

Reference List

Bhagavadgītā (2007) Translated by Swami Dayananda Saraswati. Chennai: Arsha Vidya Centre.

Bhagavadgītā with the Commentary of Śaṅkarācārya (1977) Translated by Alladi Mahadeva Sastry, Madras: Samata Books.

Brahmasūtra Bhaṣya of Śaṅkarācārya (1977) Translated by Swami Gambhirananda, Calcutta: Advaita Ashrama.

Chandogya Upaniṣad (1975) Translated by Swami Swahananda, Madras: Sri Ramakrishna Math.

Eight Upaniṣads with the Commentary of Śaṅkarācārya (1965–1966), 2 vols: *Īśa, Kena, Kaṭha,* and *Taittirīya* in vol. 1; *Aitaraya, Muṇḍaka, Māṇḍūkya* and *Kārika* and *Praśna* in vol. 2. Translated by Swami Gambhirananda, Calcutta: Advaita Ashrama.

Oddie, Geoffrey A. (2006) *Imagined Hinduism*, New Delhi: Sage Publications.

Pennington, Brian K. (2005) *Was Hinduism Invented?*, New York: Oxford University Press.

Rambachan, Anantanand (2006) *The Advaita Worldview*, Albany, NY: State University of New York Press.

Savarkar, V.S. (1989) *Hindutva*, New Delhi: Bharti Sahitya Sadan.

Swami Dayananda Saraswati (2006) *Talks and Essays*, vol. 2, Saylorsburg: Arsha Vidya Gurukulam.

Chapter 11
Is Buddhism Sensible?

Dharmachari Subhuti

It could be said that the aim of this volume of chapters, and it is a highly laudable one, is to point out where lies the truly significant fault line within the general phenomenon we call 'religion.' Of course, there are many crucial differences between particular religions, and even within each one, between its various schools and sects – I could hardly call myself a Buddhist if I did not 'go for refuge' to the Buddha, rather than to a God or Gods, for instance. Yet the differences between my own understanding and faith and that of my fellow contributors are, surely, as nothing compared with our shared differences from the moral laxity, perverted understanding, intolerance, inhumanity, and fanaticism – at times, the outright evil – of some, perhaps quite a number, of each of our own co-religionists. As Christopher Lewis tasks us in the opening chapter, we must distinguish between 'good' and 'bad' religion in general, 'sensible' religion and religion that is against reason, lacks a beneficial relationship to the wider world, and is insensitive to the happiness and well-being of all humanity.

Religion, to use that broad and ambiguous term, has been responsible for some of the worst excesses of human history, as well as some of its most noble words and deeds. Examples can be cited from all the great world religions of cruelty as well as of kindness, of ignorance as well as of wisdom. Indeed, one might be tempted, aphoristically, to assign a besetting sin to each religion, to be contrasted, perhaps, with a peculiar virtue: intolerance against charity; fanaticism against purity; inhumanity against sublimity. We cannot assess any particular religion without acknowledging both the sins and the virtues to which its followers have historically been prone, just as there can be no true religious or spiritual life without acknowledging one's own moral weaknesses as well as strengths.

Buddhism too has had its weaknesses and evils as well as its strengths and virtues. Perhaps, the greatest failing to which its followers have been susceptible, and from which many of its evils have sprung, is laziness (Sangharakshita, 1979). Most often that laziness means simply a superstitious formalism that never truly engages with the moral challenges the religion poses to our ordinary lives. Yet all too frequently has it led to the endorsement of or participation in real evil, as Buddhists have compromised with power or identified Buddhism with merely national or ethnic interests: whether in the form of those Japanese priests who blessed bombs in the Second World War or Sri Lankan monks who encourage Sinhala ethnic nationalism or, most topically and shamefully, Burmese Buddhists today, not excluding monks, who have engaged in genocidal attacks on Rohingya Muslims in Rakhine State.

Too often have Buddhists settled for a hypocritical formalism of robes and ceremonies, for pious words empty of sincerity, or for the preservation of the letter rather than the meaning. Buddhists can, all too easily, be 'sensible' in this, the worst, sense: looking to one's own immediate worldly interests or indolently drifting on the path of least resistance. '"Gross Laziness" means being attached to non-virtues like destroying enemies, accumulating wealth, and so forth' (Gampopa 1998: 215). From the religious point of view, the worst form of laziness is simply joining the rat-race, however strenuous and stressful that may be.

My purpose here, as I am sure it is that of my fellow contributors in the case of their own subjects, is to show that Buddhism has been and still can be eminently sensible in the best sense, despite the many deficiencies of some of its avowed followers over the millennia. If one is to decide whether or not Buddhism is *essentially* sensible, it is to its basic principles that one must look, at least in the first instance. I am therefore going to focus on the life and teachings of its founder, Gautama Shakyamuni, who, having been born a human being, became the Awakened One – the Buddha.

Buddhism, like other religious traditions, is today represented by a large number of schools, with diverse, and sometimes divergent, teachings. All, however, acknowledge the same basic essentials: they all trace themselves back to the Buddha, whose role and nature they broadly agree upon, and they all accept a common core of teachings deriving from him, however differently contextualized today. Inevitably there is rivalry, and even animosity at times, but on the whole all today recognize each other as fellow Buddhists – at least on the public platform. I hope that what I have to say would therefore be more or less acceptable to all my Buddhist brothers and sisters, in principle if not in detail.

The Buddha lived more than 2,500 years ago in North India and himself wrote nothing down. Accounts of his life and teachings were handed down orally by groups of monk disciples, gradually finding their way into writing after many centuries. The most easily accessible and complete body of such material available in English translation is the *Tipiṭaka* or 'Three Baskets', recorded in Sri Lanka, during the first century BCE., in the Pali language (Pali Canon: Selection). Whether this extensive collection encompasses all that the Buddha said and did is a matter of debate, although many modern scholars suggest that it inevitably amounts to a selection by a particular strand within the early Buddhist community. It nonetheless remains the best and least disputed evidence available in English of who the Buddha was and what was the core of his teaching. I shall therefore mainly base myself upon it, without in any sense wishing to dismiss what other Buddhists revere that is not found there – some of which is also precious to me personally as a source of spiritual guidance and inspiration.

So, is Buddhism, as exemplified in the life and teaching of the Buddha as found especially in the Pali *Tipiṭaka*, sensible? Inevitably this requires some defining of 'sensible'. However, I do not wish to be drawn into lexicography or etymology. In line with what Christopher Lewis says in his opening chapter, I shall rather explore a 'sensible' understanding of 'sensible', answering three questions about the Buddha's teaching: is it accessible to reason, especially in the sense of critical appraisal? Does it bring happiness and well-being to those who practice it? Is it beneficial for humanity, indeed for life as a whole?

Is Buddhism Reasonable?

Buddhism does not come from the same cultural background as the religions with which we have hitherto been familiar in the West and it has a quite different relationship to reason. Although there is much in popular Buddhist practice that is superstitious or obscurantist, the Buddha's teaching (his *Dharma* in Sanskrit or *Dhamma* in Pali) itself does not depend on revelation and therefore does not need to reconcile reason and faith. From the outset, the Buddha himself strongly encouraged critical thinking, and his Dharma makes clear the function and limits of reason. Indeed, he was later referred to as the '*vibhajjavādin*' – 'the one who teaches the doctrine of reason' or even 'the one whose doctrine is reasonable'. He is, one might say, the expounder of a sensible religion.

The clearest instance of his insistence on common sense is found in the *Kālāma Sutta* of the *Tipiṭaka* (Pali Canon, AN III.65). The story begins with the Buddha journeying on foot with a group of his renunciant disciples, as was his custom, until he arrives at a settlement belonging to the Kālāmas, a clan who lived in what are now the Indian states of Uttar Pradesh and Bihar. The Buddha's reputation as a man of wisdom has reached the Kālāmas and so, naturally, they seek him out.

It seems they are experiencing some confusion. A variety of religious teachers have been visiting them, all of whom, 'expound and glorify their own doctrines, but as for the doctrines of others, they deprecate them, revile them, show contempt for them, and disparage them'. The Kālāmas are therefore left doubting and insecure about the best way to live. How are they to tell which of these teachers are speaking the truth, and which are lying?

The Buddha first acknowledges their problem, telling them that this is a genuinely doubtful issue and therefore will lead to insecurity if it is not cleared up. He then suggests criteria for distinguishing teachings that they should accept from those they should not. There are, he tells them, ten fallacious grounds that should not be the basis for acceptance:

> Do not go upon what has been acquired by repeated hearing; nor upon tradition; nor upon rumour; nor upon what is in a scripture; nor upon surmise; nor upon an axiom; nor upon specious reasoning; nor upon a bias towards a notion that has been pondered over; nor upon another's seeming ability; nor upon the consideration, 'The monk is our teacher'.

The precise meaning of some of this is now debatable, but the general sense is clear. Don't accept anything just because you've heard it a number of times; or because it is hallowed by a religious or philosophical tradition, lineage, school, or church; or because of hearsay ('someone told me ...'); or just because it is written in a sacred book (a nice irony to find such a rejection in what is now, for some, a 'sacred' text); or because the reasoning is sound, albeit the premises unproven (logical validity is not the same as truth); or because of impressive rhetoric or sophistry; or because the idea appeals to you; or because of the speaker's charisma; or simply on the basis of authority, whether religious, cultural, or political.

Having given them a broad critique of fallacious arguments, in effect he urges them to be sensible – to use their common sense. He tells them to refer to their own moral sensibility and to the judgment of those they have found, in their own experience, to be wise.

> Kālāmas, when you know for yourselves 'These things are bad; these things are blameworthy; these things are censured by the wise; undertaken and carried out, these things lead to harm and to suffering,' abandon them.

He then catechizes them, in true Socratic fashion, asking them whether deeds performed on the basis of a mind overcome by greed, aversion, or delusion lead to welfare or to harm. They acknowledge that such mental states are harmful and similarly that they are blameworthy, censured by the wise, and that, when acted upon, they cause suffering. What then about the opposite, positive, states: non-greed or contentment, non-hatred or loving-kindness, and non-delusion –

awareness or wisdom? Again they acknowledge that these are beneficial, blameless, praised by the wise, and result in happiness when they are the basis of action.

In effect he is asking them to look at the connection between mental states and their consequence in terms of suffering and happiness. He argues that this will not only offer the best way of sorting out their doubts about the truth and falsity of the doctrines proclaimed by visiting teachers, but can be a basis for resolving their deeper sense of insecurity and confusion about the best way to live and act. He asserts further that, if one cultivates positive states of mind, one will gain a profound inner confidence. He speaks especially of developing four 'unbounded' states that are the antithesis of greed and hatred: *metta,* the desire for the welfare of all living beings; *karuṇā*, the compassionate wish that those who suffer may find happiness; *muditā*, the sympathetic desire that those who are happy continue to enjoy their happiness; and *upekkhā*, an even-minded non-reactivity or equanimity in the face of whatever temptation or provocation.

If one is living in such a loving empathy with all beings in all the directions of space, one will feel deeply confident and secure, the Buddha argues, because of what amounts to a kind of Buddhist Pascal's Wager. Either there is a future life or there is not and either our actions now affect the future or they do not. If there is a future life and that life is affected by our present actions, then dwelling in these loving states will benefit us in the future; but even if there is no future life or our present actions have no effect upon the future, at least we will enjoy pleasant states now.

The Kālāmas are deeply impressed by what the Buddha has had to say. At the start, they had addressed him with merely formal courtesy, as just another would-be guru, but at the end they recognize him for who he really is, accepting him as their teacher and placing their confidence in him as their guide – because he has given them sensible grounds for sorting out their difficulties and a basis of moral well-being:

> Wonderful! Wonderful! You have made the truth clear to us in various ways and we feel as if something upside down has been turned right side up, or something hidden has been revealed, or someone lost has been shown the way, or a light has been shone so one can see what was in darkness.

The Buddha's teaching, as revealed here, is sensible in that it is reasonable, but also insofar as it points to what can be directly experienced – it is, one might say, empirical. When we attend carefully and objectively to what is happening, both within us and around us, we recognize that the one constant of all our experience is that it is conditioned: it arises in dependence on conditions and itself forms the conditions for future arisings. We cannot experience anything that is fixed, standing unchanged outside the flow of conditions. We can never, by definition, make anything eternal the object of our perception. We never come into contact with metaphysical essences, whether eternal souls or an ultimate divine being. We live amidst ever-changing processes, of which we ourselves are constituted, as is everything else we can ever come to know. All else is speculation and conceptual construction – what the Buddha called *diṭṭhi* or views.

Reason reveals, however, that there are patterns to the flow of conditions, regularities that can allow us to predict which conditions lead to which consequences. The laws of physics, chemistry, and biology are the regularities that are most familiar to us and that underlie the most concrete aspects of our experience. The Buddha, however, pointed to other kinds of regularity, less frequently made explicit, but perhaps semi-consciously recognized by most of us – and it is to the most obvious of these that the Buddha directs the Kālāmas attention in the latter part of his discussion with them (Subhuti).

These patterns, referred to under the heading of the Law of Karma (*kamma* in Pali) are found in the relationship between our own mental volitions and their consequences, particularly their consequences for our own future inner satisfaction or frustration. Mental states dominated by greed, aversion, and delusion are painful in themselves, however much they anticipate future pleasure. If we act on them, we will, of course, be likely to cause harm to others and that will often rebound upon us, but more surely we will modify our own minds for the worse, leading to our own unhappiness, frustration, and insecurity. Conversely, if we act with generosity, loving-kindness, and awareness, we will experience satisfaction now and our minds will develop, becoming more confident, fulfilled, sensitive, refined, aware, and wisely in tune with how things truly are.

It is the recognition of these Karmic patterns and the regulation of one's life in accordance with them that is the most significant use of our intelligence and that will produce a far better life for us. The chief applications of these Karmic patterns are embodied in the *pañcasīla*, the five ethical precepts universal to Buddhism, all based on the fundamental principle of non-harm (Sangharakshita, 2010). These are to be applied not merely to the individual but to society as a whole. A truly good and just society is one that is governed in accordance with these moral principles, in which the majority of citizens are applying the Law of Karma to their relations with one another (Pali Canon, DN 17, 1.10).

Buddhist morality is then, in the first place, this intelligent adaptation of one's life to these regularities. Those who do so adapt themselves are said to act 'skilfully' (Pali: *kusala*), an interesting term adopted, like its English equivalent, from the world of professional craft: just as a skilful carpenter works with the grain of the wood, so the morally skilful person works with the Law of Karma to create a better and better life for self and for others. Being sensible then is growing in skilfulness.

But the regularities amidst which our lives are lived extend further and deeper. The Buddha did not raise this with the Kālāmas because he was dealing with their immediate problem of working out who to trust – and these further regularities are less easy to recognize. These are the processes that lead us beyond mere personal interest, processes that depend upon motivations arising within the individual that transcend the individual. They come under the broad heading of Dharma and they come into operation as Karma is applied more systematically and deeply to one's life.

Karmic development enables one gradually to recognize that the idea of self is a mental construction – one that has been essential in evolutionary terms but that has no ultimate metaphysical referent. To put it less wordily, Karmic evolution leads to letting go of selfishness – one becomes increasingly selfless, motivated by the desire to relieve suffering and to bring true happiness to others. Once a sufficient degree of selflessness is achieved, it naturally unfolds in a spontaneous way, without conscious effort. In the Buddha's terms, one 'enters the stream of the Dharma' that leads, through states of every higher happiness and understanding, to complete and final freedom from self-clinging in the blissful awakening of Enlightenment (Pali Canon, DN 6, 12). Buddhas, briefly speaking, are those who have become entirely selfless and they too arise in dependence on conditioned processes, processes that unfold once Karmic development has led to a decisive break with selfishness.

The 'religious' life, from the Buddhist point of view, is the life lived in accordance with Karma and Dharma processes – a life in which one consciously and deliberately establishes the conditions for these processes to unfold in a progressive way, leading ultimately to Buddhahood. These processes are natural, as much part of the structure of reality as are the laws of gravity or photosynthesis: they are regularities that can be recognized by an impartial observer. One could even say that they are to be found through the application of a kind of scientific method of observation, hypothesis, and experimental testing – in this case, through their application to one's own mind.

So far, so reasonable – so sensible. One can, usefully and with truth, reason about the connections between conditions and their consequences. Yet there are limits to reason and these the Buddha sets out in another famous dialogue, this time with a philosophically minded ascetic, named Vacchagotta (Pali Canon, MN 72). Vacchagotta asks the Buddha whether he holds that the universe is spatially finite or infinite, whether it is temporally eternal or limited, and whether the soul and body are identical or different. To each of these antinomies, the Buddha replies that he does not hold either view. Vacchagotta then asks him if a Buddha exists after death or not – or both exists and doesn't exist, or neither exists nor doesn't exist. Once more the Buddha says that he does not hold any of these positions. Poor Vacchagotta is completely confounded – despite the rather dry format of the texts, one seems to hear his despairing confusion at the Buddha's rejection of all possible answers. 'What's the problem', he seems to ask, 'surely you must accept *one* of them?'

The Buddha replies that each of these alternatives is just a *diṭṭhi* – a view. This is a very important critical term in Buddhist epistemology, indicating a way of thinking about things that is merely relative and does not encompass the whole, because it is an abstraction from the way things truly are from a particular perspective. Our thoughts about things are not the same as reality itself. If we overuse reason, we attach undue significance to views so they tangle us up and confine us, misleading us as to the real nature of our experience. This engenders suffering – partly because we become attached to our views and get caught up in argument or worse and partly because we act on the basis of a misreading of the way things are and collide with reality, like an unskilful carpenter spoiling his wood by failing to observe the run of the grain. Above all, such views deepen our self-clinging and we cannot then experience the unfolding within us of the Dharmic processes that carry us to complete liberation.

The Buddha speaks many times of the Dharma, here in the sense of the truth itself, as 'profound, hard to see, hard to understand, peaceful, excellent, *beyond the reach of reason*, subtle, to be experienced directly by the wise' (Pali Canon, MN 72, v. 18). To put it bluntly, there is something entirely non-reasonable about the Buddhist life: 'non-reasonable' in the sense that it is not merely about reason. There is a vast difference between having a theory about the way things are and actually *seeing* it directly for oneself. The end and goal of the Buddhist life is this direct seeing, which is called *bodhi* or awakening. And *bodhi* transcends reason – without at all denying it.

Does Buddhism Bring Happiness and Well-Being to Those Who Practice it?

A sensible religion will surely be one that benefits its practitioners, promoting their genuine well-being. Of course, what that might be is a matter of contention, but presumably pleasure, happiness, or fulfilment would be generally recognized as most desirable. The Buddha speaks of three different kinds of pleasure or happiness (Pali Canon, MN 10, 32). There is first *sāmisa sukha vedanā*, 'carnal' or worldly pleasure, both in the direct sense of pleasurable sensations and of the pleasures of getting what you want, achieving your worldly objectives, being popular, and being praised. Such happiness is dependent on circumstances, and enjoyable as it is, is always fragile, for it arises from particular conditions that cannot last. From the Buddhist point of view, this kind of pleasure is nice if it happens, but not worth living your life for.

Secondly, there is *nirāmisa sukha vedanā*, non-worldly pleasure or happiness. Such happiness arises as one begins to work more and more with the processes of karma. Through acting skilfully, on the basis of loving-kindness, generosity, and awareness, one recreates one's own consciousness, which will become increasingly suffused with happiness. There are many lists of such progressively enjoyable states to be found in the *Tipiṭaka*, but one important sequence moves from suffering to confidence as one experiences the positive effects of one's efforts, to joy born of moral innocence, to rapture as one's energies begin to flow more and more freely, to tranquility, to bliss, to a deep and highly positive absorption, called *samādhi*: each successive stage arising out of the other on the basis of progressively more subtle and profound skillfulness (Pali Canon, SN II, 12.23.)

Thirdly, there is the happiness of Nirvāna (Pali *nibbāna*), the goal of the Buddhist Path, the attainment of which constitutes *bodhi*. Here words exhaust themselves, since Nirvāna transcends our normal modes of experience. However, the Buddha, who dwelt always in that state from the moment of his Awakening, declared it to be the most desirable of ends and spoke of it as 'supreme happiness' (Pali Canon, *Dhammapada*, v. 204). One early Western scholar gathered together a number of metaphors and epithets for Nirvāna from the *Tipiṭaka* that bring out yet more richly its positive and desirable character:

> The harbour of refuge, the cool cave, the island amidst the floods, the place of bliss, emancipation, liberation, safety, the supreme, the transcendental, the uncreated, the tranquil, the home of ease, the calm, the end of suffering, the medicine for all evil, the unshaken, the ambrosia, the immaterial, the imperishable, the abiding, the further shore, the unending, the bliss of effort, the supreme joy, the ineffable, the detachment, the holy city. (Rhys Davids 2000: 172)

The practice of Buddhism is not directly concerned with worldly pleasure – although such happiness is more likely to come one's way if one acts skilfully. However, as one works more and more successfully with the processes of karma through loving-kindness, generosity, and awareness, then one will experience increasing satisfaction and fulfilment of the 'unworldly' kind. Further progress will begin to free one from self-clinging, so one's experience will have an increasing flavor of Nirvānic happiness.

The Buddha considered that his teaching was to be judged on its results: did it bring happiness and fulfilment through Karmic development and, more especially, did it bring the supreme happiness of Nirvāna? He made this clear in a famous answer to his foster-mother, Mahāpajāpatī Gotamī. Now a nun in his Order, she wanted to know how she could have confidence in a teaching so that she could practice it wholeheartedly. The Buddha's answer is entirely pragmatic, even empirical:

> You can assure yourself that a teaching is not mine, not my practice, not my message, if it gives rise to disturbance of mind not to dispassion, to mental enslavement not to detachment, to worldly preoccupations not to letting them go, to greed not to wanting little, to discontent not to contentment, to delight in mere sociability not to reflective solitude, to laziness not to creative effort, to delight in evil not to delight in what is skilful. But if a teaching is the opposite of these, you can be sure it is mine. (Pali Canon, *Vinaya*, ii.10)

This criterion can be applied to Buddhism today, as at any time. One could even say that one is only genuinely a Buddhist to the extent that one is practicing teachings that are demonstrably bringing these results.

Is Buddhism Beneficial for Humanity?

A sensible religion will surely be one that is of larger benefit. One would expect it to produce individuals who are decent, friendly, and kind – good neighbours and fellow citizens, contributing to the world. The Buddha himself exemplifies the goal of Buddhism: the Buddhist life is lived to become like him. So, what kind of a man was he?

Much of the *Tipiṭaka* is concerned with the monastic life and with the practice of meditation and the development of direct understanding of the nature of things, known as *vipassana* or Insight. The overwhelming emphasis is on breaking the false interpretation of experience in terms of a fixed and unchanging *atta* (Sanskrit *ātman*)or self, because it is through clinging to that view that we are led into suffering and evil. This self-clinging is not merely a thought or concept, but a fundamental attitude that we do not normally question because it is deeply rooted in our minds, below the threshold of ordinary consciousness. It is as much affective as cognitive: as much a mood as an interpretation. This is the cause of the problem of suffering that the Buddhist Path is intended to resolve. And the Buddha himself had found that resolution by completely relinquishing all self-clinging:

> Many a birth have I undergone in this (process of) faring on (in the round of conditioned existence), seeking the builder of the house and not finding him. Painful is (such) repeated birth:

> O house-builder, (now) you are seen! Never again shall you build (me) a house. Your rafters are all broken, your ridge-pole shattered. The (conditioned) mind too has gone to destruction: one has attained to the cessation of craving. (Pali Canon, Dhammapada, vv. 153–4)

The Buddha became free from self-clinging, from the 'house-builder', and what followed from it: the craving and hatred that fuel unskilful action. But this does not mean that he became a sort of blank, removed from the affairs of his fellow human beings. Far from it: he spent the remaining 50 or so years of his long life patiently and tirelessly trying to communicate to others his Dharma or teaching so that they too could become free, as he had done. All selfish motivations had been extinguished – indeed, they were now impossible for him: but he lived a very active life, a selfless life, based purely on compassion. So striking was his compassion that his closest companion and attendant, Ānanda, who was with him continuously and intimately through much of his teaching career, was overwhelmed with grief when the master lay dying, weeping, 'The teacher is passing away, who was so kind to me!' (Pali Canon, DN 16, 5.12).

This is important to stress, since so much emphasis is given in many modern Buddhist schools to the cognitive aspects of spiritual practice. Though these are intrinsic to development in the Dharma, they are only one side of the process: selflessness does not merely mean absence of self, but the presence of love and compassion. The Buddha himself stressed the development of loving-kindness or *metta* again and again, asking his disciples to cultivate it, together with compassion for those who are suffering, sympathetic joy towards those who are happy, and equanimity in the face of life's many ups and downs. In a famous early discourse he speaks of what one needs to do if one wants the best for oneself. One should reflect:

> Now, may all living things, or weak or strong,
> Omitting none, tall, middle-sized, or short,
> Subtle or gross of form, seen or unseen,

Those dwelling near or dwelling far away,
Born or unborn – may every living thing
Abound in bliss. Let none deceive or think
Scorn of another, in whatever way.
But as a mother watches o'er her child,
Her only child, so long as she doth breathe,
So let him practise unto all that live
An all-embracing mind. And let a man
Practise unbounded love for all the world,
Above, below, across, in every way,
Love unobstructed, void of enmity.
Standing or moving, sitting, lying down,
In whatsoever way that man may be,
Provided he be slothless, let him found
Firmly this mindfulness of boundless love.
For this is what men call 'The State Sublime.' (Pali Canon, Sn 1.8)

And he clearly asserts that anyone who develops this kind of love will achieve liberation.

Conclusion

In sum, if one practices the Buddha's teachings as he intended one will think critically about the best ends and means for human life, one will bring oneself the greatest happiness, and one will be a loving presence in the world, acting for the benefit of all. Surely a sensible religion indeed!

However, all who call themselves Buddhists are not sensible by these criteria. There is too much in modern Buddhism that is foolish superstition, harmful to the individual, and of no benefit to humanity as a whole – and in some cases, is actively inhuman. I am not here going to name and shame because that is not a simple task. One usually cannot merely look at this or that school or tradition and say, 'That is not sensible Buddhism', even if one might have doctrinal or practical differences with it. One must rather look to the behaviour of individual Buddhists in each school and tradition – in Buddhist terms: at their actions of body, speech, and mind – to determine whether or not they are sensible. Inevitably, in every school one will find examples all along the spectrum.

Nonetheless, some broad trends and tendencies are discernible among modern Buddhists that are not sensible by these criteria. The most basic kind of non-sensible Buddhism, as no doubt of all religion, is what might be called merely cultural Buddhism, which is its commonest form throughout the old Buddhist world. Here people are Buddhist simply because they were born into a Buddhist family and make little or no attempt to apply the Buddha's teaching to their lives. A sub-species of cultural Buddhism might be called magical Buddhism. Here Buddhist rituals and symbols are used superstitiously, simply to gain mundane benefits: wealth, children (usually sons), power, health and long life. The strongly conservative character of such cultural Buddhism means it is readily invoked in support of oppressive social customs, especially as regards the status of women.

These forms of cultural Buddhism, when challenged from outside, all too easily turn into religio-nationalism or religio-ethnicism/racism. Identity religion, wherein one's sense of self is closely bound up with one's religion, leads very quickly to intolerance of others and thereby to oppression and violence, such as has been exhibited very recently by Buddhists in Myanmar, Sri Lanka, and Thailand; national and ethnic identity being for many inextricably bound up with being Buddhists (*The Economist*, July 27, 2013).

Buddhism is very much on the defensive in its old heartlands in Asia, against other religions and, more pressingly, consumerism. At its worst, it is responding with this kind of atavistic defensiveness or clinging to superstition and formalism; at its best, it is re-expressing the Buddha's essential teachings, facing up to modernity, as well as to the encounter of so many, diverse Buddhist traditions and with other sophisticated, historically unforeseen religious points of view.

Buddhism is also spreading to new lands. It has returned to India, since 1956, when Dr B.R. Ambedkar, the chief author of India's Constitution and principal leader of those formerly considered 'untouchable', converted to Buddhism with millions of his followers to escape the oppressions of the Hindu caste system. Dr Ambedkar chose Buddhism precisely because it was sensible, in Christopher Lewis' full meaning, and many of his followers have taken Buddhism very seriously and practice it fully. However, for many others it is simply a new source of identity, better than their old one at the bottom of the Hindu social order, but nonetheless primarily a social identity – and therefore risks drawing them into the religious conflict and violence that is so much a part of Indian politics and society.

Buddhism is also growing in the West, where its appeal so far is primarily to the educated urban middle-classes, who are attracted precisely because it is sensible. However, herein lies a danger. Much modern Buddhism in the West assimilates aspects of the Buddha's teaching to a philosophically and culturally materialist position, accepting more or less unquestioned prevailing social, political, and economic assumptions, albeit from a somewhat liberal perspective. Buddhism, so-called, becomes the religion of a mild, vaguely reformist consumerism, an essentially selfish way of palliating the rigors of existence. Interestingly, this was Nietzsche's fear in the wake of the 'Death of God': that there would develop a 'European Buddhism', the 'passive nihilism' that would herald the twilight of Western civilization (Nietzsche). Not, in the end, sensible at all.

The Buddha presented his teaching as a 'Middle Way' between the extremes of metaphysical eternalism and nihilism. Sensible Buddhism could be said to be a middle way between the lazy passivity of the many and the nationalistic or racist violence of a few. Sensible Buddhism is reasonable and empirical, whilst recognizing the limits of reason. It is sensitive to the physical, psychological, and spiritual health of the individual. And it seeks the happiness and fulfilment of all living beings, human and non-human, the same as us or other in whatever way. This is what the Buddha himself taught.

Reference List

The Economist (2013) 'Buddhism v Islam in Asia: Fears of a New Religious Strife', July 27.

Gampopa (1998) *The Jewel Ornament of Liberation*, trans. Khenpo Konchog Gyaltsen Rinpoche, New York: Snow Lion.

Morrison, Robert G. (1997) *Nietzsche and Buddhism*, Oxford: Oxford University Press.

Nietzsche, F. (1968) *The Will to Power*, trans. Walter Kaufmann and R.J. Hollingdale, London: Vintage.

Pali Canon:

Selection: See http://www.accesstoinsight.org/index-sutta.html for an accessible selection from the Pali Tipiñaka.

AN III, 65: *Kàlàma Sutta, Aṅguttara Nikàya,* trans. Soma Thera.

Dhammapada (2011), trans. Urgyen Sangharakshita, Cambridge: Windhorse .

DN 6, 12, *Mahāli Sutta, Dīgha Nikāya.*

DN 16, 5.12, *Mahāparinibbāna Sutta, Dīgha Nikāya.*

DN 17, 1.10, *Mahāsudassana Sutta, Dīgha Nikāya.*

MN 10, 32, *Satipatthāna Sutta, Majjhima Nikāya.*

MN 72, *Aggivacchagotta Sutta, Majjhima Nikāya.*

SN II, 12.23, *Saṃyutta Nikāya.*

Sn 1.8, *Karaṇīyametta Sutta, Sutta Nipāta*: Urgyen Sangharakshita, *Complete Poems, 1941/1994,* Cambridge: Windhorse, 1995.

Vinaya: my rendering.

Rhys Davids, T.W. (2000) *Early Buddhism*, Delhi: Bharatiya.

Sangharakshita, Urgyen (1979) *Peace is a Fire*, London: Windhorse.
Sangharakshita, Urgyen (2010) *The Ten Pillars of Buddhism*, Cambridge: Windhorse.
Subhuti, Dharmachari: *Revering and Relying upon the Dharma*: www.subhuti.
    info.

Chapter 12
Buddhism: Sense and Sensibility

Hozan Alan Senauke

One day the brahman Jata Bharadvaja came to the Buddha
at Savatthi and said:
The inner tangle and the outer tangle –
This generation is entangled in a tangle.
And so I ask of Gotama this question:
Who succeeds in disentangling this tangle?

(Bodhi, 2005: 259)

Being a literal-minded fellow, I am intrigued by the implications of 'sensible religion'. Beyond or beneath the editors' generous definitions I hear other questions and murmurings. Is religion itself, whose Latin root contains the word *ligare* – to bind or tie up – a sensible undertaking? (Note that the 'goal' of Buddhism is often translated as 'unbinding'.) Are we inquiring into religious traditions that are based on the senses themselves? Within any spiritual tradition, what is the balance between rationality or sensibility and faith or beliefs?

In his introductory chapter to this book, Christopher Lewis writes that sensible religion, 'refers to reasonableness in people and beliefs: having beliefs and practices which are both consistent with what is considered to be true and which also correspond to what is seen as reality'. Lewis adds, 'Yet there is another meaning, not unrelated to the first, which refers to sensitivity, awareness, being mindful of the views of others and responsive to the world around us, both individually and collectively'.

Certainly this is moving beyond the realm of the senses or direct experience into the field of belief. As much as Buddhists often wish to underscore the empirical quality of its teachings, we can't avoid the ambiguities of belief. At the same time, Buddhism's foundational view of dependent arising, *pratityasamutpada* in Sanskrit, points directly to how we are inherently 'responsive to the world around us'. How we simultaneously engage with an interdependent reality and with at times magical-seeming doctrines and beliefs (and how we get along with others who may not share these doctrines and beliefs) are questions that often place us on the razor's edge of sensibility and dogma.

I feel fortunate to have encountered Buddhist practice. From the beginning of my practice, more than 30 years ago, Buddhism made sense to me. 'I teach only suffering and the end of suffering' (Bodhi and Nanamoli, 2005: 234). This straightforward message speaks of Shakyamuni Buddha's unique discovery of a path to awakening that is available to all beings.

After a life of princely luxury and indulgence, after six years of training with North Indian meditation masters from all the prominent schools, and after extreme austerities – mythically eating just one grain of rice daily, reduced to no more than skin stretched across bones – he took the offering of a modest meal, and sat in meditation under a Pipal tree, which ever since has been known as the Bodhi tree, the tree of enlightenment. Within a matter of days or weeks, depending on which text one reads, Siddhartha Gautama awoke to his true nature as Shakyamuni Buddha, the enlightened spiritual master of the Shakya clan. Along with his fundamental discoveries about the impermanent and interdependent nature of reality, the Buddha prescribed a way to live – the Middle Way – a path of moderation between excesses of self-indulgence and self-mortification.

Today there are many Buddhisms. One could say, as well, that there is no Buddhism, or that Buddhism is not truly a religion. Like many 'isms', Buddhism is a relatively modern word put forward by scholars, for lack of a more precise usage, trying to fit human spiritual aspirations and practices into one large box labelled 'religion'. But actually, the ancient Pali term 'Buddhasasana', meaning 'Buddha practice' or 'practicing as a Buddha' seems vivid enough for me. For the moment, as pertaining to Buddhism, let us view 'sensible' and 'religion' independently.

Among the various expressions of Buddhism today and throughout history, across many Buddhist cultures in Asia and in the West, there are common and sensible principles, which I hope to clarify. The Middle Way is one of these, along with the Four Noble Truths, the Eightfold Path, and the principle of Dependent Co-arising.

My own root practice for the last 30 years has been Zen Buddhism, a meditation-based form of Mahayana Buddhism, which developed in China and spread to Japan and other East Asian lands before leaping over oceans to arrive on Western shores. In the Chinese Zen tradition the Middle Way is brought forth in this dialogue – Case 19 in the *Gateless Gate* collection of *koans*, enlightenment stories passed down orally, then in texts from Buddhisms early days in India and in China: Master Zhaozhou asked his teacher, Nan Chuan, 'What is the way?' Nan Chuan replied, 'Ordinary mind is the way' (Aitken, 1991: 126).

This everyday approach to Zen was my door to Buddhism and to a complete, dynamic way of life.

My First Steps on the Path

In high school I began to read Chinese and Japanese poetry on my own. This was the middle-1960s, so Beat poets were my guides to the likes of Han Shan, Su Tung Po, Matsuo Basho, and other Zen poets. I was entranced by Basho's *Narrow Road to the Deep North*. In the middle of his 1,200-mile pilgrimage, Basho writes:

> I stopped overnight at Iizuka. I had a bath in a hot spring before I took shelter at an inn. It was a filthy place with rough straw mats spread out on an earth floor. They had to prepare my bed by the dim light of the fire, for there was not even a lamp in the whole house. A storm came upon us towards midnight, and between the noise of the thunder and leaking rain and the raids of mosquitoes and fleas, I could not get a wink of sleep. (Basho, 1967: 110)

In this account I could feel a transcendent sensory awareness at the ordinary heart of Basho's experience and his words. This was what I took to be Zen mind, even before I had any idea about actual Zen practice. In fact, in those days there was very little written in English that explained Zen as something one did with one's body. It seemed to be more of a philosophy or an aesthetic. You could call it a sensibility, because these Zen poets wrote in the language of the senses. There was little drama or grandiosity, but the images were vivid, clear, and plain.

I was much taken by this writing. Though it seemed far from my twentieth-century urban/suburban teenage life, I resonated with this Zen way of looking at the world. I wondered how to direct myself towards this path.

Some years passed before I was able to take up the practice itself. Two books were pivotal in my nuts-and-bolts understanding of Zen. The first was Philip Kapleau's *Three Pillars of Zen* (Kapleau, 2000), which I read in the spring of 1968. Kapleau's book, based on lectures from his own Japanese teacher Hakuun Yasutani Roshi, offered very clear *zazen* (meditation) instruction. With that as a guide, some friends and I began to meditate. Later that summer we travelled from New York City to Berkeley, California and had an opportunity to practice with communities in Berkeley and San Francisco that were led by Shunryu Suzuki Roshi. At the age of 20 I was not quite able to sustain a Zen practice, but a seed had been planted.

Suzuki Roshi's classic *Zen Mind, Beginner's Mind* was published in 1970. Reading it several years later I had very much the same kind of experience that had come with reading Zen poets in high school. Suzuki Roshi's plain language seemed to include everyone. His was not the fiery voice of 'samurai Zen', but it was seductive, in a wholesome way. He used ordinary words to illuminate the extraordinary nature of life. So again I took up cross-legged sitting. This time, when I walked through the gates of Berkeley Zen Center, I found that I was home. And I have been home there since that moment, wherever in the dusty world I might be.

Shakyamuni Buddha Turns the Dharma Wheel

Life in the Buddha's place and time, North India in the fifth century B.C.E., was different in many ways from our lives in the developed world of the twenty-first century. But human nature seems to be much the same then and now. The Buddha saw people caught in what he called the Three Poisons of greed, hatred, and delusion. He viewed the suffering of sickness, old age, death, and a multitude of social ills. He vowed to find freedom from this suffering for himself and for all beings.

When he awoke under the Bodhi tree the Buddha was liberated from the sufferings that had plagued him, and continue to arise in our own lives of craving. As a self-ministering physician, he had cured himself of the Three Poisons. Enjoying this freedom he sat in the shade of the Bodhi tree for 49 days. At first the Buddha had doubts about whether his Dharma discoveries could be taught. Celestial figures begged him to try for the sake of all beings, but even then the newly minted Buddha wondered who might be capable of understanding his teaching. Nonetheless, he set out on the road and journeyed to the small town of Sarnath. There he met five former meditation companions and preached the *Dhammacakkappavattana Sutta*, the first turning of the Dharma Wheel.

His friends were initially dubious about the Buddha's awakening. They had accompanied him through various austerities and extreme practices. Now he appeared healthy and well-nourished. To their way of thinking he had gone soft. So the Buddha addressed this question head on, advocating the Middle Way.

> There are these two extremes that are not to be indulged in by one who has gone
> forth. Which two? That which is devoted to sensual pleasure with reference to
> sensual objects: base, vulgar, common, ignoble, unprofitable; and that which
> is devoted to self-affliction: painful, ignoble, unprofitable. Avoiding both of

these extremes, the Middle Way realized by the Tathagata – producing vision, producing knowledge – leads to calm, to direct knowledge, to self-awakening, to Unbinding.

As in all of the early Pali teachings, the Buddha comes across as a man of patience, intelligence, rationality, and sensibility. His logic is always carefully constructed. In this sermon he moves from positing a Middle Way to the eight elements of that path – right view, right resolve, right speech, right action, right livelihood, right effort, right mindfulness, right concentration – which, taken together, suggest a way to live that is wholesome, enlightened, and possible. There is an elegance and logic to his discourse that is refreshingly free from the mind-bending doctrines of Indian philosophy in his time, doctrines that relied on complex and unverifiable belief systems.

Having described the Path, the Buddha then offers a set of tools for analyzing suffering and the end to suffering. We call this the Four Noble Truths:

1. the pervasive experience of suffering in all its manifestations;
2. the cause of suffering, which is variously described as desire, clinging, attachment, aversion, delusion, etc.;
3. the cessation of suffering in all its various forms;
4. again, the Path to Nibbana or suffering's end, which is the Eightfold Path – Right View, Right Thought, Right Speech, Right Action, Right Livelihood, Right Effort, Right Awareness, and Right Concentration.

'Gratified, the group of five monks delighted at his words. And while this explanation was being given, there arose to Ven. Kondañña the dustless, stainless Dhamma eye: Whatever is subject to origination is all subject to cessation' (*Dhammacakkappavattana Sutta*).

So his friend Kondañña was immediately awakened, followed shortly by the other four companions, who attained the enlightened status of *arahants*, perfected beings, and became the first members of Shakyamuni's monastic order. Within the first two months of teaching, the Buddha's order included 60 *arahants*. Their numbers swelled quickly, as whole communities of mendicants from other schools of thought and practice joined his order.

What the Buddha 'discovered' – the Four Noble Truths, the twelvefold Chain of Causation, the possibility of freedom from suffering itself – is ancient wisdom, an open secret available to each of us, though it is often hidden by our striving minds, delusions, likes and dislikes. But each of us has to make the discovery our own.

The Buddha was a patient and sensible dialectician. Travelling from village to village and kingdom to kingdom over 45 years, he was questioned by commoners and kings, wandering monks, sectarian leaders, courtesans, and warriors. These exchanges, usually dialogues, are the substance of what is called the *sutta pitaka*, the 'basket of discourses'. He broke the questions down into sensible categories:

> There are these four ways of answering questions. Which four? There are questions
> that should be answered categorically [straightforwardly yes, no, this, that]. There
> are questions that should be answered with an analytical (qualified) answer
> [defining or redefining the terms]. There are questions that should be answered
> with a counter-question. There are questions that should be put aside. These are
> the four ways of answering questions. (Bodhi, 2012: 432)

His responses were tailored to each particular person in a way designed to unlock that person's mind. Just as he analyzed their questions, he had clear criteria for his responses.

In his introduction to the *Prince Abhaya Sutta* the contemporary Western monk Thanissaro Bhikkhu writes:

> In this discourse, the Buddha shows the factors that go into deciding what is and
> is not worth saying. The main factors are three: whether or not a statement is
> true, whether or not it is beneficial, and whether or not it is pleasing to others.
> The Buddha himself would state only those things that are true and beneficial,
> and would have a sense of time for when pleasing and unpleasing things should
> be said. (*Abhaya Sutta*: introduction)

Mindfulness and the Senses

There is another way to consider Buddhism's essential sensibility. The Buddha's reasoned discourse was grounded in his view of reality. This reality arises in the internal and external world, the world of our *senses*, which reside in our bodies. In the *Satipatthana Sutta* or *Foundations of Mindfulness* he lays out a system of meditation that is remarkably straightforward (if not always easy). Bhikkhu Bodhi characterizes mindfulness meditation in this way:

> The practice of *Satipatthana* meditation centers on the methodical cultivation of
> one simple mental faculty readily available to all of us at any moment. This is the
> faculty of mindfulness, the capacity for attending to the content of our experience

as it becomes manifest in the immediate present. What the Buddha shows in the *sutta* is the tremendous, but generally hidden, power inherent in this simple mental function, a power that can unfold all the mind's potentials culminating in final deliverance from suffering. (Bodhi, in Thera, 2012: Message by Bhikkhu Bodhi)

The *sutta* maps out four areas in which we can bring mindfulness to bear:

1. Contemplation of the body. This practice includes mindfulness of breathing; mindfulness of posture; mindfulness of the material elements; and mindfulness of the body in death and decay.
2. Contemplation of feelings. In the Buddhist context, feelings are the root experience of sensation before one describes or names that sensation. Feeling is simply the discernment of pleasant, unpleasant, and neutral sensations within the body and mind itself.
3. Contemplation of consciousness. Consciousness here is akin to what we in the West think of as emotions, feelings, and states of mind. Consciousness takes the input of the senses from external sources, and internally from our body and mind itself, and makes stories of the various and transitory mind states. Out of these stories we tend to create a sense of self that we imagine to be 'real'.
4. Contemplation of Mental Objects (or Dharmas). These 'mental objects' are delineated as systems or lists of mental factors that are useful for self-reflection. Five of these systems, which are discussed at length in other early Buddhist suttas, are:
  a. the Five Hindrances are impediments to enlightenment: sensual desire, anger, sloth and torpor, agitation, and skeptical doubt;
  b. the Five Aggregates of Clinging, or the Five *Skandhas*: material form, feelings, perceptions, mental formations, and mind consciousness;
  c. the Six Internal and Six External Sense Bases: eye and sight, ear and sound, nose and smell, tongue and taste, body and touch, mind and thoughts;
  d. the Seven Factors of Enlightenment: mindfulness, investigation, energy, joy, tranquility, concentration, and equanimity;
  e. the Four Noble Truths: Suffering, its Cause, Enlightenment, and the Path – which we spoke of earlier.

Taken as a whole, this is a complex system with interesting redundancies and overlaps. Some monastics and long-term practitioners, with proper guidance, work through these contemplations step-by-step. In this chapter I don't have the space to delineate the whole system. That would entail a book, and there are several good ones available (see, for example, Analayo, 2003).

But there is a broader kind of mindfulness that involves a fluid relationship among body, mind, and world. This is what the recently evolved Mindfulness-Based Cognitive Therapy calls 'felt sense' (Teasdale, Segal and Williams, 2012). Felt sense is the kind of embodied perception described in the *Satipatthana Sutta*. It can be a kind of meditation in action. With this kind of awareness, our everyday activity, as it extends from meditation, is the field where sensible Buddhism finds its full expression.

Sensible Zen: Appropriate Response

People are often mystified about Zen. It is easy to see why. Zen has become a buzzword. There are Zen cosmetics, Zen MP3 players, Zen cafes and bars, Zen baby furniture, Zen management software, Zen hair straighteners, Zen pens, Zen soap, Zen heated toilets, and on and on. We will consider the problem of commodification, but none of these no-doubt wonderful products has anything to do with the practice of Zen Buddhism.

In the middle of the twentieth century Zen teachers from Japan, China, Korea, and Vietnam brought their traditions of Buddhism to the West. Although in each of those countries Buddhism had a monastic base, the practice in America and Europe flourished among (then) young people, many of whom were looking for spiritual paths that offered alternatives to a stultifying culture of materialism and conformism. Zen in the West did create some residential and monastic centres where one could enter a whole life of practice and livelihood. But for the most part it took root in cities and communities of lay people, who found ways to integrate the practices of Buddhism and periods of meditation into everyday activities.

The 'sensible' appeal of Zen is that one can enter a challenging and potentially liberating practice by one's own effort. While the Zen tradition is known to focus on meditation, monks and nuns in Asia worked in the fields and the kitchens of their monasteries, took care of administration, built and repaired their temples. In other words they developed an ethos of self-reliance, wholehearted effort, and attention to detail. This kind of 'ordinary' practice appealed to counter-cultural Westerners in the 1960s and 70s. Its appeal continues today.

One of those early Japanese teachers was Shunryu Suzuki Roshi, whom I mentioned above. He was sent to America to minister to the Japanese American community, which had a network of Soto Zen temples along the west coast. But Suzuki Roshi had an intuition that the West would be fertile ground for *zazen*, the Zen meditation he believed in and loved. He was right, but that ground was not in Japanese American community. When he taught meditation, he began to draw young 'bohemians', artists, housewives, and professionals. Soon he had to make a choice between his designated Soto Zen church position and the experiment of Zen in America. He turned over his ministry to a new priest from Japan and, along with his students, founded San Francisco Zen Center.

Stepping away from the Japanese American community was not an easy choice to make, but Shunryu Suzuki had an inner drive and love of Dharma as actual practice, not as an abstract system of belief. That love and acceptance seemed to be felt by all who came into his presence. He never tired of teaching *zazen* and of expressing a kind of seamless awareness. He taught this with his body, with his energy, and with his words. Week after week from 1959 to 1971 he lectured and shared his understanding with his young students, washed and unwashed. There was a sensible and down-to-earth quality to these teachings, which is immediately felt in his classic *Zen Mind, Beginner's Mind* (1970). The language is plain and simple. The practice he taught was likewise plain, but it was not and is not easy. 'A monk asked Zen Master Yunmen, 'What is the teaching of the Buddha's whole lifetime?' Yunmen replied, 'An appropriate response" (Cleary and Cleary, 2013: case 14).

This *koan* or recorded saying from the Tang Dynasty in tenth century China is a shining example of Zen's earthy wisdom. *Koans* were often dialogues that simultaneously documented an enlightening exchange between student and teacher and served as catalyst for the awakening of practitioners in the future. These enigmatic expressions, not susceptible to our usual thinking, are powerful meditative tools even today. Master Yunmen was renowned in his own time as one of the subtlest and most enigmatic teachers, drawing students from all over China.

Suzuki Roshi lectured on this *koan*. In an unpublished talk from 1963 he translated Yunmen's response a little differently: 'The teaching confronts each'. Then Suzuki Roshi commented:

> The teaching given by Shākyamuni Buddha during his lifetime was accommodated to each disciple's particular temperament, and to each occasion's particular circumstances. For each case there should be a special remedy. According to the circumstances there should even be teaching other than the teachings which were told by Buddha. In the light of this, how is it possible to interpret and pass down an essential teaching which can be applied to every possible occasion and individual temperament? (Suzuki, 1963)

So, as Suzuki Roshi points out, the Buddha's method was to offer an appropriate response to each person he encountered, according to his understanding of character, causes, and conditions. He says, 'For each case there should be a special remedy'. Again we can understand the Buddha as a physician, providing just the proper remedy to bring a suffering being into balance.

To me this is the essential purpose of Buddhist practice. The point of this *koan*, of all *koans*, is not to interpret a historical encounter, but to make it our own. Suzuki Roshi says, 'According to the circumstances there should even be teaching other than the teachings which were told by Buddha'. The truth is not contained in ancient texts and given wisdom. It has to be found and created fresh in each moment. So in our families, at our jobs, with our difficulties, we are thrown back on this question. What is an appropriate response? It's a reasonable, sensible question in any circumstance.

And the Problem Is …

The problem is that as soon as we posit 'sensible' Buddhism or Zen or religion of any kind, its opposite comes to mind: senseless, or irrational, or immoderate religion. Across all traditions present and past we find countless examples of beliefs and practices gone wrong, turning to violence, intolerance, ethnic hatred, and narrowness. I would imagine that the premise of this volume is to counter this kind of history and this all-too-common perception. Buddhism is not exempt from these pitfalls. Within recent history we see the nightmare of 'Imperial Way Buddhism', in which Japanese Buddhist schools actively supported war and civilian atrocities in China, Korea, Manchuria, and elsewhere in Asia (Victoria, 2006). The long-running civil war in Sri Lanka, pitting a majority Buddhist Singhalese population against minority Hindu Tamil, was inflamed by Buddhist monks advocating violence and even carrying guns (Tambiah, 1992). Over decades religious-based hostility resulted in armed encounters, massacres, and many thousand deaths. Most recently, even as the weight of military oppression is lifting in the predominantly Buddhist country of Burma/Myanmar, long-standing ethnic tension in the western Rakhine state has flared into hatred, communal violence, and mass displacement of Muslim Rohingyas by the majority Rakhine population, which is largely Buddhist.

In each of these cases, one can argue that religion is not entirely the issue. More to the point might be access to resources, economic and political power, land rights, etc. In many ways, there is also a matter of culture – regional, national, and local culture that predates or underlies Buddhism in its various forms. Various schools or denominations of Buddhism are often dressed – literally – in the clothing of local traditions. This is not necessarily a problem. In fact, Buddhism's ability to adapt to cultures and reframe the basic teachings in vernacular language has a lot to do with how it has been able to survive for 2500 years. So at times we feel a strong tension between sensible and superstitious aspects of Buddhism as it manifests in each particular society.

Intemperate religious values, beliefs, and tradition may be put forward – sincerely or disingenuously – as the righteous basis for violence. Religion often fuels the flame. And it is not surprising that in the countries mentioned, Buddhism is officially or unofficially the state-sponsored religion. I think that wherever religion and the nation state collude one is going to hear a lot of nonsense and find oppression in various forms.

A related problem is that religions, Buddhism included, inevitably create religious institutions, often at wide variance from the founder's vision. Religious institutions, like all organisms, tend to be self-protecting. They do so by implanting in each individual follower a particular religious identity. *I* am a Buddhist; *I* am a Christian; *I* am among the chosen people ... The individual cleaves to a religion as a member of an identity group, with clear definitions of who is in and who is not in the group. The idea of an interdependent circle of human beings breaks down into a number of smaller, more exclusive circles. Our sense of boundless connection is lost.

The miracle of modernity is that once an identity and a group has been formed and located, the masters of capitalist marketing can then sell people the very identity they cherish. Actually the true religion of the twenty-first century is consumerism and commodification, which sells us things we neither want nor need by planting and watering seeds of dissatisfaction and incompleteness. Buddhism faces these powerful forces, not always aware that they exist. So we see Buddhist magazines on newsstands month after month with glossy cover photos of the same six or ten prominent teachers. Popular and expensive meditation programs promise a short path to enlightenment. Retreat centres underscore the warm comfort of their guest rooms and their exquisite organic vegetarian food. Some even pride themselves on a kind of Buddhism that never mentions Buddhism, lest someone be made uncomfortable by the shadow of religion. Taken one-by-one none of these is necessarily a bad thing, but if we step back and look at the power of modern consumerism to coopt the sacred – its ability to sell us even the fruits of our free creativity and devotion – we should be wary. We should resist this force wherever we can.

Sensible Action

I have been completing this chapter while in residence at Upaya Zen Center, an island of Buddhist sanity in Santa Fe, New Mexico. Founding teacher Roshi Joan Halifax, resident students, and program participants who come and go are grounded in 'engaged Buddhism'. Elsewhere I have written:

> It is hard to define engaged Buddhism. But I think it has to do with a willingness to see how deeply people are suffering; to understand how we have fashioned whole systems of suffering out of gender, race, caste, class, ability, and so on; and to know that interdependently and individually we co-create this suffering. (Senauke, 2010: iii)

From this 'seeing' into the nature of impermanence and suffering – which is what the Buddha explained as Right View, the first step on the Eightfold Path, naturally there arises a sense of responsibility, an appropriate response, which we can also name as Right Action, the fourth step along the Eightfold Path.

This may sound abstract, but over the last few days at Upaya I have been listening to presentations by graduating trainees in a Buddhist chaplaincy program. These are women and men ministering in prisons and juvenile detention centres, working with nurses in emergency rooms and with people facing imminent death, guiding volunteers doing ecological restoration in Ecuador, and developing community conflict mediators. I am inspired by each of their stories and how clear they are in articulating the Buddhist base of their activity, which of course includes people of many other faiths within universal principles of sensible religion. In each situation the chaplain and his or her team are looking for an appropriate response.

I like to think that, like the Buddha, we are engaged on multiple levels. The Buddha, his disciples, and descendants often awakened beings one-by-one. But he also kept his eyes on the larger prize. In our Bodhisattva Vow we say, 'Sentient Beings are numberless. I vow to save them all'. In other words the entire map of human suffering, the multiple interlocking systems that that create individual and social suffering must go. The Buddhist chaplains I am hearing this week in New Mexico are trained in 'non-anxious presence', using meditation, listening skills, compassion, and a deep toolbox to be available and helpful to those they meet. At the same time, they also have their eyes on the prize, the transformation of dysfunctional institutions and structures – prisons, hospitals, so-called social welfare systems, corporations, the military, and more.

So I close by asking the question we began with:

The inner tangle and the outer tangle ...
Who succeeds in disentangling this tangle?

Travelling a thousand paths, may we all find the way to freedom and sensibility, living safely in our bodies and among our communities.

Reference List

Abhaya Sutta, trans. Thanissaro. Available at: www.accesstoinsight.org/tipitaka/mn/mn.058.than.html (accessed October 24, 2013).

Aitken, R. (1991) *The Gateless Barrier*, Berkeley, CA: North Point.

Analayo (2003) *Satipatthana: The Direct Path to Realization*, Birmingham: Windhorse.

Basho, M. (1967) *The Narrow Road to the Deep North*, New York: Penguin.

Bodhi, B. (2005) *The Connected Discourses: A Translation of the Samyutta Nikaya*, Boston, MA: Wisdom.

Bodhi, B. (2012) *The Numerical Discourses of the Buddha: A Complete Translation of the Anguttara Nikaya*, Boston, MA: Wisdom.

Bodhi and Nanamoli (2005) *The Middle Length Discourses of the Buddha: A Translation of the Majjhima Nikaya*, Boston, MA: Wisdom.

Cleary, T. and Cleary, J.C. (trans.) (2013) *Blue Cliff Record*, Boston, MA: Shambhala.

Dhammacakkappavattana Sutta, trans. Thanissaro. Available at: www.accesstoinsight.org/tipitaka/sn/sn56/sn56.011.than.html (accessed October 24, 2013).

Kapleau, P. (2000) *Three Pillars of Zen*, New York: Anchor/Random House.

Rewata, V. (1997) *The First Discourse of the Buddha*, Boston, MA: Wisdom.

Senauke, A. (2010) *The Bodhisattva's Embrace*, Berkeley, CA: Clear View.

Suzuki, S. (January 1963) Unpublished lecture. Available at: www.cuke.com/pdf-2013/wind-bell/wb.II.1–8pdf (accessed October 24, 2013).

Suzuki, S. (1970) *Zen Mind Beginner's Mind*, New York: Weatherhill.

Tambiah, S. (1992) *Buddhism Betrayed: Religion, Politics and Violence in Sri Lanka*, Chicago, IL: University of Chicago.

Teasdale, J., Segal, Z., and Williams, M. (2012) *Mindfulness-Based Cognitive Therapy for Depression*, London: Guilford.

Thera, Soma (2012) *The Way of Mindfulness: The Satipatthana Sutta and Its Commentary*: *Access to Insight*. Available at: http://www.accesstoinsight.org/lib/authors/soma/wayof.html (accessed on October 31, 2013).

Victoria, B. (2006) *Zen at War*, London: Rowman & Littlefield.

Chapter 13

Sikhi(sm) and the Twenty-First Century Sikh Diaspora

Opinderjit Kaur Takhar

Although the youngest of the six major world faiths, Sikhism currently has the fifth largest global following. This chapter will aim to address what makes the Sikh faith or Sikh way of life a sensible faith for millions of adherents and the extent to which Sikhi(sm) has adapted, and indeed whether adaptation is necessary, in terms of rationality and reason in the twenty-first century. Currently, there is debate amongst Sikhs whether the suffix 'ism' should be added to any references to their faith. Sikhs tend to show preference for the term 'Sikhi' which they believe is reflective of the teachings of the Sikh Gurus. Sikhs on the whole view their faith as a way of life rather than a pronounced dogma. Many also view the suffix 'ism' as a colonial invention of boxing customs and traditions together in a homogeneous category. I will explore the ways in which the central tenets of the Sikh way of life enable religious people to live Sikhi through their ordinary lives. The challenges pertaining to the transmission of Sikhi to British-born Sikhs will be addressed in the light of discussing the sensibility of Sikhi in the twenty-first century. Hence this is an attempt in providing criteria, or a 'litmus test', by which to assess the attractiveness of Sikhi to its millions of followers, with particular reference to the British Sikh diaspora. Christopher Lewis, earlier in this volume, has discussed the connotations of the term 'sensible' which extends also to an exploration of what the terms 'good' and 'bad' religion may entail. This will provide a framework for my analysis into the sensibility of Sikhi.

In the context of attempting to provide criteria for distinguishing good Sikhi from bad Sikhi, a standpoint in this discussion will be that stark aberrations from the essence of the teachings of the Gurus constitutes bad Sikhi. Good Sikhi promotes the individual's role as a good citizen both in the localized as well as global setting, hence following the aspirations of being a good human being in line with the vision of an ideal society sought by the Gurus. Good Sikhi promotes the three principles of good conduct and behavior through meditation on the

Name of God, performing selfless service and sharing with the less fortunate in society. Does this extend to the protection of one's community in taking up arms against the perpetrators, be they individuals or governments? In this respect, the actions, and subsequent reactions of Bhindranwale and Rajoana, to name but a few, would be in line with good Sikhi by acknowledging them as martyrs of the faith. Not all Sikhs would agree. This makes the task of providing criteria for 'good' and 'bad' Sikhi an arduous task. In the words of Peter Vardy 'to say that precise criteria may not be possible is true, but this does not mean that some criteria cannot be found' (Vardy, 2010: xi).

If following *bani* (spiritual teachings of the Sikh faith found in the Guru Granth Sahib and the Dasam Granth) word for word falls into the category of good Sikhi, what implications does this present in terms of the inequality which is so evidently visible within the community of Sikhs? It would follow that caste-based discrimination and gender discrimination are two criteria for determining bad Sikhi. Good Sikhi (following the ideals sought by the Sikh Gurus) lays a great deal of emphasis on treating all human beings as equal regardless of caste, gender or creed. Bad Sikhi would then also include a Sikh's exclusivist attitude towards persons professing 'other' faiths. Considering the views of others is good Sikhi, whereas arrogance is bad Sikhi. Bad Sikhi is to lose the essence of Sikhi itself which promotes tolerance towards all, regardless of creed. Significantly, the Guru Granth Sahib, also referred to as the Adi Granth (the Sikh scripture, which is seen as authoritative by the majority of Sikhs), is an epitome of love and tolerance since it contains the teachings of the Sikh Gurus as well as Hindu and Muslim devotees. Raising one's voice against aberrations which manifest themselves as the norm is a challenging task which takes great courage in standing up for one's convictions when attempting to confront elements of bad Sikhi. In order to do this, the litmus test for determining good Sikhi has to be carried out since 'the consequences of failing to challenge bad religion are simply too grave for this to be a permissible way forward' (Vardy, 2010: x). Importantly, the foundation of Sikhi is based on Guru Nanak's open rejection of what he perceived as aspects of bad religion in the socio-religious milieu of fifteenth-century Punjab.

Too often, Sikhs who cut their hair are labelled 'improper Sikhs'; this is an aberration of good Sikhi which does not condemn on the basis of mere outward show, or in this case a lack of it. Sikhs who cut their hair may be prohibited from reading the Guru Granth Sahib during public worship. So this would indicate that outward expression of one's faith takes precedence over *bani* which extols the union of the individual with the Divine essence which is immanent. An adoption of the Khalsa form is not in itself a mark of religiosity. It must be a step that has been taken as a result of one's own intentions to tread on the path of Guru Gobind

Singh's aspirations of what it means to be a *sant sipahi* (a saint soldier) and not one that is forced. Bad Sikhi is an assumption that outward identity goes hand in hand with one's spirituality. An initiated Sikh, who has not managed to shed the *haumai* (the ego-centric attitude and outlook) is not religiously more devout than an uninitiated Sikh. The mark of a 'true' Sikh, according to *bani*, is one who lives in harmony with others as a result of union with the Divine.

Although the term 'diaspora' was originally used to refer to the dispersed Jewish community, it can also be used to refer to Punjabi Sikhs living outside India. Ahluwalia aptly highlights that 'The dispersal of Punjabis and in particular Punjabi Sikhs is by no means a recent phenomenon – they have been on the move for well over a century' (2011: 96). The largest Sikh community outside India is well established in Britain. The relationships between the Sikhs and Britain 'pre-dates the imposition of British rule on Punjab' from 1849 C.E. and it is a relationship that affects the UK Sikh diaspora (Nesbitt, 2011). According to the 2011 Census, 423,000 people identified as Sikh; this equates to 0.8 percent of the population of England and Wales. Thus it does not account for Sikhs living in Scotland and Northern Ireland; the overall figure therefore of Sikhs in Britain is much higher.

The diaspora of Sikhs brings its own challenges, particularly in relation to the practice of Sikhi and the survival of the Punjabi language for the generations of Sikhs born outside India. As highlighted by Ahulwalia: 'Although culture travels, evolves and becomes hybridised, it is 'religion' that is the constitutive element of a diasporic Sikh identity forged out of a sense of displacement since the late 20th century' (106).

Although a minority faith in its Indian homeland, the Sikhs are very much visibly present due to the prominence given to the outward symbols of their faith and especially the turban. Sikhs born outside India in countries such as Britain have carved out a British Sikh identity which accommodates the demanding needs of everyday life in what appears to be a successful manner. Religious identity associated with external articles of faith through the Khalsa (created in 1699 CE) is very important to the British Sikh community. A recent example of what a British Sikh identity encompasses is perhaps best illustrated through the coverage of events relating to the wearing of the turban by a British Sikh guardsman. Jatenderpal Singh Bhullar became the first guardsman to wear a turban instead of the traditional bearskin which has been the official headdress for British Foot Guards for the last 180 years. Active campaigning has successfully taken place from the 1980s and onwards especially to allow British Sikhs the right to wear their articles of faith in public. One of the first milestones in these efforts was the *Mandla v. Dowell-Lee* case in 1983 which made it compulsory for British law to understand and accept the importance of the turban for *amritdhari* (initiated) Sikhs. The ban on wearing the turban has also been overthrown for Sikhs in France, despite France's secular values. The addressing of the religious needs of Sikhs, as necessary and sensible, by British policy-makers thus illustrates the acknowledgment, and knowledge, of Sikh religious values in twenty-first century Britain. The flaws in the secularization argument (Morris, 2012) therefore occupy a pivotal space in my discussion of Sikhi in the British diaspora.

Transmission of Sikhi to the Younger Generation

Challenges are currently being faced within all faith communities in terms of how best to actively engage the younger generation in becoming more involved within their respective communities. As future leaders of religious centers, addressing the needs of the younger generation of British-born Sikhs is particularly being explored. Sikhs are worried about the decline in Gurdwara attendance from 16–40-year-olds. Younger children are usually brought to the Gurdwara by parents and grandparents. The transmission of culture and the survival of Sikhism is a challenge that is continually being addressed by the Gurdwara management committees (Takhar, 2011). A number of projects are being run across most Gurdwaras to promote youth engagement with Sikhi and to address the demands of British-born Sikhs in terms of relating to both the Sikh and British way of life as a sensible path in the twentieth century. The challenge is how best to channel the teachings of Sikhi to the younger generation in view of the emphasis placed on rationality and logic through the British educational system. A reminder of the importance of engaging the youngsters is an often repeated appeal made by stage secretaries in most British Gurdwaras. Jasjit Singh's study (2011) of British Sikh camps overthrows the notion that the younger generation is disengaged with Sikhi. Jasjit Singh's research clearly demonstrates that younger British-born Sikhs are themselves leading camps and discussion-led activities which cater to the needs and interests of the next generation of Sikhs. He argues that young Sikhs want to learn about Sikhi out of their own persuasion rather than out of pressure from parents and grandparents and argues that the Gurdwara is not necessarily the means through which the youth prefer to engage with Sikhi. He argues that 'these camps also provide young Sikhs with a social space for learning about religion and for shaping a religious identity which may allow them to challenge and negotiate the religious and cultural norms transmitted to them by their parents' (J. Singh, 2011: 269).

Nevertheless, the importance of the Gurdwara as the hub of diasporic communities must not be overlooked. As well as functioning as religious institutions, they also serve as social centers. Activities such as sewing classes, Punjabi classes, *gurmat* (Sikh teachings and the Sikh way of life) classes, keep fit, Sikh martial arts (*shin kin* is popular in the English Midlands), cookery classes and youth groups – to name but a few – are taking place in the Gurdwara. Historically, funds have been donated by the *sangat* (Sikh community, usually in a localized sense) into the Gurdwaras as a sign of the pride that the Sikh community take in their religious institutions. Maharaja Ranjit Singh, for example, had *Harmandir Sahib* covered in gold leaf as a mark of the regency of the Sikh Empire: hence it became known as the Golden Temple. Anxiety is felt by many Sikhs who are eager, in the diaspora, to retain the communal spirit of Sikhi alive through its religious institutions.

Discussions with young Sikhs in Britain have often raised the issue of using rationality and logic when accepting hagiographical stories in Sikh tradition. This also extends to young Sikhs wanting to maintain a balance between their Sikhi and their scientific convictions. When examined closely, Sikhi addresses these issues very well. Sikh teachings have been examined closely by scholars in order to highlight that they are modern and versatile to enable a sensible approach to both religious faith and science in the twenty-first century. There are many scholars of Sikhi who have a scientific background, for example Professor Daljit Singh Virk (UK), Professor Devinder Singh Chahal (Canada) and Dr. Bhai Harbans Lal (USA). Although the Guru Granth Sahib mentions parallel universes and the Big Bang, it is important to remember that the supremacy of God overrides all systems. The concept of the Divine as the First Cause, the Unmoved Mover, to use Aristotle's terms, is also found in Sikh metaphysics. Guru Nanak, in the Guru Granth Sahib, writes:

> For countless ages there was utter darkness.
> There was no earth and no sky, but the Infinite Lord's Will alone was pervasive.
> There was neither day nor night, nor moon, nor sun, but the Lord alone sat in profound trance.
> Neither there were mines of creation, nor speech, nor air, nor water.
> Neither creation, nor destruction, nor coming, nor going …
> None else was seen but the One Lord. (Adi Granth: 1035)

The importance on the human birth with emphasis on one's relationship to the impermanency of the created universe has a prominent place for the cosmological and teleological arguments in Sikh religious philosophy. Sikhs believe that God is *Karta Purkh*, the creator of all existence but is in turn eternal, the First Cause. The concept of God's eternity is essential in Sikhi and is expressed through the steel bangle, the *Kara*, which is one of the five Ks, the essential articles of faith for an *amritdhari* Sikh.

However, an example of bad Sikhi is at times portrayed when critical analysis is discouraged under the context of confessional Sikhi which in its most conservative expression does not allow room for critical enquiry (Oberoi, 1997). This also extends to hagiographical accounts and stories as recounted in Sikh oral tradition. A growing number of younger generation British Sikhs will challenge what they hear in terms of it making sense to them through their critical analysis lens. This does not mean that they ridicule what they hear but rather prefer to enter into discussion with teachers and *Gianis* (one versed in Sikh philosophy). *Gianis* are occasionally referred to as 'priests'; this is misleading and incorrect as Sikhi does not have a 'priesthood'. So whether the Gurdwaras actually accommodate this level of metaphysical enquiry is a matter of debate. Guru Nanak encouraged discourse with learned individuals; however, philosophical discussions within Gurdwaras are too often discouraged – this is bad Sikhi. Whether or not Sikhs actually believe in the metaphysics of the entirety of Sikh religious philosophy is also a measure of sensibility. Some Sikhs, with their rational hat on, find it difficult to comprehend that God 'talked' to Guru Nanak during his three-day religious/mystical experience. How can a formless, *Nirankar* God actually 'talk'? Nevertheless, teachers and *Gianis* within the Gurdwara setting are adamant that nothing is beyond the powers of the Divine *Waheguru*. If, however, the emphasis be placed on Sikhi as *dhur ki bani*, revealed insights into the truth, then there is no need for a 'speaking' God; rather the experience will encourage the individual to speak of her/his feelings and emotions arising from the numinosity of the experience. Sikhi must therefore be understood and *experienced* from an 'appropriate understanding of its scripture' since the 'Gurus aimed to convey experience through feelings and moods because they make up an aspect of consciousness which cannot be reduced to conceptuality' (Shackle and Mandair, 2005: xxiii). In the spirit of Guru Nanak's revolutionary spirit, using ones intellect to challenge accepted norms and ritualism is not a sign of a 'bad' Sikh (Adi Granth: 163). As remarked above, Jasjit Singh's research has indicated that non-Gurdwara attendance is not necessarily a reflection of disengagement with Sikhi.

The issue of addressing the challenge of how Sikhi will survive in the diaspora is thus the focus of much activity within the British Sikh community. The British Sikh diaspora (as is the case amongst all diasporic Sikh communities) are concerned about the survival of the Punjabi language. Pettigrew (1994) discusses the role that religion, particularly Sikhi, has in secular values. She explores in depth the campaign to have Punjabi, in the Gurmukhi script, as the official language of Independent Punjab. Punjabi in the Gurmukhi script became specifically the language of the Sikhs. Projectors displaying translations of passages from the Guru Granth Sahib into English are increasingly becoming popular in British Gurdwaras. Some Sikhs, however, see this as a threat to the future of the Punjabi language, since in their opinion youngsters may not learn Punjabi if translations are readily available. The 'catch 22' situation, however, is further exacerbated in line with the thought that attendance from the younger generation is declining because they simply do not understand what is being recited during communal worship. A sensible way forward in terms of transmitting the linguistic tradition is currently being negotiated in all Gurdwaras.

Maintaining a connection with Punjabi ethnicity is also imperative for many British Punjabi Sikhs. This reflects into lifestyles and accepted norms amongst Sikhs which emanate from the Punjabi culture. The notion of *izzat* 'family honor' remains dear to most Punjabi Sikhs across the globe. However, attitudes are changing, for example in finding suitable spouses for children. Many Sikh parents continue to play a significant role in the choice of partners for their children. However, the term 'arranged' marriage is becoming out of date and rather old-fashioned. It should be replaced by 'assisted' marriages whereby one is introduced to prospective spouses and is entitled to make up one's own mind. 'Love' marriages are also becoming more acceptable amongst Sikhs where the couple meet of their own accord rather than having being introduced to each other by family or extended kinship networks.

Numerous mobile phone applications are available to bring about confidence in speaking and reading the Punjabi script. The daily *hukamnamas* (thought for the day) are instantly received through such applications as well as the Internet. This supports Turner's point that: 'In many societies, in youth cultures and popular culture generally, there have been important hybrid forms of religiosity, often employing the Internet to disseminate their services and beliefs' (2006: 440).

Thus, the youth can make their own sense of religious teachings and apply them as they see fit within the context of their own experiences. 'Khalsa Clubs' are also catering to the needs of younger British Sikhs in encouraging nurture of Sikhi through enquiry, interactive activities and discussion. Many British Khalsa Clubs, run by Gurdwaras, follow an internationally agreed syllabus. The objective is to encourage the younger generation to attend the Gurdwaras by listening and catering to *their* needs, rather than a traditional dogmatic approach to fostering a love for Sikhi. The *langar* (the free vegetarian meal which all attendees eat to symbolize equality with fellow worshippers and visitors) on such occasions consists of pizza, pasta and chips in addition to traditional Punjabi food. Nevertheless, Gurdwara attendance is not entirely the most reliable litmus test by which to assess individual approach to Sikhi.

Transmitting the culture of 'home' whilst being well established and permanently settled in Britain is an emotional and often challenging task for the older generation of Punjabi Sikhs. The 'myth of return' makes no sense to British-born Sikhs. Indeed, eventually returning to India was a notion that fast disappeared once the earliest Sikh emigrants had purchased property, reunited with family members and secured employment in Britain. Nevertheless, cultural heritage means some ties (though with differing degrees across the generations) to the Punjabi/Indian 'homeland'.

Issues and events in the Punjab affect the Sikh diaspora, especially in countries with significant Sikh populations such as Britain, Canada and the USA. Many British Sikhs are involved in political movements concerning the state of affairs in the Punjab. Major political parties (Jathebandis) are represented in all British Gurdwaras. Many of the Jathebandis have been highly influential in forging a sense of Sikh pride amongst British-born Sikhs. The recent Rajoana case is particularly relevant. The case of Rajoana is a prime example of the power of communication in the twenty-first century. The Internet had a major role to play in arousing Sikh sentiments, especially amongst the younger generation of Sikhs in the diaspora, over the execution of Rajoana. Members of the British Parliament, as well as Members of the European Parliament, showed support for Rajoana's well-wishers by highlighting that his proposed execution would be a breach of human rights. Sikh Channel and Sangat TV kept millions of viewers constantly updated with the case. Sikhs who had never heard of Rajoana soon become involved – either in agreement or disagreement – but involved nevertheless. This further strengthens the fact that politics in the Punjab are very much tied in with the sentiments of the diasporic Sikh community. What happens in the political arena has strong connotations for the global Sikh community and, indeed, for Sikh identity. Following the case of Rajoana, many young British Sikhs adopted the outward Khalsa identity by not cutting their hair. There was a noticeable increase in Britain of turban-wearing females and males. Hence religion and politics go hand in hand for many Sikhs and are reflective of Christopher Lewis' discussion of politics in general and nationalism in particular. Turner's assertion is particularly relevant in this respect, he writes: 'By the end of the 20th century, with the collapse of the Soviet Union, the rise of fundamentalism, and the retreat of assertive humanism, sociologists abandoned the secularisation thesis; religion, far from declining, is central to modern political life' (2005: 441).

Equality and Sikhi

Feminist movements are increasingly becoming popular amongst Sikh women in the diaspora. These women take inspiration from the egalitarian teachings of Sikhi. Gender related discussions are central to determining the sensibility or reasonability of religion. Sikhi is no exception; gender discourses and feminist theology are very relevant. Gill (1995) highlights the importance of Sikh women through history; she lays emphasis on depicting particularly the supporting roles played by the wives of the Sikh Gurus (3–14). Sikh teachings emphasize that the essence of the Divine is imminent in the hearts of all human beings; this in turn entails that all human beings are equal. Guru Nanak and succeeding Gurus rejected discrimination towards the lower castes and women in a society where both were deemed second-class citizens. Although Sikhi in its religious context gives total equality to both females and males, the cultural context often overlooks this egalitarianism, especially in the communal and public realms. Gender discrimination amongst some Sikhs is purely cultural and has no justification from a Sikh metaphysical or existential point of view.

Sikhi offers a sensible approach to family life whilst in the midst of temptations and false attachments. The stage of the householder, the *grihast*, enables a Sikh to live by the philosophical ideals on the practical level. Sikhi rejects celibacy and encourages full participation in the community. Sikhi encourages a loving, trusting and supportive relationship between man and wife in their joined pursuit towards *their* salvation. The practice of *Nam Simran* (mediation on the Name of God) through the life of a householder further promotes the family life. Guru Nanak's use of *Nam* reflects the formlessness of God. Sikhi leaves no scope for physical conceptualizations of the One formless Divine: 'Wherever I look, I See the One Compassionate Lord: The Merciful God, neither comes nor goes in reincarnation ...' (Adi Granth: 1038). Caution needs to be used when using the term God in reference to Sikhi since the term may have strong masculine connotations. Often Sikhs will talk of the Divine in masculine terms; this is an aberration and is incorrect since the Divine Being according to the teachings of the Gurus is gender free. Thus Sikh ontology challenges 'the powerful male-female binarism' (Gurnam Singh, 2006: 148).

The aberrations amongst Sikhs in respect to the practical application of the egalitarian teachings need addressing. It is evidently visible that the public realm within the Sikh community is dominated by men. It is rare to see a female leading the service in a Gurdwara; females are seldom visible in Gurdwara management committees. Young British Sikh females are currently challenging patriarchal dominance in Gurdwaras and actively seek female representation beyond the *langar* hall (the communal kitchen).

Although there are no obvious teachings about ritual pollution attached to menstruation and childbirth, it is important to make the point that many Sikh women themselves prefer not to touch the Guru Granth Sahib or indeed, prepare *langar* whilst menstruating. They themselves are endorsing notions of ritual pollution associated with such natural processes. This may be an inevitable aspect of the Punjabi culture. Some Gurdwaras however, explicitly debar a menstruating woman from carrying out certain roles in the Gurdwara. This is a blatant aberration of Sikhi.

The egalitarian nature of Sikh teachings also extends to rejecting caste-based discrimination. Although on a spiritual level the teachings of the Sikh Gurus reject the notion of ritual purity and conversely ritual pollution through one's birth, the eradication of the caste system, per se, from society, is open to many interpretations (Takhar, 2005). The establishment of Gurdwaras along caste-based followings is an example of bad Sikhi. Young British Sikhs are overthrowing traditional attitudes associated with the caste into which one is born. Increasingly, younger Sikhs are drawing reference to Sikh teachings which denounce caste-based discrimination, which for many extends to the caste (or indeed faith) of one's prospective spouse. Although endogamy is observed by many Sikhs, inter-caste marriages are on the increase amongst British-born Sikhs. Non-observance of endogamy, in traditional Punjabi society, would be detrimental on the *izzat* of the extended families concerned. Rejection of such attitudes is increasingly being challenged by the younger generation of British-born Sikhs. Hans (2008) is critical of the fact that caste equality has not been applied on the practical level, despite the egalitarian teachings of Sikhi, especially with regard to Sikhs who came from Dalit (historically oppressed) castes. The remuneration of Ravidassias, many of whom adopted the Sikh faith in the hope of eradicating the stigma of untouchability, as numbering 11,000 in England and Wales according to the 2011 Census cannot be ignored. This is a stark reminder that teachings emphasizing the irrelevance of caste distinctions are not actually practiced by all Sikhs. Many of the Ravidassias might have identified as Sikhs in the previous 2001 Census (see Takhar, 2011).

Earlier in this volume, Christopher Lewis highlighted the importance of deeds and free will in good religion. Birth in the human realm alone, according to Sikhi, provides the 'golden opportunity' for the individual to work towards salvation. Hence this is sensible in making the most of this life, not wasting it on material temptations and attachments. Self-discipline, which can only be acquired through one's efforts offers a *chance* of salvation. Interestingly, Singh makes parallels with Sikhi and the Hegelian notion of reason, he states:

> Notwithstanding the problems associated with particular conceptions of human rationality, one can see some interesting parallels with the Hegelian idea of rationality and the importance of the capacity to reason with the Sikh idea of *manukhi janam*, or human birth, as the only form whereby salvation is possible. (2006: 139)

Sikhi and Other Faiths

Earlier in this volume, Christopher Lewis posed the question as to what are appropriate relationships between religions and how indeed, religions should treat each other. Sikhi is an inclusivist faith which has no conversion rite. The steady but noticeable influx of non-Punjabi Sikhs (especially in the USA) strengthens the notion that Sikhi is a sensible path for modern living and spirituality regardless of one's ethnicity. Neither does Sikh history have accounts of Sikhs carrying out crusades against 'other' faiths. Sikh history and tradition is replete, however, with the heroic acts of its martyrs, ranging from the age of five upwards, in the face of forced conversions to Islam from the Mughal invaders in India. The followers of the Sikh faith identifying as distinct from the followers of the Hindu faith is a debate that has continued from the period of the Singh Sabha movement in 1873. Today, the majority of Sikhs define themselves as belonging to a distinct faith which does not allow for hybrid religious boundaries within the context of the many Indian faiths.

Guru Nanak was the pioneer in inter-faith relationships way back in the fifteenth century. His emphasis was for individuals to be 'good' and moral beings without necessarily being over-burdened with religious dogma associated with one faith or another. His famous words: 'There is no Hindu, There is no Muslim ... I will follow God's path' have been interpreted in a number of ways. One interpretation is that the emphasis in Guru Nanak's teachings was the liberation of *all* human beings, regardless of one's faith, gender or caste. This was not a purely philosophical concept but applied in practice through the composition of the *Adi Granth* (which assumed the title *Guru Granth Sahib* in 1708 CE) under the leadership of the fifth Guru, Arjan, in 1604 CE The *Guru Granth Sahib* is the only world scripture that contains the teachings of individuals from more than one faith. In addition to the teachings of the Sikh Gurus, it also contains the religious philosophical teachings of Hindu and Muslim *Sants*.

In this respect, Sikhi is positive towards claims of truth in all faiths. It is truly inclusivist in acknowledging that all religious paths lead to the same goal. Hence many Sikhs are involved in inter-faith matters around the globe.

The Sikh place of worship, the *Gurdwara*, is open to all. An important feature of the egalitarian principles of Sikhism are clearly portrayed through the distribution of *karah prasad* and *langar* in the Gurdwara. The concept of eating together illustrates that all visitors to the *Gurdwara* are equal. Furthermore, although not all Sikhs are vegetarian, the food served in the *Gurdwara* is meat-free, so as not to offend the dietary laws of different faiths. Sikhism teaches the immanence of God within the hearts of all human beings. This entails the principle that all human beings are equal, regardless of their faith or gender. Sikhs are encouraged to speak out against any form of racism. An aberration of the principle based on the equality of all individuals, however, relates to the ongoing debate as to who is a Sikh. Although the term 'orthodoxy' is alien in Sikh thought, it is too often misleadingly applied by both Sikhs and non-Sikhs to refer to *amritdhari* Sikhs. The 'non-orthodox' category in this respect are labelled the *sahajdharis*, or 'slow adopters', for whom the aspiration (as set by *amritdharis*) would be to at least keep the hair unshorn and ultimately become *amritdhari*. There are a number of problems associated with the use of the term 'orthodoxy' for elements of Sikh belief. Sikhi does not have a religious hierarchy with the ordained at the top and the laity below. Guru Nanak was strictly against such elevation of individuals and was particularly critical of the position of the *brahmins* as the intermediaries between the Divine and the individual. Furthermore, Sikhi is interpreted differently by different scholars, although not a word of the Guru Granth Sahib has been changed since the time of Guru Gobind Singh (the final human Guru). However, the language of the Scripture is no longer a spoken language. Most Sikhs are agreed on the metaphysics of Sikhi; however, differences occur in terms of the practices amongst Sikhs such as emphasis on intermediaries through the roles of *Sants* and Gurus (in addition to the ten human Gurus) and the level of authority accorded to the Guru Granth Sahib, and indeed *Sants* as well as Gurus (as in the case of Namdharis who continue the line of human Gurus to the present day). Hence one can talk of mainstream and 'sects', who deviate from what is considered mainstream amongst the Sikhs (Takhar, 2005). Thus, the Sikhs are not a homogeneous, monolithic community. There is much diversity, some of which falls into the category of good Sikhi, some of which falls into the category of bad Sikhi, as determined by the majority.

In this chapter I have attempted to explore a number of themes in the Sikh religion in order to support my contention that Sikhi is a sensible religion which caters for a good lifestyle, attitude and world view in the twentieth century. As a Sikh, it is Sikhi that inspires and encourages me to live a fruitful, happy and fulfilling life. Aberrations are present within all faith communities, praxis amongst Sikhs are not alone here. It is a very thin line between religion and Punjabi culture which may lead to visible hypocrisies between Sikhi and actual practice amongst Sikhs. The three key principles of Sikhi – *Nam Japo* (meditation on the Name of God) *Kirt Karo* (hard work) and *Vand ke Chakko* (sharing with others) – enable a devout Sikh to be a good citizen whilst remembering God at all times. Good citizenship in this respect involves carrying out selfless service (*sewa*) to help the community, both local and global. Donating a tenth of one's income (*dasvandh*) cares for those who are less fortunate. It is because of these principles that Sikhs are encouraged to take part in charitable events, without any attachment to egoistic outcomes or fame. A fine example is of the Sikh organization 'Khalsa Aid' flying out to Haiti from Britain to perform *sewa* with the victims of the abhorrent earthquake, regardless of the faith (or non-faith) of the recipients. One who works hard and shares both their income and time with the needy in society is a good person by all accounts.

Reference List

Ahluwalia, Pal (2011) 'At Home in Motion: Evolving Sikh identities', *Sikh Formations*, 7(2), 95–109.

Gill, Mohinder Kaur (1995) *The Role and Status of Women in Sikhism*, Delhi: National Book Shop.

Hans, Raj Kumar (2008) 'Dalits and the Emancipatory Sikh Religion'. Paper presented at Dalit Challenges to Academic Knowledge: The Great Paradoxes Conference, University of Pennsylvania, December 3–5.

Jacobsen, Knut A. and Myrvold, Kristina (eds) (2011) *Sikhs in Europe: Migration, Identities and Representations*, Aldershot: Ashgate.

Morris, Jeremy (2012) 'Secularization and Religious Experience: Arguments in the Historiography of Modern British Religion', *The Historical Journal*, 55(1), 195–219.

Nesbitt, Eleanor (2011) 'Sikh Diversity in the UK: Contexts and Evolution' in Knut Jacobsen and Kristina Myrvold (eds), *Sikhs in Europe: Migration, Identities and Representations*, Aldershot: Ashgate, 225–52.

Oberoi, Harjot (1997) *The Construction of Religious Boundaries*, Delhi: Oxford University Press.

Pettigrew, Joyce (1994) 'Growth of Community Consciousness among Sikhs, 1947–1966' in Dharam Singh (ed.), *Sikhism and Secularism*, New Delhi: Harman Publishing House, 1–31.

Shackle, Christopher and Mandair, Arvind-pal Singh (2005) *Teachings of the Sikh Gurus*, Abingdon: Routledge.

Singh, Gurnam (2006) 'Sikhism's Emancipatory Discourses: Some Critical Perspectives', *Sikh Formations*, 2(2), 135–51.

Singh, Jasjit (2011) 'Sikh-ing Beliefs: British Sikh Camps in the UK' in Knut Jacobsen and Kristina Myrvold (eds), *Sikhs in Europe: Migration, Identities and Representations*, Aldershot: Ashgate, 253–77.

Takhar, Opinderjit Kaur (2005) *Sikh Identity: An Exploration of Groups among Sikhs*, Aldershot: Ashgate.

Takhar, Opinderjit Kaur (2011) 'The Valmiki, Ravidasi and Namdhari Communities in Britain: Self-Representations and Transmission of Traditions' in Knut Jacobsen and Kristina Myrvold (eds), *Sikhs in Europe: Migration, Identities and Representations*, Aldershot: Ashgate: 279–304.

Turner, Bryan (2006) 'Religion', *Theory, Culture and Society*, 23(2–3), 437–55.

Vardy, Peter (2010) *Good and Bad Religion*, London: SCM Press.

Chapter 14
African Traditional Religion

Nokuzola Mndende

The purpose of this chapter is to examine the current situation of African Traditional Religion (ATR), to give an account of the main tenets of the religion and to demonstrate that it is a sensible and truly African response both to God as Creator and to God's creation. While giving this account, I will also look at some of the problems faced by ATR, both in response to the missionary religions (especially Christianity) and to the challenges of the modern world.

The Context

The history of ATR, or any discussion about the religion in southern Africa, cannot be dealt with in isolation from its history and, in particular, the manner in which its practitioners have been treated. In any debate involving aspects of this religion, one cannot avoid first examining its context and also discovering from its practitioners their understanding of their beliefs and practices. It is therefore important for the reader to understand that in order for this religion to move forwards and participate with others, without being suspicious of the intent of missionary religions, it must be acknowledged that the religion has suffered marginalization and distortions because of the introduction of a new religion whose agenda, as some Africans believe, was to destroy the existing indigenous way of life of the Africans.

The dawn of democracy in a post-colonial and post-apartheid South Africa has brought many changes in the understanding and scope of the term 'religion'. Because religion was previously narrowly defined in the light of the Abrahamic faiths (Judaism, Christianity and Islam), anything outside their scope was not regarded as a true religion, but was labelled as a false one. As a result, those who brought their understanding of religion (the white missionaries, anthropologists and colonial officials) were at liberty to use terms in relation to the indigenous religion of the country that were not known to the practitioners: terms like

Animism, Paganism and Ancestor Worship; alternatively these visitors just saw a manifestation of 'culture' which had no knowledge of God at all. In this way, a particular understanding of the term 'religion' was imposed, stemming from a racially partisan view. Unfortunately this 'holier than thou' approach was inculcated into the minds of local African people as a result of what was a Judeo/Christian approach, and was used as a measuring rod for assessing religious and moral behaviour. Anything outside biblical discourse was regarded as immoral and ungodly: a biblical text had to be cited to justify the authenticity of someone's questions or comments. This is often how 'religion' is understood today, even though the country is free.

On account of the process just described, South Africa was incorrectly declared a Christian country, and many Africans had to live a double standard. For example, an African might use indigenous names at home, while pretending to be Christian at school or at work and using so-called 'Christian names'. This practice is reflected in identity and other government-related documents, for example in the names Rholihlahla Nelson Mandela, Mpilo Desmond Tutu, Nyameko Barney Pityana, Nokuzola Oscarine Mndende. The indigenous names were publicly called 'heathen names'. This situation was a consequence of a colonial state of affairs and led to an 'acceptance', under duress, that this new religion was the only one that could enable people to relate to God. It also led to an association of Christianity with higher social status.

Although ATR practitioners have now emerged and publicly declared their beliefs, they are often received with suspicion and their intelligence is doubted. This suspicion has roots in the treatment of Africans at the time when Christianity was introduced into the country. Religion, Western schooling and Christianity were a package. Anyone who went to Western school was automatically a convert; baptism with a 'Christian' name was a prerequisite for entry to school. These converts (*amagqobhoka*) were regarded as superior to those who did not attend Western schools (*amaqaba*) as explained by Philip Mayer (1971). *Amagqobhoka* (people with a hole) and *amaqaba* (those who smear ochre) were derogatory names used by one group when referring to the other. *Amaqaba* called their rivals *amagqobhoka*: people who have holes which let something foreign into their religion, making them untrustworthy. On the other hand *amagqobhoka* called their rivals *amaqaba* implying that they are primitive and heathen.

Even though the dawn of democracy brought some hope for those who were formerly excluded (the so-called *amaqaba*), they were treated as inferior and expected to explain and justify their faith before they could participate in multi-faith debates. They had to accept an imposed definition of their identity and way of thinking. These foreign definitions of the indigenous people and of their way of life have been used in such a way that many have been convinced that God created the ATR practitioners on a level closer to animals and plants, their spirituality being labelled 'secular' (Du Toit, 2006).

Because of the scarcity of theologians from within the religion itself and the dominance of African theologians who belong to other faiths, ATR still lacks its own breathing space. Instead of the development of the religion as an independent faith in a multi-religious society, its practice and discourse are contested. Much contemporary literature is presented in the third person and voices from within the ranks of ATR itself are seen as irrational and naive. Publishers make sure that other religions are defined by their practitioners, but often accept the view that ATR is syncretistic and inferior. The South African government is biased against the practitioners of traditional spirituality.

In interfaith debates, adherents of ATR are still made to feel that they are not permitted to use certain terminology, with terms like 'God', 'religion' and 'spirituality' treated as if 'owned' by the Abrahamic faiths. Adherents are told that their Creator is less the biblical Triune God with capital letter 'G' and more of a small-letter (g)od; hence, many theologians speak of gods and goddesses when referring to ATR. Even today, with the advent of African leadership and theologians, many consider that ATR is a matter of 'culture' rather than of spirituality.

Such a two-tier understanding of ATR is also widespread in African society in general. It may be believed that dissatisfaction by ancestors results in punishment: sickness, misfortunes or unnatural deaths. When such things occur, many though professing to be Christians in public, secretly perform rituals to appease ancestors, classifying what they do as 'cultural': culture for this world and Christian religion for the next. Some African theologians are happy to use derogatory terms like 'deities', 'spirit possession', 'witchcraft', 'witchdoctors' and 'secular spirituality' when discussing ATR. Thus Africans have accepted that what is theirs is incomplete until mixed with an imported religion.

Another challenge to ATR as a whole way of life is the imposed and assumed superiority of the Roman/ Dutch Law over the indigenous law of the country. This approach leaves little room for a revival or adaptation of the indigenous law of the country, since the indigenous law is judged from the perspective of foreign law, irrespective of the value it has for maintaining the communal way of life in communities. Zvabva blames colonialism:

> The worst type of colonial enslavement is the cultural spiritual one where the colonised is given a distorted image of himself and of his God by his oppressors and he accepts that image, and continues with it unquestioningly despising

himself, his culture and his religion and slavishly aping the culture of his colonizers. (Zvabva, 1991: 76)

Today there is some wish to bridge the gap between the previous legal system, altered though it is, and the foreign legal system. The 'owners' of the previous legal system, which was the indigenous law of the community, were not first asked to say how they would like to proceed to democracy without compromising their roles as custodians of African culture and spirituality. Many had one foot in their own traditions and another in foreign traditions, and unfortunately it is the foreign traditions that have dictated ways of incorporating the law into a democratic model. The indigenous traditions are regarded as 'other' and their custodians have both to plead for recognition and to make many adjustments in order to be incorporated into modern structures.

The consequence is that equality has not been given to the various traditions within a multicultural and multi-religious society; the status of an indigenous spirituality has been compromised. Chinweizu advises us on how we should approach our history, pointing out that we should read our past with great care, for otherwise we will misdirect our efforts to shape our future (Chinweizu, 1987).

When it comes to the content of ATR, there are several challenges; most of the studies have been written by scholars of religion who belonged to other faiths and have not done it justice. Scholars who were Christian clergy (Mbiti, 1969; Idowu,1973; Magesa, 1998; Parrinder, 1976; Olupona, 1998) to mention but a few, had the opportunity to be employed in the Departments of Religious Studies as Christian theologians or as anthropologists. Perhaps because they felt some guilt concerning recent history, they were sympathetic towards ATR and started to write about it. They wrote as detached observers and their approach was from a Western or a Judeo-Christian perspective. Often they wrote using the assumptions of their new-found religion and they used the past tense, as if ATR was no longer practiced.

Characteristics

Having been critical of the past and of the present, it is important that I now describe ATR and demonstrate what it stands for. What exactly is ATR? Until fairly recently, of course, it had no name. The practitioners did not bother about a name because it was their way of life, integral to the communities in which they lived. When other religions arrived and when people started to study indigenous religion, some called it 'African Religion' or 'African Religions', others called it

'African Traditional Religion' or 'African Traditional Religions'. Some call it 'Ancestor worship' or any name that suited their purposes. Sometimes they saw it only in the light of missionary religions. In this chapter I am using the term that I myself find most appropriate, namely African Traditional Religion (ATR).

There is some agreement among scholars, but below I have specifically cited Awolalu, because he relates his analysis to contemporary material. Awolalu explains ATR as follows:

> When we speak of African Traditional Religion we mean the indigenous religion of the Africans. It is the religion that has been handed down from generation to generation by the forebears of the present generation of Africans. It is not a fossil religion (a thing of the past) but a religion that Africans today have made theirs by living it and practising it. (cited by Dopamu, 1991: 21)

Idowu (1973) is very specific, as he always includes the geographical area where the religion is practiced, which is Sub- Saharan.

A Unified Religion

The use of a plural (African Traditional Religions) is common in the writings of some scholars of the religion (Mbiti, 1969; Okot, 1970; Ferguson, 1978), but the majority of scholars believe that there are many similarities between all the religious practices of the sub-Saharan Africa, so the religion can be seen as one (Idowu, 1973; Parrinder, 1976; Dopamu, 1991; Oladimeji, 1980). Despite the differences, there is an underlying identity. There is a distinct regular rhythm in the general pattern of the people's beliefs and practices, namely belief in the Creator. Although it is not necessary to justify whether the religion is singular or plural to those who are curious (as it does not affect what the practitioners of the religion do) I will cite those who agree that the religion is singular. Idowu argues:

> We find that in Africa, the real cohesive factor of religion is the living God and that without this one factor; all things would fall to pieces. And it is on this ground especially – this identical concept that we can speak of the religion of Africa in the singular. (Idowu, 1973:104)

Basic Beliefs

As explained above, until the religion gets full recognition, it is important that one exercises some patience and that one explains the basic beliefs as if for the first time, before engaging in any debate. Practitioners of the religion believe that their religion consists of spiritual beliefs and practices that are in their blood from birth. ATR practitioners believe that these beliefs and practices were handed down by their forebears and have survived, despite the many changes that the continent has experienced. ATR has no founder; it is believed that it was revealed to the first generation by the Creator. The first humans were given all the laws of how to live in harmony with the Creator, with other human beings and with nature.

The story goes on to say that when the first generation died, they joined the Spiritual World where the Creator lives. In other words, the death of the first generation marked the beginning of ancestors. Ancestors then became the messengers of the Creator and also the supervisors of the physical world. The ancestors look to the welfare of the living, mainly through the elders who in turn teach the youth orally and through ritual performances. This is how the religion gets passed on from generation to generation.

There are therefore three basic beliefs, namely belief in the Creator, in Ancestors and in communal life.

The Creator

People who practice ATR believe in the existence of the Supernatural Power who created life and the earth. Neither science nor human beings can explain the powers of the Creator. The Creator is the Spirit and is neither male nor female. Although the Spiritual Power is believed to be everywhere in creation, it is also believed that creation began in the Spiritual World which is holy and is where the laws, rituals and taboos that control the welfare of the physical world originate.

Africa is made up of many nations and each nation has a name or names for the Creator depending on the attributes that these communities believe are associated with the Creator. Some groups may share a common name.

Ancestors

Ndlovu summarizes the concept of ancestors concisely when he says that the way in which African languages speak of ancestors points to five fundamental beliefs and principles:

- a recognition that each human being is made up not only of flesh, bones and blood, but also of spirit or soul;

- a belief that whereas the human body dies and decomposes, the spirit (soul) does not perish;
- an understanding that human relationships, especially within the family circle, do not die, but once established, continue forever;
- a recognition of the unique relationship that exists between the 'Creator Spirit' and the human;
- the fact that in the light of the above, the spirits of the departed play the vital role of intermediaries, linking the world of those who are alive with the world of the Creator (Ndlovu, 1991: 34).

Communal Life through Ritual Performances and Social Upbringing

Rituals are extraordinary communal practices performed by the living for the Spiritual World. Rituals take place at special gatherings of the clans. They are performed for particular purposes such as rites of passage (birth, initiation, marriage and death), thanksgiving, divination processes, and also because of requests by ancestors, for example in order to bring back the spirit of some family member who has died far away from home. In these religious gatherings the community acts out its various forms of worship. Through these rituals, unity and healing are achieved.

African Communities

The unit which makes up African communities is the family. Depending on the nature of the society, the family may be patrilineal or matrilineal. Mbiti (1969) refers to this basic structure and says that: '... kinship is reckoned through blood and betrothal (engagement and marriage). It is kinship which controls social relationships between people in a given community, it governs marital customs and regulations, it determines the behaviours of one individual towards another' (Mbiti 1969: 104). During ritual performances the members of the clan come together and perform the ritual collectively. An African community is understood as being made up of every member of the family: the living members and those of the past and of the future. Mbiti again explains this community as follows:

> The kinship system also extends vertically to include the departed and those yet to be born. It is part of traditional education for children in many African societies to learn the genealogies of their descent. The genealogy gives a sense of depth, historical belongingness, a feeling of deep rootedness and a sense of sacred obligation to extend the genealogical line. (Mbiti, 1969: 105)

Every transformation in the development of the living individual must be announced publicly in order officially to inform both the living and the ancestors, all of whom are members of the community.

The Role of Elders

In ATR it is compulsory that an individual perform the rites of passage, as each stage allows a person to be taught about the expectations and responsibilities of the next stage. Instruction and the rituals themselves are led by the elders of a particular clan; they must support and witness the events. In ATR no one is allowed to be part of a ritual if a person, irrespective of age, has never performed that particular stage. This is because the elders must teach by example; for instance a bachelor, of whatever age, can never admonish a couple during the marriage ritual, as he has never been married. A boy can never be part of the admonishing, or indeed play any part, in the seclusion and passing-out parade of male initiation rituals.

During all rituals, the elders lead the whole process, which is characterized by speeches and ritual acts. Their obligations are both to give a lead so that there is moral stability and proper guidance as to what is expected by those in the Spirit World, and also to ensure that their wisdom is passed on to the next generation.

As ancestors are believed to be intermediaries between the living and the Creator, they play a crucial role within the affairs of the living. Since ancestors are near to God in the Spiritual World, they are also believed to play a part in protecting, healing, rewarding and punishing the living. Ancestors reveal themselves to the living through dreams or visions and sometimes use certain animals as channels of communication. There are different categories of dreams as understood by ATR adherents: ordinary dreams (*amaphupha*) and dreams that carry messages from ancestors (*amathongo*). It is the elders who interpret the meaning of *amathongo* through symbols in particular contexts, such as round houses, beads, ochre, grasses and animals (for example, leopards, dogs, goats, cattle and bees). Sometimes the elders are not sure what the dreams mean and consult a spiritual healer (diviner) who then interprets what ancestors are saying.

Relationship with Nature

ATR has very close relationship with nature. As explained above, ancestors in the Spirit World reveal their messages using natural objects and certain animals. Nature is expected to be treated with respect as it is believed that all creation is God's creation. Some people are chosen by ancestors to heal, and these are the diviners. They undergo ritual initiation as prescribed through dreams by ancestors. A diviner can never graduate without having been in seclusion in particular sacred places like rivers, forests, seas, mountains and caves.

During ritual performances, natural symbols are used: branches of olive or sneeze-wood trees, clan medicines and particular grasses.

ATR has no special day of worship. All days are believed to be created by God, so it is regarded as disrespectful to make one day holier than the others. All days are holy. For communal worship people gather together for rituals, but such days are not understood as more holy than other days. What is regarded as holy is the ritual itself; it can be performed on any day of the week.

Ethical values within ATR are 'people-centered' or anthropocentric. Evil originates with humans and not with God. ATR focuses on oral transmission of norms and values, acted out in practice. The emphasis is on the daily practice of these values and also on rituals, rather than on texts as sacred authority. Practitioners know whom to consult within the clan as guidance will vary with the times, whereas a book is static. In their communal way of life, practitioners are constantly reminded of all the aspects of their religion. Rituals, together with the normal social interaction of daily life are where respect and morality are practiced and reinforced.

The Future

Despite the situation described at the beginning of this chapter, ATR practitioners are becoming part of the multi-faith debates in South Africa, having made inroads into broadcasting and with the religion being part of the education curriculum. Several books have been written in order to give ATR members confidence about their spirituality and about their roots.

Some institutes have developed on a small scale in order to teach the young about the religion. The Icamagu Institute, in particular, is arranging advocacy programs and has conducted many seminars and conferences on the revival of ATR. The Institute is the only institution in South Africa that has produced ATR clergy, and it has participated in policy-making in such national government departments as Education, Correctional Services, Defence, Arts and Culture.

So there are hopeful developments; yet there are also new problems. Prior to colonization, ATR had been part of the way of life of sub-Saharan Africans. It was practiced within the family and was communally acted out by each individual, by members of the family and by members of the community. It was an oral tradition that was characterized by practice in order to instil it in the younger generation.

Because of the outside factors which tried to intermingle with the religion, ATR lost the confidence it had before and contemporary practitioners face the challenge of renewing ATR for the modern world. In the past the clan was the basic structure of the religious practice. Today's clans are not homogeneous as far as religion is concerned, for there is a mixture of ATR and Christianity, sometimes using the term 'culture' for ATR and 'religion' for Christianity. Syncretism has created tensions among family members and, of course, among those who believe in the centrality of the doctrines of their respective religions.

We are also experiencing a lot of moral decay leading to alarming rates of rape, murder and deaths by unnatural causes, like accidents and the so-called muti-killings. Muti-killing is murder in order to mutilate the body for incorporation into medicines by people who claim that the parts are useful for curing diseases. All of these are actions of the forces of darkness. Anyone involved in crimes is believed to be neglected by his ancestors and, after facing the might of the law, will also have to undergo spiritual cleansing in order to be able to relate to his or her ancestors.

The liberation of ATR in the post-colonial country has not only brought joy to ATR adherents but has also given freedom to charlatans who cause distortions regarding the content and significance of the religion, especially in the field of divination.

Although in principle ATR is regarded as a faith that promotes a communal way of life with full participation of the genders, the patrilineal nature of most communities means that the ideal is not realized. Women are defined in two categories, that is *iintombi* (lit. a girl) and *umfazi* (a married woman). During ritual performances, women who are born within that particular clan and have married into other clans are called back to be part of the ritual as they have their roles to play. At their biological homes they are called *iintombi* (girls) irrespective of age and there is no gender discrimination. But in many situations males use patriarchy in a selective manner and deny women their right to participate. This situation leads to conflicts among family members and is despised by ancestors.

Conclusion

As in every modern society, the situation is mixed. Yet we need to focus on the nature of ATR and on the way in which it is practiced in much of sub-Saharan Africa today. In ATR no one is irreligious; every person is a bearer of religion or spirituality. From the time of conception until death and even beyond the grave (as an ancestor), individuals are engaged in actively maintaining close contact with the Spirit World of the Creator. Every human being in ATR belongs to a larger community. This belonging is demonstrated by a person's participation in the religious and cultural ceremonies, the rituals and festivals of that particular community. Belief and action cannot be separated because what one does is motivated by what one believes, and what one believes springs from what one does and experiences.

We should realize, however, that the world is not static and the religion must change, although the main principles of ATR must be retained. Also governments must recognize the challenges when more than one religious group is active in a particular society.

In the terms of this book, the development of ATR since its origins in the mists of time, needs to be recognized. It is a religion which reaches out in worship to the Creator from a deeply African context and has strong distinguishing characteristics: a powerful sense of the sacredness of the creation; the place of kinship and community; the role of ancestors and of ritual; a knowledge of nature and its intimate connection with the Spirit World. The dangers and problems facing ATR have been described and are similar to those facing other religions. At its best, ATR is a profound and sensible response to the divine, to the world around us and to each other.

Reference List

p' Bitek, O. (1970) *African Religions in Western Scholarship*, Nairobi: African Literature Bureau.

Chinweizu (1987) *Decolonizing the African Mind*, Nigeria: Pero Press.

Dopamu, P.A. (1991) 'Towards Understanding African Traditional Religion'. In e m Uka, *Readings in African Traditional Religion*, New York: Peter Lang.

Du Toit, C.W. and Mayson, Cedric (eds) (2006) *Secular Spirituality as a Contextual Critique of Religion*, UNISA: Research Institute for Theology and Religion.

Ferguson, J. (1978) 'African Religions'. In Francis Clark and John Ferguson, *The Religious Perspective: African Religions*, Maidenhead: The Open University.

Idowu, E. Bolaji (1973) *African Traditional Religion: A Definition*, London: SCM Press.

Magesa, L. (1998) *African Religion: The Moral Traditions of Abundant Life*, New York: Orbis Books.

Mayer, P. (1971) *Townsmen or Tribesmen*, Cape Town: Oxford University Press.

Mbiti, J.S. (1969) *African Religions and Philosophy*, London: Heinemann.

Mndende, N. (2006) *African Spiritual Journey: Rites of Passage among the Xhosa Speaking of South Africa*, Cape Town: Icamagu Institute.

Mndende, N. (2009) *Tears of Distress: Voices of a Denied Spirituality in a Democratic South Africa*, Idutywa: Icamagu Institute.

Ndlovu, J.J.M. (1991) 'The Place of African Traditional Religious Heritage in Religious Education Curricula'. In S.J. Nondo (ed), *Multifaith Issues and Approaches in Religious Education with Special Reference to Zimbabwe*, Utrecht: Rijksuniversiteit.

Oladimeji, O. (1980) *African Traditional Religion*, Nigeria: Hesanmi Press & Sons.

Olupona, J. (ed) (1998) *African Traditional Religions in Contemporary Scholarship*, New York: Paragon House.

Parrinder, G. (1976) *African Traditional Religion*, Westport, CT: Greenwood Press.

Zvabva, O. (1991) 'Development of Research in African Traditional Religions'. In S. Nondo (ed.), *Multifaith Issues and Approaches in Religious Education with Special Reference to Zimbabwe*, Utrecht: Rijksuniversiteit.

Chapter 15
Conclusion: Sensible Religion Matters

Dan Cohn-Sherbok

In recent years religion has been under severe attack. Secularists, humanists, scientists and others seek to demonstrate that humankind's religious quest is an illusion. Some critics focus on religion's pernicious influence on human behaviour, citing religious wars as examples of the consequences of such delusional conviction. Yet at the same time, throughout the world millions of believers are intent on shaping society to conform to their religious ideals. This is especially the case in Muslim countries where fundamentalist Islam is embraced by millions. In Israel, the religious parties are determined to ensure that the Torah serves as the blueprint for Jewish living. Christian fundamentalists in Western countries and elsewhere similarly champion Jesus' message, believing that society should embrace Christian values. In our pluralistic world, religion is on the march. At the same time, supernaturalism is under attack. What sense can we make of it all? Is all religion good? Is all religion bad? Is it possible to differentiate good from bad religion? That is the key question this book seeks to address. Are there criteria which can be used to distinguish between religions that are sensible, and religions which are not?

Evaluating Religion

In the opening chapter of this volume, Christopher Lewis stresses that there are two central areas which should be explored in attempting to evaluate modern religion. He writes:

> The contention of this book is that to follow the religious path is a sensible response to the fact of life in our world, and that the vast majority of religious people are leading ordinary loving lives. The concerns addressed here are therefore related to the philosophical question of whether religious belief or at least religious belief in some of its forms is intellectual acceptable; reasonable, justifiable and

therefore what Alvin Plantinga, after lengthy and thorough examination, calls 'warranted'. 'Sensible' has a number of connotations. The most common refers to reasonableness in people and beliefs, having beliefs and practices which are both consistent with what is considered to be true and which also correspond to what is seen as reality.

Here Lewis highlights the rational dimension of religious conviction – the test is whether religious belief is theologically tenable. He goes on then to call attention to a second dimension:

Yet there is another meaning, not unrelated to the first, which refers to sensibility, awareness, being mindful of the views of others and responsive to the world around us, both individually and collectively.

Such considerations are ethical in nature. Judgment of religion, he stresses, must ascertain whether a religion is followed by rounded and loving people in the modern world, indeed that the traditions enable people to be altruistic, as well as fulfilled.

This conviction – that it is possible to evaluate both the rational and the ethical dimensions of religion – has been a contention of a number of philosophers of religion. John Hick (1981) discusses this issue. In his view, religious concepts and practices are not all on the same level of value or validity. This is so, he writes, among the different religions and even within individual religious systems. Indeed, he notes, throughout history the most significant religious figures have been critical of various ideas and attitudes. The Buddha, for example, rejected the notion of the eternal atman. The Hebrew prophets criticized mere outward observances and practices. Jesus attacked the formalism and insincerity of the scribes and Pharisees. Muhammad rejected the polytheism of Arabian society. Guru Nanak and Martin Luther were critical of the traditions into which they were born.

Hence, Hick maintains that assessing religious phenomena is a central feature of religious seriousness and openness to the Divine. It is legitimate to grade aspects of religions and place them in some order of merit. No one, he believes, is going to think that all the features of the world's religions are on the same level of value or validity. Different aspects have to be regarded as higher or lower, better or worse, Divine or demonic.

Yet, Hick is anxious to emphasize that while it is proper to assess religious phenomena, it is not realistic to grade the world's religions as totalities. According to Hick, it is the theologian's task to ascertain what aspects of a tradition are belief-worthy. In making such a judgment, he outlines four criteria. The first is theological coherence. Allied with the notion of internal coherence is a second criterion of religious adequacy, namely its adequacy both to the particular form of experience on which it is based and to the data of human experience in general. What is being referred to here is the question whether the theology or philosophy within a religious tradition is adequate to the originating religions vision as well as its success in interpreting that vision to a new age.

The third criterion Hick suggests is spiritual in nature. Here the test consists in ascertaining the extent to which religious ideas promote or hinder the aims of salvation and liberation. In explaining this principle, Hick gives examples from several religions: Christians give themselves to God in Christ in a total renunciation of the self-centred ego and its concerns; Muslims give themselves in total submission to God; Hindus strive for union with the Ultimate through meditation and selfless action.

The final criterion Hick proposes is moral assessment. In recommending this standard, Hick extols the lives of various saints of the world's faiths, yet he emphasizes that the actual histories of religious traditions frequently fall short of moral ideals. In this context he catalogues what he considers modern moral evils engendered by religious faith: the lethargy of Eastern countries in relation to social and economic problems; Hindu and Buddhist otherworldliness in retarding social, economic and technological progress; the unjust caste system of India; the burning of widows in India; the cutting of a thief's hands under Islamic law, and so forth. In making these judgments, Hick wishes to illustrate that in the history of all religious traditions there is both virtue and vice.

Another approach to grading religions was formulated by Paul Knitter (1982). According to Knitter, there are three guidelines for determining the truth-value of any religion or religious figure:

1. Personally, does the revelation of the religion or religious figure – the story, the myth, the message – move the human heart?
2. Intellectually, does the religion also satisfy and expand the mind? Is it intellectually coherent? Does it broaden one's horizons of understanding?
3. Practically, does the message provide for psychological health of individuals, their sense of value, purpose and freedom? Does it promote the welfare, the liberation of all peoples?

Peter Vardy (2010) argues that it is possible to differentiate between what he regards as good religion and bad religion. The need to separate good from bad religion, he writes, is an urgent task. At the conclusion of his book, he outlines a number of observations about good and bad religion:

1. Authority can react to challenges with arrogance and by coercion because the priority is perceived as preserving and enlarging the religious community and keeping it from error in matters of doctrine and religious practice. This is a feature of bad religion because it encourages seeing religion as a matter of social cohesion rather than individual transformation.

2. Religious imperatives that are not subject to rational scrutiny and interpretation are features of bad religion. Claiming the supposed command of God without any rational basis for determining whether such commands are of divine origin is no longer acceptable. Textual fundamentalism should be resisted. A refusal to acknowledge the discipline of hermeneutics or the influence of the cultural context of any text is misguided.

3. Good religion is not afraid of science; rather it is committed to the view that religion and science are both seeking truth. A resistance to scientific discoveries and insights is a feature of bad religion.

4. The demand to practice justice is one of the strongest, most powerful and most universal of all religious demands. Good religion must be willing to challenge the preconceptions and assumptions of the culture of which it forms a part, and should provide an independent voice that seeks to foster justice.

5. Good religion must aim to foster human flourishing, to help human beings to develop their full potential, however this may be defined. Any religion that cannot show itself as fostering the fulfillment of potential of all human beings should be resisted.

6. Good religion respects human freedom. It does not seek to coerce people, is willing to educate youth into alternative perspectives other than its own, while being confident in its own positions. Good religion rejects indoctrination and is not frightened of alternative possibilities (Vardy, 2010: 170–73).

Sensible Religion and Rationality

Adopting an approach similar to Hick, Knitter and Vardy, the contributors to this volume are convinced that it is possible to make a case for a rational and moral framework for living from within the various world's religions. With regard to rationality, Keith Ward focuses on the concept of reason itself in making a case for the reasonableness of Christian doctrine. Here he points out that it is a mistake to define reasonableness simply as requiring good public evidence. Rather, a reasonable view should be aware of its own basic principles and be consistent; in addition, it should recognize relative alternative views. Further, it should be self-critical, always open to reasoned objections and cognizant of relevant facts and arguments and the strength and limits of expert option. A reasonable view should be open, empathetic, critical and engaged.

Ward makes a number of key observations. First, he stresses that some atheists as well as believers fail these tests. They do not realize the fragility and contestability of their basic axioms, fail to take other views seriously or state them accurately, are unwilling to be self-critical and ignore expert opinion in relevant disciplines. Scientifically informed atheists, for example, sometimes do not bother to read works of classical theology, while some theologically trained Christians remain ignorant of the strength of scientific claims. Second, Ward contends that it is untrue to say that there are no considerations that count for or against belief in God. For example, the existence of suffering and randomness in nature count against belief in a benevolent Creator. In addition, the elegance of physical laws, the fine-tuning of fundamental laws and constants of nature, the appearance of directionality in evolution, the existence of consciousness, as well as the frequency of religious and moral experiences count in favour of the existence of a spiritual basis to reality.

Reflecting on the notion of rationality, Mary Grey offers a comprehensive understanding of reason. Rejecting the enlightenment paradigm which has sidelined religion, she argues that there is another form of knowing based on personal participation, engagement and involvement. According to Grey, there is a way of connected knowing that comprehends a diversity of factors. In this regard, she notes that there is an ecological element in the process of knowing and a dimension of care. The ethics of care, she writes, spring from a knowing which is 'tending' and 'attending', cherishing and nourishing the many interconnections between all living things. Connected knowing is not adversarial in nature; rather it invokes a wide basis of knowledge. It holds together perceptions, feelings, sensations, images and ideas. Knowing at this level also involves the activity of listening.

Such a broadened reinterpretation of listening has far reaching implications for Christian belief. According to Grey, human existence is enriched, not impoverished, by the discovery of many ways of knowing. In her view, the opening up of different, more inclusive ways of knowing frees up eternal doctrinal truths. Once knowledge is recognized as clothed in time-bound language and images and linked with the exercise of power and vested interests, the task of reinterpretation becomes critical. In conclusion, she writes that with a widened concept of rationality including the language of emotion with its links with materiality, the Christian faith may be seen to speak to some of the key issues of our times with a wisdom born of listening and humility.

Tim Winter carries on the discussion of what is meant by a sensible religion. Mainstream Islamic affiliation, he writes, can add significant value to citizenship and social cohesion. This is fundamentally different from radical Islam which supplies its polar opposite. Islam's mainstream, he writes, offers adherents a sensible form of religious life. Here he reflects on the idea of a sensible faith. To be sensible, he notes, is all too often to be perceived as prudent, moderate, consensual and cautious. Yet, what religion offers – at its most prophetic and authentic level – is a different notion of sensibleness. A truly sensible religion will have liberative and awkward things to say about the world, offering some of the most trenchant, counter-cultural and difficult critiques of society. In his view Islam, as the West's most salient counter-narrative, can help save the West from materialism, introspection and intellectual and moral decline.

Reflecting on the characteristics that make Islam a sensible faith, he points out that mainstream Muslims lay claim to a wealth of alternative perspectives to offer to Westerners who are prepared to learn from cultures other than their own. Explaining mainstream Islam's appeal as a sensible faith, he notes that Islam is vastly diverse, and thereby supplies homes for humans of a vastly divergent range of tastes and orientations. It has no orthodoxy as does Christianity. Rather, like Hinduism, it is polycentric. There is no high priest, no sacraments, no hierarchy. The Sharia is not a law; it is an ever-evolving tradition of legal, moral and ritual interpretation. Islamic theology is similarly diverse. Because of the openness to widely divergent readings of the Qur'an and Hadith texts, there are a variety of different theological schools – all are seen as acceptable by the major traditional centres of learning. Continuing this discussion, he maintains that a sensible religion does not treat the mind in isolation; rather it integrates the body into the mind's activities. The highly embodied nature of Islam's ritual, he believes, is well suited to maintaining this holistic form of life. Further, he argues that a sensible religion celebrates nature: in the Qur'an the nature of God is entirely focused on the contemplation of his signs in the world.

Anantanand Rambachan in his discussion of Hinduism argues that a sensible religion must fulfil a number of criteria:

1. It must explain and offer reasonable grounds for looking to an authoritative source or sources of knowledge other than those that are generally accepted.

2. It requires that the claims of such authoritative texts are not opposed to fact.
3. It must justify the need for religion by identifying clearly the human problem or problems that religion uniquely addresses.
4. The truth claims of sensible religion must be universally accessible and valid.
5. A sensible religion must make the case for itself by a willingness to speak with clarity about its fruits and its transformative impact on human life.
6. A sensible religion must demonstrate how its teachings foster a deep sense of human community and a unity of humanity that transcends boundaries of nationality, race, ethnicity and culture.
7. Sensible religion must advocate teachings that support the equal worth, value and dignity of all human beings.
8. Sensible religion must offer values that motivate human beings to lives of compassionate engagement, generosity and justice in the world.
9. Sensible religion, though affirming its own truth clams, must acknowledge the limits of all human symbols in relation to the limitless.

With regard to Hinduism, he points out that the Advaita tradition recognizes that people are different and look to religion for different ends. Those who aspire exclusively after finite things are not condemned but instructed to pursue goals with attentiveness to basic ethical values such as non-injury, truth, non-stealing, generosity and self-control. In the Chandogya Upanisad the human condition is likened to a person forcibly taken away from her beloved home, blindfolded and left in the wilderness. A compassionate response is to remove the blindfold and show the person the way back home. Similarly, a teacher liberates the ignorance-bound individual by teaching about that person's identify with brahman. Hence, through the instruction of scripture and teacher, it is possible to discover that the self which we assumed to be finite and subject to time and space, is in fact identical with the limitless brahman. Advaita is a teaching tradition that aims to instruct about the true nature of the self.

There are, however, interpretations of the Hindu tradition and practices that do not reflect the true understanding of human unity and worth. Many Hindus, Rambachan argues, continue to define the meaning of Hindu identity in the context of a hierarchal caste order. The doctrine of karma is interpreted in ways that justify case inequalities. Such views justify violence against persons seeing as belonging to lower castes and promote a passive acceptance of violence. No incentives are offered for social reform. Sensible religion, he stresses, cannot condone such oppression: it is contrary to Advaita teachings about human unity and value.

Adopting a different approach to Hindusim, Rita Sherma in her chapter stresses that a sensible religion must be an open system, with permeable boundaries and a dialogical dynamic where currents of information and insight flow in and out much like an ecosystem. When religion reacts in this way, she writes, it is supported and nourished by feedback loops that move and transform information from the natural world, other religious traditions, and human experience. Such an open system approach allows for respectful and non-defensive dialogue. There are, she contends, significant resources in the Hindu tradition that support such a view of religion as an open, interconnected system. The challenge for Hindu thought and practice today lies in positing a religious identity no matter how fluid, re-envisioning a faith that is embedded in geography in a way that is meaningful to a global civilization, and rejecting customs of inherited injustice. Hinduism, she concludes, is at a crossroads. Tomorrow's Hindu ethos will be different from today. What is uncertain is what form it will take. It may be that Hindus will forget their own history throughout which religion has been perceived as an open ecosystem, supported and nourished by feedback loops. Alternatively, the ecosystem approach to religion will be rediscovered and reformulated for a new age.

Alan Senauke focuses on Buddha's enlightenment. In all of the early Pali teachings, the Buddha is presented as a person of patience, intelligence, rationality and sensibility. Advocating the Middle Way, he stresses the importance of right view, right resolve, right speech, right action, right livelihood, right effort, right mindfulness, right concentration. Taken together, these elements suggest a way to live that is wholesome, enlightened and attainable. According to Senauke, there is an elegance and logic to his discourse, free from the mind-bending doctrines of Indian philosophy that relied on unverifiable belief systems. Having described this path of living, the Buddha then offers a set of tools for analysing suffering and the end of suffering. These Four Noble Truths involve perceiving suffering in all its manifestations, the cause of suffering, the cessation of suffering, and the path to Nibbana.

Yet, as Senauke points out, alongside sensible Buddhism, there has existed a form of Buddhism which is senseless, irrational and immoderate. Within recent history, for example, there has been the nightmare of Imperial Way Buddhism, in which Japanese Buddhist schools actively supported war and civilian atrocities in China, Korea, Manchuria and elsewhere in Asia. Again, the civil war in Sri Lanka has pitted the majority Buddhist population against minority Hindu Tamil – this was inflamed by Buddhist monks. Most recently, there has been long-standing ethnic tension in the western Rakhine state which has flared into hatred, communal violence and mass displacement of Muslim Rohingyas by the majority Rakhine population which is largely Buddhist.

Echoing Senauke's endorsement of sensible Buddhism, Dharmachari Subhuti stresses that Buddhism does not depend on revelation and hence there is no need to reconcile reason and faith. From the outset the Buddha strongly encouraged critical thought. In this respect, he can be regarded as the expounder of a sensible religion. Continuing this discussion, Subhuti stresses that the Buddha encouraged his followers to ask themselves whether deeds performed on the basis of a mind overcome by greed, aversion or delusion lead to welfare or harm. He then asks them to consider the opposite: non-greed or contentment, non-hatred or loving-kindness, and non-delusion – awareness or wisdom. In making this assessment, the Buddha encourages his disciples to approach these questions in a rational fashion. This, Subhuti believes, is the hallmark of a sensible religious life. In conclusion, he maintains that if one practices the Buddha's teachings as he intended, one will think critically about the best ends and means for living a human life and attain the greatest happiness possible.

Ethics and Sensible Religion

In the opening chapter Christopher Lewis highlights that a sensible religion seeks to foster altruism and promote human welfare. Such a view is echoed by various contributors in assessing their own traditions. Concerning Judaism, Melissa Raphael maintains that even illiberal forms of Judaism are conducive to a well-regulated life that is attentive to the needs and interests of the vulnerable and universalist in its commitment to the flourishing of human beings, animals and the natural environment. Turning to biblical teaching, she stresses that the prophets demanded the justice that is predicated on the servanthood of all earthly powers. Repeatedly the prophets railed against the hubris of rulers' self-aggrandizement. The covenant, she notes, is opposed to a theocracy that would put the dispensation of the divine will into the hands of a religious hierarchy claiming to be God's regent on earth. Instead, the prophets envisaged a religious democracy where the law is inscribed in the hearts of human beings without intermediaries. In conclusion she asserts that Judaism's iconoclastic dynamic prevents the world being taken captive to authoritarianism. Judaism, she writes, has a practical activist sensibility to the most deeply rooted human concerns.

Michael Lerner extols a theology of love. Within religious traditions including Judaism, there is what he refers to as the Right Hand of power and control. Yet, by contrast there is the Left Hand of compassion based on a very different understanding of human nature. Instead of regarding human life as a struggle for domination, the Left Hand recognizes human beings as fundamentally desiring loving connections with others. Human beings, he asserts, can achieve their goals best when they they learn how to treat each other with love and a generosity of spirit. Referring to the Jewish tradition, Lerner outlines an emancipatory tradition of love. When God's voice is received by Moses or the Israelites or by those who composed the biblical narrative in later centuries it is received as a voice challenging existing systems of domination.

Judaism, he states, entered the world with a revolutionary message: the social world is not fixed. The one God of history is a force for transformation. The cruelty of slavery as well as all other forms of domination, are not the products of nature, but the distorted creations of human beings. The God of the universe is the force that makes possible the overcoming of these distortions. The God of Israel is the God of love. The Jewish faith insists that the world can be based on love, and it is the task of the Jewry to create a world based on such principles.

Throughout history, the Jewish people have sought to follow this redemptive path. Today, there are elements within the Jewish community who seek to ignore this central dimension of the faith. Instead of embracing the Left Hand of love, they are preoccupied with power and domination in the Holy Land. The struggle between Israel and the Palestinians has overshadowed the rich spiritual tradition. In Lerner's view, the Left Hand of Judaism must be reclaimed if Jews today are to be authentic to their tradition. In conclusion he highlights the importance of the Network of Spiritual Progressives which includes Jews and others in the quest to be the voice of sensible religion for the modern age.

Sara Khan stresses that within Islam belief is not sufficient – it is connected to proactive action, establishing justice and developing selflessness, tolerance and forgiveness. Although ritual is essential, Islam emphasizes that worshipping God can only be accomplished through service to others. From the outset, Muhammad called his followers to free slaves and liberate women. Even in times of conflict, he gave clear instructions that civilians including the elderly, the young, women and non-combatants should not be harmed. Khan notes that Islam is frequently translated to mean peace and submission to God, but a more accurate translation would be the act of peace-making. As a counter-extremism and women's right's activist, Khan contends that it is Islam's message of justice, equality and dignity which drives her to defend human rights, challenge social injustice, and contribute to the well-being of humanity.

Throughout her chapter, she focuses on Islam and women's rights. As far back as the seventh century, she points out, Muslim women had more rights available than they do in many Muslim majority countries today. The Qur'an not only banned female infanticide, it also gave women the right to choose their own marriage partner as well as the right to education, to inherit, to vote, to work, to own property, to contribute politically and to participate in war. Today, however, there is the danger that the dominance of literal, decontextualized readings of Islam's scriptures and a misuse in the application of doctrines and traditions of Islamic law will overshadow the essentially liberating dimensions of the faith. According to Khan, it is vital that the true liberating voice of Islam is heard. Through a combined struggle of religious, scholarly and activist endeavor, she argues, it is possible to fulfill Islam's promise to women and humanity.

Dawoud El-Alami is highly critical of currents within the Islamic world which foster violent forms of jihad. Contrasting such an interpretation of the faith with a traditional understanding of jihad, he stresses the ethical dimensions of the concept. The basic meaning of jihad is struggle. Correctly interpreted, it refers to a spiritual quest. It should not be understood as a religious concept that justifies acts of terrorism or suicide bombing. Rather, the term designates the daily struggle of all Muslims to be better persons, to listen to their consciences, to resist greed, deception, immorality, prejudice and hatred. Muslims are to cultivate themselves in faith, moral virtue, honesty, integrity, compassion and understanding. Further, jihad implies the struggle to spread knowledge, education and understanding. One who carries out jihad works for social reform. Properly conceived jihad should encourage followers to work against corruption, discrimination, abuses of human rights, and the eradication of social ills. Allied to such activities is the desire to alleviate poverty and improve the life of the poor. Finally, jihad refers to just warfare in accordance with a number of conditions including the provision that non-combatants should be spared.

Anantanand Rambachan points out that the end of Advaita instruction is liberation. This is possible because the human problem is related to ignorance of the self. The most immediate fruit of a new understanding of the self is freedom from greed. According to Advaita, the root of greed is self-ignorance which causes a false sense of incompleteness and inadequacy. Yet, the understanding of the identity of the self with brahman leads to the discovery of one's fullness and the overcoming of the suffering occasioned by a sense of insignificance. Such liberation does not isolate individuals from the community; rather, since brahman is the self of all, liberation results in the deepest identity that we can have with others. We recognize ourselves in all beings. Such an identification with others transcends the boundaries of nationality, religion, race and ethnicity. Hating and oppressing other human beings on the basis of caste, sex or race is unjust, a consequence of blindness to the truth of brahman's non-dual nature and identity in all. To hate another, Rambachan argues, is to hate oneself, to hurt another is to hurt oneself. Advaita advances a teaching that enables human beings to be both altruistic and fulfilled.

In this context, Rambachan is critical of Hindus who continue to define the meaning of Hindu identity in the context of a hierarchal caste order that labels others as impure and denies them dignity and worth. The doctrine of karma is interpreted in ways that justify caste inequalities by contending that the birth in a lower case is the deserved consequence of evil actions in past lives. On such a view there is no freedom from its indignities without rebirth into a higher caste. Such views, he notes, justify violence against individuals who are perceived as belonging to lower castes.

No incentives are offered for social change and reform. In his view, the oppression and injustice of caste and patriarchy cannot be justified. They are contrary to core Advaita teachings about human unity and equal value.

Alan Senauke stresses the moral imperatives at the heart of Buddhist teaching. From seeing into the nature of impermanence and suffering – which is what the Buddha explained as the first step on the Eightfold Path, there naturally arises a sense of responsibility. This is the fourth step along the Eightfold Path: right action. This, he believes, should lead to the transformation of dysfunctional institutions and structures including prisons, hospitals, social welfare systems, corporations, and the military. Echoing such views, Dharmachari Subhuti focuses on Buddha's teaching. For 50 years he tirelessly sought to communicate to others his Dharma so that they too could become free as he had done. All selfish motivations were extinguished so that he was able to live a life of compassion.

According to Subhuti, this aspect of Buddha's message needs to be stressed since so much emphasis is given in modern Buddhist schools to cognitive aspects of spiritual practice. Though these are intrinsic to the development in the Dharma, they are only one side of the process. Selflessness does not mean simply absence of self: rather it leads to the presence of love and compassion. Continually the Buddha emphasized the development of loving-kindness, asking his disciples to cultivate it together with compassion for those who are suffering. In conclusion, Subhuti states that if one practises the Buddha's teachings properly one will think critically about the best ends and means of human life, acting for the benefit of all.

Opinderjit Takhar stresses that the Sikh way of life promotes an individual's role as a good citizen in the localized as well as the global setting. Here she makes a clear distinction between what she refers to as 'good Sikhi' and 'bad Sikhi'. As opposed to bad Sikhi, good Sikhi embraces principles of good conduct and behavior through meditation on the Name of God, performing selfless service and sharing with the less fortunate in society. Such a perspective has profound implications for the inequality that exists within the community of Sikhs. Caste based discrimination and gender discrimination are two criteria for determining bad Sikhi. Good Sikhi, on the other hand, lays emphasis on treating all human beings as equal regardless of caste, gender or creed. Bad Sikhi also includes an exclusivist attitude towards persons professing another faith. Of particular concern in Takhar's chapter is the treatment of women and caste. As she notes, feminist movements have increasingly become popular among Sikh women in the diaspora. These women take inspiration from the egalitarian teachings of Sikhi. The egalitarian nature of Sikh teachings also extends to rejecting caste distinctions. Increasingly younger Sikhs are drawing reference to Sikh teachings which denounce caste based discrimination.

In the final chapter of the book, Nokuzola Mndende highlights the ethical dimensions of African traditional religion (ATR). Ethical values within ATR are people-centred. Evil originates with humans and not with God. ATR focuses on the oral transmission of norms and values acted out in practice. The emphasis is on the daily practice of these values and also on rituals, rather than on texts as sacred authority. Practitioners know whom to consult for guidance within the clan. In their communal way of life they are constantly reminded of all aspects of their religion. Rituals together with the normal social interaction of daily life are where respect and morality are practiced and reinforced. Such ideals are of critical importance in facing the moral decay in African society (including rape, murder and muti-killing). All of these actions are the result of the forces of darkness which can be combated by the ideals of ATR.

Conclusion

In various ways then the contributors to this volume follow the same path as Hick, Knitter and Vardy in defending what they consider sensible religion. Few, however, are as explicit about laying down specific criteria for differentiating good from bad religion. A notable exception to this pattern is Anantanand Rambachan's list of nine Advaita criteria for sensible religion. In his view the truth claims of sensible religion must be universally accessible and valid. Again, he states that a sensible religion must offer values that motivate human beings to lives of compassionate engagement, generosity and justice in the world. Other writers are less specific. Instead of formulating precise criteria, they lay down general principles that a sensible religion should fulfill. Keith Ward, for example, argues that a sensible religion should be aware of its own basic principles and be consistent. In addition, it should recognize alternative views, be self-critical and open to reasoned objections. Similarly Rita Sherma maintains that a sensible religion should be an open system with permeable boundaries and a dialogical dynamic whereby currents of information and insight flow in and out. Dharmachari Subhuti focuses on Buddha's encouragement of critical thought.

Other contributors stress that the concept of rationality be expanded to embrace a more comprehensive understanding of reason. Mary Grey, for example, rejects the enlightenment paradigm and offers instead another form of knowing based on personal participation, engagement and involvement. In a similar vein, Nokuzola Mndende is highly critical of the ways that ATR was suppressed by Christian missionaries. The dawn of democracy has brought about a new understanding and definition of religion. Previously, the concept of religion was narrowly defined in a dogmatic manner based on Western culture. As a consequence, indigenous African religion was viewed with distaste. Today, however, ATR should be regarded as an authentic expression of the spiritual life. In her discussion Mndende offers a non-Western model of a religious faith which is spiritually sensitive and sensible in the lives of believers.

Turning to ethical criteria, contributors similarly offer general guidelines. Appeals are made to a wide variety of concerns. Here they are united in affirming that sensible religion fosters human growth, fulfillment and welfare. Stress is constantly made on the ways that religion addresses material and spiritual needs. Melissa Raphael emphasizes that a sensible religion should be attentive to the interests of the vulnerable and universalist in its commitment to the flourishing of human beings, animals and nature. Michael Lerner warns against what he refers to as the Right Hand of oppression. The one God of Judaism, he states, is a positive force for the transformation of earthly life. It is the God of love who can combat the distorted creations of human beings. Sara Khan maintains that Islam advocates justice, selflessness, tolerance and forgiveness. Extending this discussion, Dawoud El-Alami contends that jihad in a moral concept designating a spiritual struggle to bring about a more just world. In the view of Anantanand Rambachan, human liberation is a paramount importance in Hinduism. Alan Senauke argues that moral imperatives are at the heart of Buddhism. In a similar vein, Opinderjit Takhar focuses on the ways in which Sikhism fosters selfless service to others.

Good religion fosters such virtues. Yet, as a number of contributors point out, there are currently manifestations of bad religion in contemporary society. Michael Lerner's critique of the Right Hand of Judaism illustrates the dangers of the quest for power and domination within the Jewish world. Mary Grey is critical of the narrow understanding of rationality in Christianity. In the conclusion to her chapter she argues that by excluding the language of the body and the emotions a distorted understanding of reason has created inadequate forms of the Christian faith.

Tim Winter points to the distorted version of Islam which is shaped by terrorism and Islamist political totalitarianism. At the margins of the Islamic world, radicalism fosters a distorted interpretation of the faith. In his presentation of Hinduism, Anantanda Rambachan warns against those beliefs and practices that do not reflect the true understanding of human unity and worth. Rita Sherma stresses that Hinduism must be supported and nourished by information from the natural world, other religious traditions and human experience. When Hindus forget their own history throughout which the faith has been nourished by such experience and encounter, they are unfaithful to the past. Buddhism, too, comes in for criticism in Alan Senauke's chapter. Here he emphasises the terrors unleashed in the name of Buddhism.

Good – as opposed to bad religion – thus has a fundamental role to play in the modern world. As never before religion is under attack. Critics maintain that the world's faiths have substantially contributed to human suffering and evil. Religious belief, they argue, is nothing more than fantasy and wishful thinking. The clash between belief and disbelief is portrayed as a struggle between the forces of light and darkness. The contributors to this book seek in different ways to demonstrate the rationality and ethical integrity of their traditions. It is their conviction that through the centuries religious faith has enriched human existence and continues to do so in modern society. Yet, in their view it is imperative to differentiate between good and bad religion.

A sensible religion is one which is rational, reasonable and coherent, affirming the centrality of absolute standards of justice and goodness. Sensible religions are passionately interested in improving the life of all individuals, respecting the essential value of human life. In summary: if religion is to be defended from the attacks of modern critics, good religion must be distinguished from bad religion. Bad religion lacks humility; it is coercive; it fears freedom and scientific discovery. Good religion, however, provides a framework for human flourishing in a world torn by conflict, misunderstanding and bloodshed.

Reference List

Hick, J. (1981) 'On Grading Religions', *Religious Studies*, 17, 451–67.
Knitter, P. (1982) *No Other Name*, Maryknoll, NY: Orbis.
Vardy, P. (2010) *Good and Bad Religion*, London: SCM.

Index